HOW TO STUDY THE CITY CHURCH

INSTITUTE OF SOCIAL AND RELIGIOUS RESEARCH

HOW TO STUDY THE CITY CHURCH

BY

H. PAUL DOUGLASS

GARDEN CITY, NEW YORK

DOUBLEDAY, DORAN & COMPANY, INC.

INTRODUCTION

The Institute of Social and Religious Research began to publish studies in the field of the city church in 1924. Numerous inquiries and requests have since been received relative to the making of first-hand investigations and surveys in this field. In response to this demand the present book has been written.

A widespread interest has been revealed by these requests, some of which have come from important and representative sources. They testify to the growing strength of the conviction voiced in a report of the findings committee of the Methodist Council of Cities, representing the nearly one hundred city extension societies of this largest of the Protestant denominations.

"In too large a measure the Church of to-day is governed by the blessed trinity of chance, accident and mistake. Building upon unconfirmed belief has been her most costly error. In other realms whim and caprice have been replaced by scientific and accurate surveys. The Church, too, must accept this method if she would have the largest measure of success. The A. B. C. of her task is thoroughly to examine herself and the community in which she works. The discovery of the largest number of facts concerning the Church and the community is fundamental to the formation of a program."[1]

Two classes of men are primarily concerned in locally undertaking first-hand studies of the Church; namely, parish ministers (with their associated lay officials), and denominational executives in charge of minor territorial districts, with whom may be grouped secretaries of city extension societies and of church federations.

The parish minister may want (1) to make an all-round study of his church; or (2) to intensify the investigation of some one or more limited aspects of its life and work; or (3) he may feel the need to investigate the religious antecedents and affiliations of the population of a city or particular area to determine his church's responsibility.

The first three chapters of the book give directions for making studies growing out of these three typical situations. It is assumed in all three cases that the proposed research is to be carried out by the church's own leaders with very little expert assistance, if any; that it will be conducted in connection with regular duties and without the setting up of elaborate special machinery. In brief, self-surveys are contemplated.

[1] *The Council of Cities of the Methodist Episcopal Church, Fifth Annual Meeting* (Philadelphia: Department of City Work, The Board of Home Missions and the Church Extension of the Methodist Episcopal Church, 1922), p. 281.

INTRODUCTION

The city or district executive, or the Federation secretary, who may be interested in studying the city church, naturally wants to investigate the collective institutional life of some group of churches with which he is concerned. If his object is primarily ecclesiastical, he may be satisfied (1) to deal with strictly institutional phenomena, omitting the larger setting in which the church group finds itself; or (2) he may wish to explore the relations of churches to the particular neighborhoods or communities to which they belong. The second division of the book tells how to make these studies. Chapter v tells how to make two types of studies of groups of churches, one historical, the other contemporaneous; while chapter vi shows how to fill in the study of the community background.

The processes involved in these studies are not too difficult technically to be carried out by such church executives as are in mind, provided the church group under investigation is fairly small, the survey schedule simple, and the community not too extensive or complicated. When, however, the data are extensive and the church group has an entire city or metropolitan area for its social background, it is assumed that even the limited survey will be under expert professional direction. Chapter vii outlines the practical conduct of complete community surveys of organized religion definitely requiring extensive organization, large budgets, and a corps of professional research and survey workers.

The methodology proposed for making the above studies generalizes methods successfully pursued in actual projects of the Institute of Social and Religious Research. In the discussion of each study, expositions of the point of view will be found. These, it is recognized, involve judgments on many debatable issues which the reader is at liberty to challenge at any point. The imperative form in which the subsequent directions for carrying out the several researches are couched, is, of course, merely a device to aid definiteness and save space. Many passages of the book will reveal its purpose to provoke thoughtful consideration of its assumptions and methods rather than to urge their wholesale adoption; and it should be understood that very often the forms of research here offered can be bettered in detail by those who may attempt to use them.

BIBLIOGRAPHY AND REFERENCES

Burns, *A Program for the City Church* (pamphlet) (Philadelphia: Department of City Work Board of Home Mission and Church Extension, Methodist Episcopal Church, 1920).

The Council of Cities of the Methodist Episcopal Church, Proceedings of Annual Meetings (Philadelphia: Department of City Work, Board of Home Mission and Church Extension, 1922 and 1923).

INTRODUCTION

Reports of Conferences on City Church Work (New York: Union
Theological Seminary, Reprints from Union Theological Seminary
Bulletin, Nov., 1923, Jan., 1925, June, 1925; mimeographed reports
1926 and 1927).

SEARS (ed.), *Baptist City Planning* (Philadelphia: The Judson Press,
1926). Reports of 15 committees prepared for a national denominational conference on city work, with the findings of the conference.

CONTENTS

LIST OF CHARTS

LIST OF SCHEDULES

LIST OF TABLES

A Scheme of Study is appended to Chapter II, and to each succeeding chapter, to serve in each case as an aid in the conduct of surveys of the kind described.

PART I: HOW TO STUDY ONE CHURCH

CHAPTER I

THE SEMI-INTENSIVE STUDY OF A SINGLE CHURCH

The purpose of this chapter and of chapter ii is to tell how to conduct a study of a single church. It is assumed that the church wants to make a comprehensive institutional self-examination that shall be scientific and thoroughgoing so far as it attempts to go; but that shall require only a limited amount of time and labor and not be carried into exhaustive detail at any point. It seems fair to designate a study with such limitations as a semi-intensive one.

In assuming a situation calling for a semi-intensive self-study of a single church, it is not necessary to attempt to set forth any particular method of organizing for the practical administration of the project. It may be possible for the minister to carry it out in connection with his ordinary routine as a means of understanding his task better. At any rate, no special research organization or resources from outside the church are proposed as essential to the situation.

It will be better, however, if from its inception the self-study is formally made an undertaking of the church as such. This view is in interesting harmony with a report of the findings committee on the study of the local church adopted by the conference on The City Church at Work held at Union Theological Seminary in 1925.

> The committee recommends the formation of a "research commission" to study the problems of the church and help develop a program to meet the needs. This should be officially elected, if possible, and include the most expert talent in the church and also some of the leading members who through lack of vision or adequate knowledge might oppose the plans to be undertaken. To put them on the commission will develop in them a sense of responsibility and lead them to take part in putting the plan into action. "Only as a new plan truly rises out of the constituency of the church is it good leadership. If it is your own private scheme it is poor leadership."[1]

From the outset, too, the advice of reliable experts should be sought. Such experts may be looked for in the departments of city church work or of church surveys at denominational headquarters; in local ecclesiastical officials who may have had training and experience in first-hand studies of churches; sometimes in offices of church federations or councils of churches; or in the departments of

[1] *The City Church at Work* (New York: Union Theological Seminary, 1925).

1

social research in near-by universities. It should be accepted as an implied condition of a self-survey that all possible help should be drawn from such sources as these.

It will now be assumed that whatever steps are judged necessary to initiate the proposed study with the church have been taken; and the following paragraphs will indicate and describe the characteristic stages and methods of carrying on, as well as the typical forms into which the results of the work should be cast.

PLANNING THE STUDY

The first step is to reach a preliminary determination of the scope, content and phases of the study. Briefly stated, what one has to determine are the fundamental ways of regarding the subject of study from the standpoint of the particular investigation. By the fundamental ways of regarding the subject, are meant valid and fruitful ways. These are partly determined by what is assumed as the nature of the subject in itself. The church, for example, seems to possess certain distinctive characteristics which identify it in contrast with other subjects. It stands in its own continuous and determining relations. Common sense has already identified its most practical aspects; and thoughtful observation and analysis discover what are the exact traits and relationships to be studied.

But the point of view of those making the study also partly determines what ways of regarding a subject are to be considered as fundamental in any given case. A fact becomes more or less important according to the use that is to be made of it. Ways of regarding a subject are always weighted by the mind that does the regarding. Even a study intended to be objectively inclusive and perfectly balanced will have its particular objectives; or else its results will be far too indefinite to be worth while. The persons concerned in the work, instead of deluding themselves into thinking that a particular piece of research has no special point of view, should know that it has one, and should determine, accept and confess it.

A good plan of research will satisfy both the objective characteristics of the facts with which it deals and the purposes of the people who are studying them. There can be no best plan; but only one most suitable from a given point of view.

The following outline for the study of a single church is accordingly proposed primarily for the purposes of illustration and exposition. No church should start a study of itself by accepting the outline just as it stands. Instead, the outline should be criticized, modified and adapted from the viewpoint of the church's own interests and purposes. This requires that it be examined in a way to show what it is and how it was arrived at.

OUTLINE FOR A SEMI-INTENSIVE STUDY OF A
SINGLE CHURCH

I. *Preliminary Study*
    Reconnaissance of current activities
    Historical evolution

II. *Factual Study of the Present Church*
    A. Basic Factors
        (1) Members and constituents
        (2) Parish and geographical relations with constituency
        (3) Effective environment and relation to structure of city
    B. Aspects of the Church in Action
        (1) Organization and activities; program
        (2) Professional leadership; the ministry
        (3) Staff organization and relationships
        (4) Plant and equipment
        (5) Finances
        (6) Public services
        (7) Religious education
        (8) Methods of growth and conservation
        (9) Current church life
        (10) Relation of the church to its community
        (11) Relation of the church to its denomination

III. *Study of Adaptations*
    Evidences of problems or experiences which have challenged to new
      adaptations
    The specific adaptations attempted or effectuated
      Institutional—organizations, workers, finances, plant, etc.
      Modifications of objective—change in the church's thinking and purpose
    Success of the adaptations as measured by common sense criteria of institutional progress and enlarged service
    The general trend of the church consequent upon the fusion of old elements and new adaptations

ANALYSIS OF OUTLINE

The ways in which it is proposed to regard the church for the purposes of this study appear most plainly in the second division of the outline headed "Factual Study of the Present Church." The more fundamental aspects are here distinguished from certain secondary ones. Included among the former are these facts: that a church is identified with a social group—a constituency; that it is related to a certain distribution of the people of this constituency in a parish; that it is conditioned by a larger social whole—a community—of which its constituency and parish are partial aspects. The secondary aspects of the church are distinguished from the primary as those that are more easily and directly affected by conscious decisions and short-time policies—as, for example, its program, its leadership, its finances and methods.

Within the group of secondary topics, sub-classifications occur. The first seven deal with separate forms in which the church expresses itself; the eighth and ninth with institutional processes going on continuously; and the tenth and eleventh with the chief relations in which the church stands.

The outline is also based on the assumption that the study is to follow three different phases characterized by distinct points of view.

In the first, or preliminary, phase comes a rapid preview of the case, intended to give quickly a limited understanding of the church, present and past. The second phase is painstakingly factual. The church is to be described in one after another of the aspects outlined above; and an understanding of it is to be reached in the light of such natural comparisons as may follow from the long series of approaches to the facts.

In the third phase, it is intended to restate and summarize the whole factual study from the viewpoint of an explanatory hypothesis; namely, that the present church is the result of a series of adaptations to its situation as revealed in past and recent experience.

Thinking into a project in these or similar terms precedes any movement toward actual research processes. It should result in a very definite product of thought and planning, even before a choice is made of the technical instruments of research.

But any plan of research, since it is confessedly the result of thinking and choosing, and not a demonstration of the only best way, is open to challenge by any one with a different viewpoint. The principle of classification and the phases of approach may be indefinitely varied. A church should work over the basic plan of study until it has made it thoroughly its own, adding or subtracting items, reconceiving relations and reorganizing topics in order to reach the most fundamental ways of regarding the subject in the light of its purposes in the investigation.

PLANNING TIME, COST AND WORKERS

The best of topical planning, however, yields merely the bare outline of a possible study. This being tentatively fixed, the next stage is to devise practical means for carrying on an actual investigation limited by a certain allotment of time, workers and financial resources. Planning for a self-study should cover these points just as faithfully as though the church were having the work done by outside investigators.

Experience proves that in a "semi-intensive study" of a single church, such as is here outlined, the assembling and recording of the existing data on the topics outlined for investigation can be covered by an amateur investigator of good education with a non-professional clerical assistant, in from ten days to two weeks, provided the church has made certain preparations in advance. The subsequent processes of tabulating and studying the data and of embodying the results in a written report will probably require one person's time for two months.

Taking so considerable an amount of time from a busy minister, or getting it contributed by volunteers, is no slight undertaking. It is strongly recommended that a church definitely bind itself to release the necessary time within specified dates and to provide the resources; otherwise the project may drag indefinitely to failure.

Among the things that should obviously be arranged in advance of the actual study, to economize time and assure uninterrupted progress, are the following:

1. Bring together in one place complete lists with addresses of the members of the church and the members of each subsidiary organization that has a definite membership, together with all records kept of their relationship to the church; also similar data for all financial supporters.

2. Bring together in one place the complete annual reports of the church and of all subsidiaries and stated activities for the last ecclesiastical or financial year, together with all current church publications issued within the same year. These can be used as a basis for the study unless the church wishes to make up special reports for the twelve months immediately preceding the survey. (All these required data are already in existence but are generally scattered in many hands. The survey cannot easily be completed within the time limits unless they are assembled in advance.)

3. Supply clerical assistant who can give time practically upon demand for period aggregating two weeks. One of the paid staff of the church is frequently assigned as clerical assistant, or a lay person who can fit in with the available time of the chief investigator.

4. Provide those who are studying the problem ample place to work. The place is usually provided in the church office or some available room adjacent. Storage and filing space for data and desk-room sufficient for many documents are primary requirements.

5. Supply a reasonable amount of transportation for the sociological study of the parish and to save time in securing interviews. Members of the church who own cars may be secured to take the investigators around in the study of the field and for the more distant interviews.

6. Arrange for brief regular interviews, preferably daily, between the investigator and his associates, and schedule appointments in advance with all persons from whom information has to be received, so that the progress of the work may be continuous.

7. Provide the cost of necessary stationery and supplies—such as a reasonably large scale map of the parish, a set of membership cards for entire constituency (cost approximately $10 per thousand); paper properly ruled for tabulation of statistics; materials for such charts and diagrams as may be needed to show the results of the study. The cost of these incidentals is not likely to exceed $25 per church.

ACTUAL PIECEMEAL PROCEDURE

Even after all these preliminary preparations, actual steps of procedure will bear almost no relation to the logical framework of the study. The work will have to proceed piecemeal and be varied from day to day as it can be sandwiched in to suit the convenience of the coöperating church workers and the numerous individuals from whom information has to be secured. Lists of members will not be forthcoming when promised, or will have to be sent back for revision. Data ostensibly complete will be found to be fragmentary and will have to be supplemented. This is sure to be the case whenever such a study is made by professional persons whose time is subject to frequent interruptions or by lay volunteers. The investigator will have to turn to this or that particular part of the study that can go forward at any given moment.

METHOD OF CHECKING PROGRESS

This necessity makes it imperative to discover a method of checking daily progress. The following form provides a memorandum for the purpose:

MEMORANDUM OF PROGRESS—STUDY OF .... CHURCH

TOPICS	DAYS AND DATES				Degree of Progress
	1st	2nd	3rd	4th	
I. Preliminary Study					
1. Reconnaissance Study					
2. History					
II. Factual Study					
A.					
1. Members and Constituents					
2. Parish and geographical relations					
3. Environment					
B.					
1. Organizations and activities—etc.					

Columns standing for each day of the survey period are ruled opposite the several items of the study as previously outlined. A tentative schedule of investigation covering the proposed steps from day to day should be entered against each item. Thus the second preliminary topic, the church's history, may be begun on the first day and require parts of four days to complete; on the first, one may review the data and make a digest of it; on the second, examine the parallel statistics; on the third, decide upon the epochs in which that history is to be set forth; and, on the last day, complete the historical write-up. These four proposed stages of the work should be entered under the first four days. If the work is completed as proposed it may be crossed off. If not, the item should be carried forward for another day and its degree of completeness entered. The same thing may be done for every item of an outline.

The degree of completion of the study of each item, and of the whole study, should be summarized every third or fourth day as "not begun," "one-tenth done," "one-fourth done," "half done," as the case may be. By these means, close track may be kept of the progress of the study topic by topic, and loose ends may be brought up as rapidly as possible, even though the actual order of processes cannot be determined in advance.

The succeeding paragraphs of this methodology ignore the actual order in which the field work of a study may be done, in order to show the steps involved, what has to be done with each element of the data, and how results are summarized and findings and conclusions reached. That is to say, the exposition follows a logical order rather than any proposed chronological order of investigation.

Technical Methodology and Detailed Procedure

The general plan of the semi-intensive study of a single church calls for the investigation of some two dozen topics. A specific plan and technical procedure have to be devised under each of these topics, just as though each constituted a separate research; and frequently several plans under subdivisions of a single topic. A statement of the precise procedures to be followed under each topic makes up the main body of this chapter.

PRELIMINARY PHASE

1. *Reconnaissance Study*

After much preparation the investigator is now ready to begin his actual research in the sense of dealing with concrete data about the church. But there is still a preliminary phase to spend time upon in order to save time in the end. The purpose of this phase is to reach a quick understanding of the general scope and contents of the phenomena that the church actually presents for study, and to relate them provisionally to the main plan.

The first step is to compile a list of all the details necessary to complete the significant picture of the institution; that is to say, to inventory the ultimate units of investigation, the recurrent activities, organizations, methods and practices, uses of facilities, etc., that enter into the concrete reality of the church's life.

As an aid toward such an inventory, a check-list of activities, organizations, etc., characteristic of city churches should be used. The following list, compiled from studies of many churches, will serve for this purpose. Every item of the list that is found present and actively operative (within six months, say, of the date of the study) should be starred or checked against; the rest should be left blank.

HOW TO STUDY THE CITY CHURCH

Check-List of Church Organizations, Activities, Practices and Facilities

* Outside bulletin board with weekly notices
* Young People's Society, League, Union or equivalent
* Church office open daily
* Sunday school completely graded (class for every three years)
   Annual every-member financial canvass
* Calendar or bulletin issued weekly
* Organized athletic teams or contests
* Boy Scouts or equivalent
* Confirmation class or Catechetical instruction
* Organized Welcome (by ushers or others definitely delegated)
* Regular paid newspaper advertising
* Church choir (eight voices or more)
* Formal coöperation with organized churches (Church Federations, etc.)
   Religious education formally organized as separate department (with special
     board)
* Young Women's Clubs (Service League, Girls' Friendly, etc.)
   Gymnasium instruction
   Girl Scouts, Camp Fire Girls or equivalent
* Children's congregation meeting separately for services
* Women's Missionary Society (Home, Foreign or both)
* Men's Club, Brotherhood, or equivalent
* Daily Vacation Bible School (two weeks or more annually)
   Sunday school financed by church as part of regular budget
* Women's Guild—Ladies' Aid Society, etc.
* Girls' Clubs (other than Scout type)
* Sunday evening social gatherings or teas
* Dramatic organization
   Regular use of motion-pictures
   Concerts (periodic or frequent)
   Boys' Club (other than Scout type)
   Church receptions or dinners (four times a year or oftener)
   Library (general or reference) in regular use
   Mission Study Classes (separately organized)
   Lectures (periodic or frequent)
   Unified woman's organization (combining missions and parish aid)
* Mothers' or parents' organization
   Church open daily for private devotions
   Vacation farm or country property used for outings
* Employment agency
   Music classes
   Dramatics (as phase of social service interest)
   Local church paper (issued monthly or oftener)
   Week-day religious school (two days weekly, three months or more)
* Sewing or millinery classes
   Orchestra or band
* Domestic Science or home-making instruction
   English classes for foreigners
   Forum (public discussion by general audience or large group)
   Health classes
   Children's sermons regularly
   Kindergarten
   Systematic vocational advice
* Dormitory or boarding facilities for constituents
   Civics or economics classes
   Services in more than one language
   Visiting nurse
   Dispensary or clinic
   Branch church (served in whole or in part by church staff)
   Day Nursery

Special services for industrial or other employees
Outdoor or street preaching (periodic or frequent)

The next step is to classify the items of the check-list under the categories of the main outline of the investigation. Some will need to be considered from the standpoint of program; others from that of leadership or facilities or finance. The more important ones will need to be considered from more than one standpoint. When all the items have been distributed provisionally within the main outline, it will be found that most of the subtopics for investigation have been naturally suggested.

The next probable discovery will be that there are now too many topics in the outline for every one to get separate treatment within the limits of a semi-intensive study. This condition will require that some be combined, or relegated to mere mention in the text of the report, others eliminated. The process of generalizing the too prolific details, and of balancing up the plan of study according to their relative importance, must then take place. At this stage, which is still provisional, results are reached by a trial-and-error process rather than by any method that can be scientifically formulated. It will be a safe thing for the beginner to confine himself rather closely to the ground covered in subsequent paragraphs; at the same time he ought to feel that he has far more right to follow his own vital thinking than the author has to suggest limitations to him.

At any rate, when these preliminary processes are faithfully carried out, the investigator will be well oriented with respect to his entire remaining task. He will also find the organization of his study in detail much simpler and closer to the facts than if he had not painstakingly built up its structure out of a multitude of separate items. Finally, he should be able to retain a sensitiveness to the many facts that have been obscured or omitted from statement as a result of the necessary compression of the plan of study. For, after all, these facts continue to exist, and the church remains more varied than are the items that can be investigated and talked about.

2. *Historical Phase: Method of Securing Historical Data*

Data in strictly historical form do not exist for most churches. All churches, however, have records more or less carefully preserved. Nearly all churches publish brief historical notes from time to time, often in connection with the celebration of their more important anniversaries or achievements. A few possess histories distinguished by worthy literary quality and real social insight. All well-established denominations issue annual statistics for local churches in somewhat comparable form (some in national yearbooks, others in the minutes of the territorial districts). Their statistics include such items as church-membershp, Sunday-school

TABLE I

TABLE —SUMMARY OF A CHURCH'S HISTORY BY PERIODS OF DEVELOPMENT

Dates	Characteristics and Epochal Events of Period	Length of Period in Years	Status at End of Period		
			Approximate Population of City	Number of	
				Church-members	Sunday-school Pupils
1853–1866	Mission Sunday school preceding church	13	100,000	45	Not known
1866–1872	Organization of church; erection of building	6	160,000	112	225
1872–1901	Growth, culmination and decline of development	29	575,000	842	266
1901–1907	Agitation of removal; erection of present church	6	650,000	748	267
1907–1926	Development in present location	19	825,000	1,264	575

enrollment and financial expenditures. Files of such yearbooks are usually to be found in the custody of the district administrators of the several denominations. It is assumed that these historical sources have been brought together for the church under investigation so that their study may go forward without delay or interruption.

The first thing to be decided is how far to go with the available data. A semi-intensive study may well be limited to a compressed summary of the church's history indicating its most important turning points and the trends of development from point to point. This will be enough to furnish a background for the contemporary factual investigation.

3. *Determination of Epochs*

History is commonly written by epochs, which date from one to another of the turning points. It necessarily generalizes many thousands of events under a few categories and classes. The essentials are, accordingly, to find the right turning points and to devise the most adequate classification.

With respect to the church, it is most natural to consider, among matters likely to be recorded, such things as institutional growth in members or financial resources; church-building epochs; removals; other striking changes of fortune or of policy.

Table I shows how the story of a church from such standpoints may be compactly summarized by epochs.

When the annual growth of the church and that of the Sunday school are charted, three trends are clear: (1) The church's rapid development for the years following the completion of its original building; (2) its subsequent checking and decline, and (3) new growth, at a rate almost paralleling that of the first period, following its relocation.

How does one know that the above table presents true epochs for the church in question? Provided the criteria chosen represent really important functions in a church's life, the real test of any proposed epoch is whether it can be proved that a variety of significant aspects of the church actually changed their trend at the times fixed upon to mark the beginning and the end of the epoch, and whether the direction of the development of all or most of them generally coincided during the period in question.

The assumed epochs in the illustrative case are further tested by these criteria in the following chart, which covers the last three epochs of the particular church's history.

It will be noted that the curve of Sunday-school growth went up with that of the church, but that it went down sooner and faster. The Sunday school also recovered much less completely than did the church after the removal, and it did not grow as fast as the church did after the post-war period.

In other words, the turning point for one part of the church's life may not be exactly that of another's. One part advances while the other lags. History thus has to be more or less arbitrary in its discrimination of epochs. In the illustrative case, the fortunes of the church were considered primary, those of the Sunday school secondary, in the choice of exact turning points. But since the two

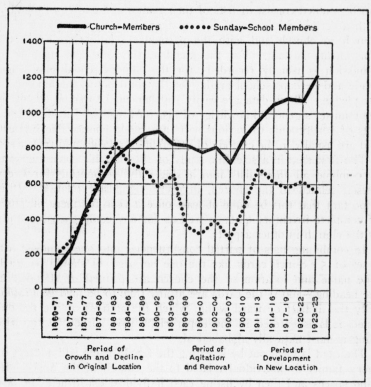

CHART I—INCREASE AND DECREASE OF CHURCH-MEMBERSHIP AND SUNDAY-SCHOOL ENROLLMENT OF A ST. LOUIS CHURCH, 1869-1925.

followed generally similar courses, and since available resources, prestige, etc., largely followed the course of membership-growth, it is doubtful whether any other system of epochs would more nearly do justice to the facts.

In applying such methods to the study of a particular church, the development of the church in a variety of aspects should be charted, and the periods in which the agreement of trend is greatest should be chosen as historical epochs.

With such a framework arrived at, it is easy to write in from the source material the brief historical sketch that a semi-intensive study requires.[2]

1. *Members and Constituents*

The existing data by means of which members and constituents can be studied consist of lists of their names and addresses together with a certain minimum of information about them, varying from church to church and with the particular relationship which the constituents sustain. For the member, the date and manner of admission is usually recorded; for the Sunday-school pupil, age, grade and perhaps school grade; for the contributor, the amount of his pledge. These data are easily supplemented to some extent by the minister's general knowledge of his constituents. But the several lists of constituents of various sorts are rarely comparable in form and are usually in the custody of different secretaries and treasurers.

The first step in a scientific study of the church's constituency is to combine all these lists into a single list accounting for every person related to the church, in every significant relation. It is important that this be done at least once a year for mere purposes of complete inventory quite as well as for any comprehensive study of the church in other aspects.

In combining lists of partial constituencies into one complete list, a set of 5 x 8-inch cards like the one on page 14 should be used. The name and location of the church are printed or stamped in the heading—and if the cards are at any time to be filed geographically the district or ward within which the address of the persons listed falls is entered in the upper right-hand corner. Otherwise filing is most naturally alphabetical.

The card is filled out by inserting the family name and address of every family or individual related to the church in the upper left-hand spaces and then by listing each individual constituent, in case of families according to relationship to the family, sex and age; in the case of minors in the spaces of the first column. The data called for in columns 2 and 3 are rarely available from church records; and there will not be time in a semi-intensive study to circulate the questionnaire necessary to get it. For the present study, these columns should therefore be ignored.[3]

Check-marks should next be entered in columns 4 to 16 against

---

[2] In the preceding chart, averages for three-year periods are presented instead of the exact figures for single years. The reason for this frequent statistical practice is that the presentation of data by single years is unnecessarily extensive, that the method of averages avoids the blurring of general tendencies by reason of exceptional changes occurring in single years, and that the resulting figures tend to represent results lasting over a considerable period of time. See chap. v, pp. 129 f., on the value of condensing presentation of results.

[3] For directions for the use of these columns, see pp. 75 f.

SCHEDULE I

Church Members and Adherents

CHURCH

ADDRESS

DISTRICT Nº

WARD Nº

		1	2	3	4	5	6	7	8	9	10	11	12	13	14	15	16
		FAMILY NAME	WHERE BORN	OCCUPATION (See Key on Back of Card)		SUNDAY SCHOOL MEMBER	MEMBER CHURCH ORGANIZATIONS										PLEDGED CONTRIBUTIONS

WHERE BORN: U.S. — CITY / RURAL; OTHER COUNTRY (Give Name)

OCCUPATION (See Key on Back of Card)

CHURCH OFFICER / CHURCH MEMBER / REGULAR ATTENDANT

SUNDAY SCHOOL MEMBER

MEMBER CHURCH ORGANIZATIONS:
6 ADULT MIXED — 1 2
7 ADULT MEN'S — 1 2
8 ADULT WOMEN'S — 1 2 3 4
9 YOUNG PEOPLE'S MIXED — 1 2
10 YOUNG MEN'S — 1 2 3
11 YOUNG WOMEN'S — 1 2 3
12 CHILDREN'S MIXED — 1
13 BOYS' — 1 2 3
14 GIRLS' — 1 2 3
15 CHILDREN UNDER 5 YEARS — 1 2

PLEDGED CONTRIBUTIONS

A FAMILY NAME
B ADDRESS
C DISTANCE / DIRECTION
D FATHER'S NAME
E MOTHER'S NAME
F —M / F OTHERS
G
H
I

CHILDREN UNDER 21: BOYS / GIRLS / AGE
J
K
L
M
N

Signed......................

Date......................

each name, showing every membership that any person may have in the church or any of its subsidiary organizations. The amount of each contributor's weekly pledge (in the size-group to which it belongs—as, under five cents weekly, five to nine cents, nine to fifteen cents, etc.) should be entered in column 16.

For columns 6-15, a key-card will have to be prepared showing the particular organizations which the church maintains for each age and sex. Such a key for a St. Louis church is illustrated in the following list:

Type of Organization	*Name*
Adult Men's	Men's Triangle Club
Adult Women's	Women's Foreign Missionary Society Women's Home Missionary Society Business Women's Missionary Society Ladies' Aid Society Mothercraft Club
Young People's Mixed	Epworth League Dramatic Club
Young Men's	Kappa Sigma Pi Luccock Lodge House Organization Phi Beta Phi
Young Women's	Queen Esthers Standard Bearers
Children's Mixed	Intermediate-Senior Epworth League Junior Church (two groups) Home Guard Heralds Daily Vacation Bible School and Craft School
Boys'	Boy Scouts
Girls'	Camp Fire Girls
Children under Five Years	Mothers' Jewels Little Light Bearers

When the cards are filled out for all a church's constituents, Column 4 constitutes a complete church-membership roll, Column 5 a complete Sunday-school roll, and successive columns are complete lists of all subsidiary organizations.

One then sees at a glance just what relations each listed individual has to the church; and by counting the check-marks one can tell how many relations each individual or family has.

Probably some cards will bear names without check-marks. They will represent persons whom the church lists because it has some sense of responsibility for them, or feels that some sentimental tie exists, though they do not belong to it in any determinate way. These indeterminate adherents may then be distinguished from the determinate ones.

Again, of recorded adherents, some belong to adherent families while others are detached individuals whose families do not adhere to the church. In brief, the card enables one to distinguish a number of classes of adherents apart from the classes already indicated by column headings. The next step is to count the constituents of each class the church has. Suppose the first count is to discover the number belonging to family groups or detached individuals who are determinate and indeterminate adherents, according to sex and to broad age-groups.

This will be accomplished through two processes: first by sorting the cards of adherents from adherent families into one pile and those of detached individuals into another. The names in each pile may then be counted and the number in each entered. (It will facilitate this process if cards of different colors are used for the two classes to start with.)

Further counting requires tally sheets, because the names of more than one class of adherents may occur on a single card. Tally sheets in the following form should be drawn up, one for family group adherents and one for individuals.

TABLE II

TALLY SHEET —NUMBER OF ADHERENTS

	ADHERENTS		
	Total	*Determinate*	*Indeterminate*
Class of Adherents			
Total			
Adult			
Adolescent			
Child			
Infant			
Male			
Total			
Adult			
Adolescent			
Child			
Infant			
Female			
Total			
Adult			
Adolescent			
Child			
Infant			

In filling out the tally sheet, two persons should work together. One, the reader, should read off the class of constituent that each name on the cards represents: as, "determinate adherent, male, adult," "indeterminate adherent, female, child," etc. The other, the scorer, makes a score-mark in the space corresponding to the classification read for each name. As each name is read, the reader should make a light check-mark above it so that none may be repeated or omitted, and the scorer should repeat the classification after him to be sure that it is correctly understood.

When the scores are all entered they are counted, the totals arrived at by addition (and confirmed by the previous count of the cards). A tally sheet of the same form may now be used as a table showing the result of the count by the substitution of figures for check-marks. A similar table should be made for detached individual adherents and the two combined into a table for total adherents.

Similar counts by means of sorting cards and the use of the tally sheets should be made and tabulated on the following points:

(1) Number of members of church; Sunday school; of each subsidiary; number of financial contributors, officers, regular attendants

(2) Number of exclusive memberships
    a. in church only
    b. in Sunday school only
    c. in subsidiary organizations only

(3) Number of overlapping memberships
    a. in church and Sunday school
    b. in church and subsidiaries
    c. in church, Sunday school and subsidiaries, all three

(4) Number of adherents belonging to the church in one, two, three, four, five, six and seven or more ways

This covers generally the topics of size and composition of constituency and the number of the several kinds of constituents; and carries this phase of the study as far as can be expected in a semi-intensive project.[4] The scientific gain is that the church now knows accurately how large is the human social group that has been gathered together in its name, and of what sort of units it is composed. The practical gain is that, with all the factors before it, the church can begin to reconsider how to make any given constituent's status more valuable to him and more satisfactory to itself.

2. The Church Studying its Parish

In a semi-intensive research, the study of the parish may reasonably be confined to the making of such spot-maps as are desirable anyhow from the standpoint of parish records and administration, and to counting the number of constituents of various sorts who live at given distances and directions from the church. These processes show the geographical distribution of the church's individual units.

The basis of the spot-map is the constituent's address as given in the upper left-hand corner of the card shown in the last section.

Each address must be located on a map. This may be done with approximate accuracy by means of a street directory giving the

---

4 The same subject is dealt with more intensively in chap. iii, pp. 78 ff.

numbers of all houses on each street block by block. Such directories are on commercial sale in all important cities.

The map should be of sufficient size to make the location clear. If not printed on durable paper, it should be mounted on cloth. Maps may sometimes be secured inexpensively by borrowing originals from city engineer's offices or city planning boards and having copies made photographically; or they may be bought from commercial map makers. A scale of one inch to at least two hundred feet is desirable. In a large parish the map may need to be mounted and handled in sections; but arrangements should be made so that these may be displayed together when necessary, showing the entire

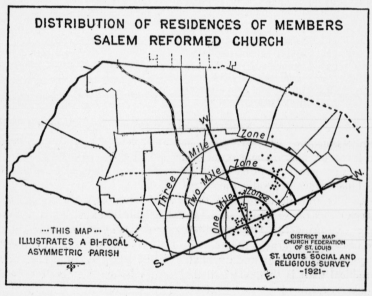

DISTRIBUTION OF RESIDENCES OF MEMBERS
SALEM REFORMED CHURCH

···THIS MAP···
ILLUSTRATES A BI-FOCAL
ASYMMETRIC PARISH

DISTRICT MAP
CHURCH FEDERATION
OF ST. LOUIS
ST. LOUIS SOCIAL AND
RELIGIOUS SURVEY
-1921-

CHART II—A PARISH SPOT MAP.

parish at once. Where, as frequently happens, parishes overlap city boundaries, getting maps of the same scale may be difficult. Regional planning boards, however, may have mapped these larger districts; or special drawings may have to be made.

The base map for use in the parish study should show only streets and their names, with a very few major structural features of the city, like rivers, railroads and physical barriers to growth. Greater detail than this confuses the eye unnecessarily. The best way of mapping a constituent's home is to indicate it by a spot or circle, which, on a map of the scale suggested, may be one-fourth of an inch in diameter. The best means of making the spot is by the use of a special spotting pen applied in the manner of a rubber stamp, but leaving a clear-cut impression in solid ink. In case too many constituents live in a given block to permit the mapping of enough spots within the block boundaries, a few spots can be located in adjacent blocks and connecting lines drawn to show where they ought to be. This will not happen often if the map is of the size suggested.

The number of individual adherents living at the address indicated by each spot may then be entered in white ink upon each spot, or in black within each circle.

One who is willing to take the pains, can, instead, ink in small dots of different colors to indicate the manner of adherence of each constituent as distinguished in the previous section. But over-elaborate maps are hard to read, and it is really better to make a series of spot maps, one for each of the major constituencies, as follows:

(1) Church-members
(2) Sunday-school pupils
(3) Members of subsidiaries (indicating the particular organization by colored dots)
(4) Church and other officers
(5) Contributors, etc.

As an alternative to the method of mapping here suggested, maps indicating the addresses of different constituencies by means of colored pins are often used. Their advantages are presumed to be that pins can be located more accurately and changed as addresses change.

TABLE III

TABLE   —TOTAL RESIDENT CONSTITUENCY, BY THE DISTANCE AND DIRECTION OF THEIR RESIDENCE FROM THE CHURCH BUILDING

DISTANCE	ALL DIRECTIONS	DIRECTION				
		North-east	*South-east*	*South-west*	*North-west*	*Address not Reported*
Total Constituency						
Less than ½ mile						
½ to 1 mile						
1 to 2 miles						
2 to 3 miles						
3 to 4 miles						
4 to 5 miles						
Over 5 miles						
Out of city						
Not reported						

NOTE: Family Group Constituents and Individual Constituents may be recorded in the same way, their sum automatically checking the totals.

But one ought not to try to use a map as a directory of exact addresses; besides, pins are rarely changed often enough to keep the locations fully up to date. Again, one chief use of the parish map

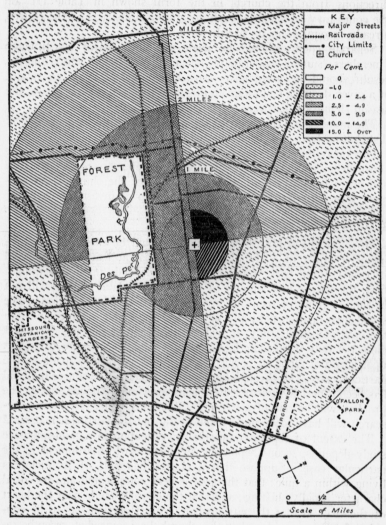

CHART III—A PARISH MAP SHOWING DISTRIBUTION OF A CHURCH'S ADHERENTS BY ZONES AND SECTORS.

is to preserve the record of the distribution of constituents in the past so as to compare with that of future years. This cannot be accomplished by changing pins.

It is really better to go to the expense of securing enough base maps of proper scale, to spot them by the rapid methods suggested, and then to keep them for comparison.

Parish data as derived from spot-maps may be summarized after simple counting of constituents' residences according to distance and directions from the church, in the form shown in Table III; or the count may be made by such geographical districts as the church already recognizes in its parish work.

Separate counts should be made for each major constituency (members, Sunday-school pupils, officers, contributors, etc.), and the results should be compared to see whether one of them is stronger at a given distance or in a given direction than the others. If so, the reason should be discovered if possible.[5]

The number and character of the constituency and its geographical distribution have now been covered by the study.

Obviously, however, the geographical distribution of the church's constituency cannot be understood without reference to the structure and characteristics of its city. The study of the church's environment thus necessarily becomes the next step of investigation.

3. *Environment and Relation to the City*

How far the study of environment should be carried in a semi-intensive study of a church (assuming that at least the minimum necessary for a background is secured) depends upon two things: first, the nature and amount of the available data. There will not be time to think of securing any really first-hand information; since social investigation naturally takes much time and is expensive. In the environmental study, it will be necessary to depend, for exact data, not only upon material commonly available in large cities, but upon any inventory of social investigations previously made in the particular city. If, through happy circumstances, the source material has been especially assembled for some previous religious survey, the problem will be one of selection. Otherwise a piece of literary research will have to be undertaken to dig out the pertinent material.[6]

The extent of the environmental investigation in a semi-intensive study depends, second, upon the significance of environment in the particular case. Suppose that a church has half of its members living within a mile; that the area is very complicated and its social character rapidly shifting; and that the church stands near the heart of the city, so that the city's whole central portion has to be considered. Suppose also that the church has somewhat recently removed to its present location, that it is discussing both the further adaptation of its program to the needs of the locality and the erection of a new building. These conditions would warrant a very extra emphasis upon the environmental study. If, on the other hand, a

---

5 For a more intensive parish study, see pp. 167 ff.

6 For a further discussion of commonly available environmental and social data, see pp. 161 ff.

church occupies a static neighborhood to which it is well adapted and which offers it no acute problems, then the environmental study may well be limited.[7]

Sources

The specific data usually available in an environmental study are as follows:

(a) Statistics of population for the whole city and by wards derived from the Federal Census (see *1920 Census,* Vol. III, Table 13 under all states), which gives the total population by age and sex and by nationality, as native white, foreign-born and Negro, etc.

(b) School statistics, for the whole city and by school districts (usually found in published reports of the Board of Education), sometimes indicate the place of birth of pupils and enable one to trace the location of incoming rural population as well as of foreigners. Most progressive school systems carry on occasional social researches showing, for example, the relation of race and nationality to school attendance and standing. These should be carefully studied.

(c) The physical structure of the city and of the areas falling within the parish boundaries of the church as determined by the original topography of the land and the occupancy by railways, industries, parks, etc., together with the major street plan and calculation of traffic density, will be set forth in the various reports of the City Plan Commission or by maps in the City Engineer's office.

(d) The economic character of the church's environment may frequently be determined from housing and rent maps calculated by small enumeration precincts. Such maps are often made by commercial agencies to show the buying power of different districts served by retail trade. For example, a five-months study (in which thirty canvassers were employed) was made by the *St. Louis Post Dispatch* in 1925 in connection with an advertising campaign.

(e) The relation of rents and assessed values of land to parks and open spaces, on the one hand, and to business and industry on the other, may be observed by comparing the City Plan structural and use maps with economic maps. This comparison will show how far the church's constituency occupies desirable spots or areas, and how far its environment is unfortunate.

(f) The geography of the city's social evolution will probably have been studied by the City Plan Commission, which may have mapped population, industries, etc., as they were located ten and twenty years ago, and may have shown structural changes by periods. Geographi-

[7] The making of social surveys as a background for religious investigations on a community-wide scale is discussed in detail in chapter vii. The present paragraph does not therefore attempt to give adequate directions for making environmental studies in the investigation of the individual church. It simply points out the sources of information that are typically available to a city church, so that they may be consulted, digested, and used in the interpretation of the parish data already secured.

cal evolution may have been implied in the church's own history. Its successive removals will show the path along which the major growth of the city has proceeded and suggest its most acute changes. The attempt of the zoning ordinance to control the evolution should be studied from the zone plans. Maps showing all the churches of the area at present and ten and twenty years ago should be compiled from lists found in old city directories.

(g) The social structure of the environment as determined by the location of distinct populations, such as Negro, Jewish and rural colonies, Irish and German clusters, and solid areas of native white population, should be mapped from the census data and from field observation. The economic status of these social groups may be judged by the appearance of their houses and streets; and the observation may be checked by reference to the rent and housing maps for the same areas.

(h) The social quality and relative social levels of the people in different parts of the parish area may also be discovered through the records of philanthropic and social agencies. Either the central Council of Social Agencies or the separate agencies may have spot-maps showing such pathological conditions as dependency, delinquency, tuberculosis and infant mortality, and bad health of school children. These will show how far the parish area is identified with these evils, and whether conditions are better or worse than elsewhere.

As these sources are consulted, accurate notes will, of course, be made. As a means of transcription and record, the investigator is urged to provide himself with a plentiful supply of cheap maps on which he may roughly express the facts as he finds them. Such maps are frequently issued for advertising purposes and may be had for the asking; or base maps, showing little detail, and hence better for such use, may be bought from commercial map makers. The amateur must simply imitate the methods of mapping data that he finds on the source maps consulted. He should have a set of child's colored crayons. He should work fast, not trying for great accuracy but simply to catch the essential facts and to transcribe them as aids to his memory and as illustrations of his notes. Then, too, striking environmental conditions that have been discovered in the ordinary cultivation of the parish should be photographed.

As a result of the study, by these methods, of such typical sources as have been suggested, a clear statement should finally be drawn up concerning the church's social background. It should cover the following points:

1. General characterization of the parish area, as to physical structure; use by business, industry, transportation, homes; function within the general life of the city; subdivisions into smaller areas having uniform characteristics.

2. Population; number by total and by age and sex; number by age and sex of church's adherents relative to total population.

3. Character of population; by race and nationality; and by economic status and occupation.

4. Extent and form of parish as affected by character of population. With what sorts of people is it identified, and how exhaustively with each? Does it occupy its territory totally or selectively? What special affinities does it show—for high-rent areas? for vicinity of parks? for neighborhood of former site? What avoidance does it show—for Negro and industrial areas? for apartment-house sections?

5. The parish area as it was five and ten years ago (determined by old membership and address lists), and the character of the present parish area, as to physical extent and structure, population, etc.

6. The nature and direction of the social changes now going on in the parish area; e.g., growth or decline of population and character of population, derived from comparing United States census figures for wards for the last census and for previous censuses, *provided the ward boundaries have not changed,* foreshadow their probable effect upon the fortunes of the church in the future.

Such a study of the church's environment as has been outlined will carry one as far as one can reasonably hope to go in a limited comprehensive investigation. Its results ought to suggest numerous points to be considered in practical church policies, and to afford the understanding a more profound grasp upon the underlying forces that make or unmake the church on levels deeper than those of deliberate effort.

4. *Organizations and Activities*

The number and relationships of members and constituents, the parish and geographical distribution of constituency, and the larger environmental relations of the church, are aspects of it that show the consequences of large forces, chiefly of instinctive origin, operating according to long-time trends; so that to alter them significantly is beyond the immediate control of the church's purpose at a given moment, or of such relatively short-time policies as church plans usually have to do with.

The study of organizations and activities, on the contrary, passes over to aspects of the church in action. It now begins to deal with matters immediately subject to control by the every-day decisions of ministers and church bodies.

As considered in the earlier section, the church in the largest sense consists of a social group united by ties that may in many instances be largely nominal; and exhibits a fringe of adherents bound to it by merely psychological bonds, such as sentiment and religious predilections. These things, however, are recognized as expressing latent attitudes and as having real significance in defining the institution.

In contrast with this view, the church is now to be considered as a body of active participants identified through their relations with specific organizations and activities. In the highly organized church these organizations are very numerous. For example, a St. Louis church announced sixteen meetings for organized activities during a sample week studied. The meetings stood for a wide range of objects and the use of a great variety of methods. The sum total of these organizations and activities constitutes the totality of the church in what may be called its motor aspects; that is to say, in contrast with its hidden sentiments and motives. Activities do not, of course, reveal the whole of the church but merely its characteristics as a purposefully organized group.

The natural measure of the church in this aspect is attendance. There may be spiritual unity without the assembling of the constituent body; but participation in the active program is, in the main, expressed by getting people together (not always in the church building) in services, meetings and group exercises. It is obviously important to understand and measure the church in this respect.

Methods

The two most fundamental steps in the method of study are:

(1) A complete inventory of all organizations and activities, followed by the gathering of data concerning them.

(2) A method of classification and definition that enables one to simplify and summarize the whole for purposes of presentation and comparison.

These two steps are taken by filling out, in the following form, a schedule of attendance on all regular services and meetings of organizations and stated activities.

Definitions

A schedule such as the foregoing involves categories that have to be given precise definition. By regular services and meetings of organizations and stated activities, it is meant to include everything that a church carries on regularly as frequently as once a month throughout the active church season (whether or not the activity has a determinate membership, provided that the activity is recognized by the church and that there are regularly appointed officers and leaders); also whatever the church regularly does seasonally through several consecutive days or weeks, such as operating a summer camp or a Daily Vacation Bible School.

But it is meant to exclude all special or merely occasional activities or single events, even though they occur annually. A separate schedule in the same form is used to summarize these extras so that the church's total attendance, both on regular and on special events, may be shown.

The study assumes that the most significant distinctions within the total activities-program are those between Sunday and week-day

SCHEDULE   —ANNUAL ATTENDANCE ON REGULAR SERVICES AND MEETINGS OF ORGANIZATIONS AND
STATED ACTIVITIES

Church................., Denomination................, City................, Date................

	CHURCH'S TOTAL MEMBER-SHIP	STATED ACTIVITIES						
		WEEK DAY			SUNDAY			TOTAL
		Weekly Attendance	Weeks in Operation	Total Attending	Attendance per Sunday	Sundays in Operation	Total Attending	Weekly Attendance	Total Attending

Total

I. Formal Religious Services
 Sunday morning
 Sunday evening
 Other Sunday services
 Week-day
II. Sunday School
 (Branch Sunday school included)
III. All Other Meetings and Activities
 Church officers
 Standing and important special
  committees
 A. Classified by Age and Sex
  Mixed organizations for adults
  Organizations for adult men
  Organizations for adult women
  Mixed organizations for young
   people (15-23)
  Organizations for young men
  Organizations for young women
  Mixed organizations for boys
   and girls
  Organizations for boys
  Organizations for girls
  Mixed organizations for children
 B. Classified by Function rather
  than by Age and Sex
   a.
   b.
   c. (etc.)

activities; between church, Sunday-school, and subsidiary activities; and, within the subsidiary group, between the various age- and sex-groups included in the activity, on the one hand, and activities defined by function rather than by age and sex, on the other.

Filling Out the Schedules

The names of each particular service of the church and of each subsidiary organization and activity are to be entered upon the schedule under the proper classification. Average weekly attendance will then be entered according to week-day and Sunday activities, and the total annual attendance in each activity arrived at by multiplying the average attendance by the number of weeks in the year in operation. It should be noted again that the total reached through this method does not purport to give total attendance, but rather comparable attendance on stated activities that definitely characterize the church and its operations over significant periods of time. They thus constitute a fair basis of comparison between one year and another; which would not be the case if extra and occasional events were included, since the latter are more apt to fluctuate.

The accuracy of estimated average attendance in the case of activities for which no attendance records are systematically kept needs, of course, to be carefully guarded. Whenever possible, the estimates of several informed persons should be compared, and original records should frequently be resorted to. Any church that attempts such a summary of attendance on its total program of activities is likely to discover at how many points its records are vague or absent; and will naturally institute an actual count over a series of months to check the estimate with the facts.[8]

Summary

The following example indicates how to take the second step of method; namely, summarization.

TABLE IV

TABLE —DISTRIBUTION OF ESTIMATED ANNUAL CHURCH ATTENDANCE

Occasion	Attendance	
	Number	*Per Cent.*
Total		
Sunday		
Week-day		
Formal religious services (Sunday and week-day)		
Sunday school		
All other stated activities *		

* Include meetings of church officers and committees.

8 One should avoid the impression that carefully checked estimates are not valid in statistics. On the contrary, they may be very important. The whole scheme of government reporting on crop prospects, for example, is based on estimates.

The classified summary of attendance on subsidiary organizations may be made in the form shown for a St. Louis church by the following table.

TABLE V

TABLE —ESTIMATED ANNUAL ATTENDANCE ON SUBSIDI-
ARY ORGANIZATIONS AND STATED ACTIVITIES

ORGANIZATION	ATTENDANCE		NUMBER OF ORGANIZATIONS
	Number	Per Cent.	
Total	17,586	100	19
Mixed organizations for adults	0	0	0
Organizations for adult men	400	2	1
Organizations for adult women	2,900	16	4
Mixed organizations for young people (ages 15–23)	4,960	28	2
Organizations for young men	675	4	2
Organizations for young women	975	6	3
Mixed organizations for boys and girls	6,140	35	3
Organizations for boys	960	5	1
Organizations for girls	450	3	1
Mixed organizations for children	126	1	2

The relative magnitudes of the various parts of the church program should next be studied. The church just used for illustration had no subsidiary activities that could not be classified by the age and sex served. Numerically speaking, the boys' and girls' program was shown to constitute a large third of the total subsidiary activity of the church, the mixed young people's organizations coming second, and women's organizations third. Summarizing the entire subsidiary program with respect to sex alignment, it was found to classify as follows: of activities for men, 11 per cent.; of activities for women, 25 per cent.; and of activities for mixed groups, 64 per cent.

It is probably unwise to attempt to summarize the church's activity program according to the professed objectives or dominant interests of the organizations: such as devotional, educational, recreational, missionary, etc.; the reason being that on any fair analysis all organizations perform multiple functions. A public church service, for example, is obviously a mixture of devotional, instructional, and social activity; and whatever its announced purpose, its actual purpose covers all three.

Value and Limitations

The value of such a summary and classification of the church's total activities program as have just been shown is, first, that it throws light on the problems of balance and proportion in the internal organization of the church; and, second, that such analysis repeated from year to year enables the church to trace the growth, not only of its separate departments and activities, but of their proportions and relationships to the total program over a period of time. Some of the problems that such a study raises are: (1) What is the desirable balance between the Sunday and the week-day program in a given church? (2) What is the desirable balance between the church, the Sunday-school and the subsidiary program? (3) What is the right balance between activities for the different ages and sexes? (4) Is it better to have more organizations and meetings, or fewer with broader and more adequately carried out functions? (5) How far are the ostensible objects of church activities the real objects? When are the moral and religious values of activities equivalent and when not equivalent? (6) Has this church organizations and activities that it does not need, or has it omitted some that it does need? Could any be recombined to advantage?

5. *The Study of the Ministry*

The semi-intensive study of the ministry in a church will be covered in two main divisions: first, by securing the personnel records of the paid workers; second, by a comparative study of the duties these workers performed during one or more sample weeks.

The Personnel Record

It is to be assumed that at the time each worker was engaged the church had looked into his experience and qualifications, and that the various salaries were a matter of annual consideration and record. The collection of these data in systematic form is obviously a vital phase of the scientific study of the present church. They may be regarded as in the nature of a review of the facts with reference to comparison and a consideration of their relations to other aspects of the church as revealed by study.

An outline of the schedule to be used in this part of the study follows on page 30.

Summary: A convenient method of summarizing the findings of the personnel record is shown in the illustrative data on page 31.

Method of Studying the Staff at Work

A rigidly statistical study of the staff at work, on the basis of careful work-records, would be so intensive as to be disproportionate compared with the treatment of other topics included in this semi-intensive study. The statement of the full method is therefore reserved for presentation under the head "Intensive Topical Studies" in chapter iii. But even in a limited study, it would be well to have each member of the staff keep a work-record for a week according to the form shown on page 90, to tabulate the results as shown on page 121, and to try to interpret them in common sense terms.

Schedule III

SCHEDULE —OUTLINE OF PERSONNEL RECORD

(To be filled out for each Paid Worker of the Church Staff)

Name .... Sex .... Position.................. Approximate Age ....

Education

Academic: (1) secondary school completed............; (2) college—two or more years (?)..........; graduated (?)..........
Professional: (1) theological course (number of years)..........; (2) post-graduate (number of years)..........; (3) religious training school—(kind.........., number of years attended..........; graduated..........); (4) other schools—(kind.........., number of years attended.........., graduated..........).
Continuation: education via short courses, etc. (Number and kinds specified)................................
(1) taken in regular institutions..........; (2) or reading courses, institutes, etc. ....;

Experience and Tenure

Gainful employment before entering religious work:
Kinds ....
Number of years spent in each ....
Religious work other than in present profession:
Kinds ....
Number of years spent in each ....
Present profession (years spent in)......................
Years with present church:
(1) In position prior to this one..........
(2) In this position..........

Pay

Amount of cash salary..........; allowance for board and lodging..........; other perquisites..........
Additional pay: parsonage with rental value..........
(estimate cash value of each)

Vacation

Length of vacation on pay..........

Pension

Does office entitle worker to an ecclesiastical pension?..........

30

Some of the questions that may be answered from the record by means of simple calculation are:

How long is the minister or other worker on duty during the average day or week?

How much of his time is spent in cultural pursuits not immediately related to any other specific duty, but which must be allowed because necessary for an effective ministry in the long run?

TABLE VI

TABLE —QUALIFICATIONS, EXPERIENCE AND SALARIES OF
A CHURCH STAFF

	STAFF		
	Pastor	Director Religious Education	Children's Worker
Sex	Male	Male	Female
Degree of Education			
Academic	None	College	Secondary school
Professional or special	None	None	Kindergarten training school
Years of employment			
Prior to this position			
Secular work	8	0	2
Religious work	38	5	0
In this position	3	2	2
Present salary			
Cash	$5,500	$2,400 *	*
Perquisites			
Nature	None	House, auto, heat, light, laundry	
Value	None	$760	*
Entitled to ecclesiastical pension	Yes	Yes	No
Length of vacation	4 weeks	2 weeks	2 weeks

* The director of religious education and his wife, the latter holding the position of "children's worker," receive this salary and perquisites jointly.

As measured by the length of time spent upon each of the recognized chief divisions of the minister's work (preaching, pastoral work or administration) which is primary in the sense of consuming a fourth or more of the entire day's time and which secondary or less?

Judged on the same points, how does the assistant minister's work differ?

Is the Director of Religious Education chiefly employed in professional duties peculiar to his office or in general church work? What are his specific professional duties and how is his time distributed between these and his other work?

How much of the church secretary's work is distinctively clerical and how much administrative work of a minor sort? Does some of it require her to counsel and comfort people who come to the church office? In these cases is it pastoral?

The use of the work-record also enables one to go back of the nominal designations of workers and to reclassify them according to actual functions. This is often necessary. In one case, for example, the duties of the "children's worker" were found to be exceedingly miscellaneous, the main ones being those of church hostess for many social activities and not a few of the duties of a working house-keeper; while group work for children was quite secondary. The record also enables one to compare workers with one another and with those in similar positions elsewhere whose records may be known.

6. Staff Organization and Relationships

For the church that has no paid worker except a minister, this topic will have no meaning. But where a staff exists, the study of relationships of the members to the governing bodies and internal organizations of the church, and to one another, is obviously significant.

Schedules covering these points follow. Their categories are largely self-explanatory, and clearly indicate the tangible relationships that it is regarded as important to record.

The following schedule concerns the relationships of paid workers to the lay governing bodies of the church. (See page 33.)

The theoretical status of the minister in his church differs with the denominations and often from church to church. In general he may be "under" or "over" the several local lay boards of the church; or he may have concurrent authority with them in their respective spheres of operation. The forms in which these relationships are commonly expressed are suggested in the first column of the schedule; and the classified list of the boards and governing authorities of the particular church is written in at the head of the succeeding columns. The schedule is filled out for each worker by checking each relationship that pertains with each board, etc.

Subordinate church workers (unless themselves ordained) may have very slight relation to the machinery of church government unless they report to some special departmental committee.

A second schedule, similar in form and filled out in the same way, relates to the subsidiary organizations of the church. It is constructed by writing in the left-hand column the classified list of these organizations as shown on page 26, and in adding columns representing the possible formal relations that can grow out of the position of, or fall to, a paid worker, viz., (1) president of organization, (2) secretary, (3) treasurer, (4) superintendent, (5) technical director, (6) regular group leader, (7) teacher, (8) unofficial leader, (9) expected-to-be member of, (10) other. Some of these terms require definition. A technical director is one who has charge of an organization from a particular standpoint; as, for example, a coach with respect to athletics or dramatics while the ordinary operation of the organization is left to its officers. An unofficial leader

SCHEDULE IV

SCHEDULE —MINISTER'S (OR OTHER PAID CHURCH WORKER'S) RELATIONS TO LAY BOARDS, COMMITTEES, ETC., WITHIN LOCAL CHURCH*

NOTE: Check L (by law of denomination or constitution of local church), or C (by custom but not by definite law) in each appropriate space.

Relation Sustained	Chief Spiritual Officers (Deacons, Elders, etc.)	Chief Business Officers (Trustees, Stewards, etc.)	Other Regular Boards or Committees†	Subsidiary Church Organizations	Special Committees	Church Cabinet‡
Name of Worker						
Is member of						
(a) Ex-officio						
(b) By election						
Is ex-officio president or chairman						
Holds other office in						
Habitually meets with in formal sessions						
Makes stated formal reports to						
May be assigned specific responsibilities by						
Works concurrently with in some part of function						

* Provide a column for, and write in name of, each particular board or committee of the church.
† Created by constitution or by-laws of church.
‡ Consisting of officers or representatives of all interests.

33

is one designated by the church to advise or "keep an eye" on a subsidiary organization without being elected to such a position by the organization itself. "Expected-to-be member of" stands for a situation in which a church worker without official relations to an organization would nevertheless be criticized if he did not belong to it. This is often a very real situation. Calculate the number of ways in which each staff member is related to subsidiary organization, and compare the staff members as to the kinds of relationship sustained. The study of this schedule reveals the extent to which the work of members of the staff of the church is tied up to, and occupied by, the affairs of subsidiary organizations, some of which were previously conducted entirely by lay workers.

Relationships expressing authority and subordination within the staff are recorded by checking on the following schedules.

SCHEDULE V

SCHEDULE —PRINCIPAL WORKER'S RELATION TO SUBORDINATE ON STAFF

Principal Worker's Name............................ Subordinate's Name............................

1. Recommends for

   a. Employment

   b. Discharge

2. Makes direct assignment of work

3. Supervises by personal inspection of work

4. Supervises by conference and receipt of reports

   a. Formal

   b. Informal

5. Intervenes in case of unsatisfactory work

6. Coördinates work with other Departments but does not

   a. Direct

   b. Supervise

7. Has no responsibility for fellow worker because

   a. Fellow worker reports to some other staff member

   b. Fellow worker reports to some one outside Church

   c. Fellow worker is under direction of Lay Church officer or Board

   d. Fellow worker is employed to work independently

   e. Fellow worker's conditions determined by staff action

   f. Other reason

SCHEDULE VI

SCHEDULE —SUBORDINATE WORKER'S RELATION TO PRINCIPAL WORKER

Subordinate's Name..Principal's Name.................................

1. Is recommended for

   a. Employment by

   b. Discharge by

2. Receives direct assignment of work from

3. Work is personally inspected by

4. Makes reports to

   a. Formal

   b. Informal

5. Unsatisfactory work is criticized by

6. Is not directed by

7. Is not supervised by

The results show the lines of authority in the staff, and the outward ways in which it is expressed. Calculate the frequency with which each phase of superior or subordinate authority occurs in the staff, and note the predominant forms. These studies are useful in clarifying relationships, and often suggest their possible modifications.

CHAPTER II

THE SEMI-INTENSIVE STUDY OF A SINGLE CHURCH (*Cont.*)

7. *Plant*

The study of the church's plant and equipment can best be made by means of the Interchurch thousand-point score-card for rating city churches. This was developed for the Interchurch World Movement by a group of experts, and was used in the well-known Malden survey.[1]

The complete study of the church plant by means of the apparatus cited carries one into an intensive topical study. But by the use of the score-card without the accompanying elaborate measurements, it may be kept proportionate to the other topics of the semi-intensive study.

The Interchurch score-card contains 121 items, grouped under the major and secondary headings shown in the following summary of the score of a St. Louis church. Each item and group of items (as shown in the first column) is assigned a numerical value, the total adding to the perfect score, 1,000.

In the application of this method to a given church, the church plant is carefully inspected and independently scored, item by item, against the standard score by three competent judges, the final figure being the average of the three scores.

The method of entering the score is illustrated for the St. Louis church in the column headed "Allotted Score" in the following table.

In the illustrated case, the church scored nearly three-fourths of the possible score with respect to site, and more than two-thirds of the possible score with respect to building and church rooms. On the other hand, it scored only a little more than one-third of the possible score on service systems and religious school rooms, and only one-fourth of the possible score on community service rooms, the resulting total score being less than half the possible one.

An explanation of the discrepancy between the ideal and the actual score should be appended to the score-card. In the case just cited, the explanation read as follows:

> The lot has 240 foot frontage on Delmar Boulevard, with a depth of about 120 feet. It is terraced and stands high above the street; and the buildings, erected in the roomier era of the city's growth,

[1] *Standards for City Church Plants* (New York: Interchurch World Movement, 1920); Athearn, *Malden Survey* (New York: Interchurch World Movement, 1919); Athearn, *The Indiana Survey of Religious Education* (New York: Doran, 1924), Vol. I, p. 93; Vol. II, chap. v.

have ample space about them. This situation permits the high score shown with respect to location, nature and condition, and size and form of the site.

TABLE VII

TABLE —SUMMARIZED SCORE-CARD FOR CHURCH PLANT

ITEM	STANDARD SCORE (a)	ALLOTTED SCORE (b)	RATIO OF (B) TO (A) %
Total	1,000	481	48
I. Site	130	96	74
A. Location	55	44	
B. Nature and condition	30	20	
C. Size and form	45	32	
II. Building or buildings	150	102	68
A. Placement	20	16	
B. Gross structure	80	57	
C. Internal structure	50	29	
III. Service systems	160	56	35
A. Heating and ventilation	40	20	
B. Fire protection system	40	4	
C. Cleaning system	10	6	
D. Artificial lighting system	15	6	
E. Water supply system	15	4	
F. Toilet system	25	11	
G. Other service systems	10	3	
H. Service rooms	5	2	
IV. Church rooms	170	113	67
A. Convenience of arrangement	20	16	
B. Auditorium	100	69	
C. Chapel or small assembly	15	7	
D. Parlor and church-board room	5	3	
E. Church office	10	7	
F. Pastor's study	15	11	
G. Church vault	5	0	
V. Religious school rooms	200	67	34
A. Location and connection	15	7	
B. Assembly room	60	20	
C. Classrooms	90	36	
D. Cloak rooms and wardrobes	15	0	
E. Superintendent's office	10	2	
F. Supply rooms	10	2	
VI. Community service rooms	190	47	25
A. Rooms for general use	60	30	
B. Rooms for social service	70	17	
C. Recreation and athletic rooms	60	0	

The church is a dignified stone structure of more or less consistent Romanesque architecture, and well built according to the standards of its time. The rooms for public worship are ample and dignified without being churchly in the oppressive sense. These conditions permit the relatively high scores on building and church rooms. The fact that the service systems are those of forty years ago is obvious explanation of the low score on that point. The church is equally out of date with respect to modern Sunday-school construction, though its quite ample chapel and social rooms give a fair opportunity for departmentalization. A limited amount of equipment has been secured for community service, but there has been no extensive reconstruction of or addition to the church with special community functions in mind. In brief, the church was built for a different program from that which is now going on in it. The score merely reflects this fact.

To carry out the scoring of the plant, it will be necessary to get the full score-card and directions for its use in one of the books cited in the first footnote in this chapter. The judges should read and talk over the directions together and then do their work independently. Suitable judges for a self-survey would be the pastor of the church, a good architect, and a competent local builder.[2]

8. *Finances*

It is fair to assume that a semi-intensive study of church finance cannot be expected to go back of the periodical summary statements resulting from church bookkeeping; it will not examine the books of original entry. Accuracy, so far as such summaries go, will have to be presumed. But, on the basis of sad experience, completeness cannot be counted on; and comparable form from year to year is not to be expected.

The first data of the study will be found in the summarized (and perhaps published) financial reports for the last church or conference year. One may hope that this summary will distinguish the major accounts: such as (1) the current account of the church; (2) the permanent property account; (3) the current benevolent account; and (4) an account of any commercial activities involving outgo as well as income, only the net results of which should be admitted to the final summary. If several accounts are kept, rather than one subdivided account, it will be necessary to combine the results into a summary statement for the church as a whole; and into this must be brought also the accounts of all subsidiary organizations, which are sometimes very numerous. If separate accounts are not kept, it will be necessary to analyze the general summary so as to derive them.

The chief shortcomings of church accounting are: (1) Duplicatory items that, in the various accounts, stand for the exchange, between

2 While the Interchurch thousand-point score-card provides a very valuable vehicle for the study of the church plant, and while nothing yet developed is better for this purpose, a church, before applying its standards directly, should criticize the conceptions of what a church's program ought to be as held by those who made the standard, and should determine whether it agrees with them. Plant and equipment obviously ought to reflect the functions it is proposed, or desired, to carry on by means of them; and not all churches will agree to the theories of the experts who constructed the scale.

departments of the church, of debits or credits that are not formally adjusted and in consequence of which the relations of the accounts are not always perfectly clear. Under such circumstances there is danger of counting certain items twice in attempting to make up a combined statement. (2) Balances at the beginning and at the end of the year are not formally accounted for, either in the individual or the combined accounts. An attached note may call attention to the fact that the statement is thus incomplete. It is likely that in the cases of a good many of the subsidiaries no balances are given at all. (3) The total receipts and total expenditures may thus not balance by considerable amounts because of defective bookkeeping on one side or both.

The specific problem of a semi-intensive financial study is that of organizing the data at hand into a comprehensive whole, throwing the maximum light on the total finances of the church enterprise from the points of view most practical for church administration. Absolute scientific accountancy can not always be applied to the existing data; and will be possible only when accounts are kept according to standard forms over a period of time.

The inclusive financial statement should be based on a few fundamental categories of church accountancy; that is to say, those that tell what most needs to be known. Therefore the major items of receipts and expenditures must first be arranged in grand divisions. The arrangement should ignore the particular separate accounts that churches keep according to the type of denominational organization or their own varying administrative methods. In determining the categories and forms on the receipt side, two points of view ought to be adopted: namely that one wants to know (1) from what *sources* the church derives support, and (2) for what *objects* it makes separate financial appeals to its supporting constituents. Considering the latter point first, it is a matter of common knowledge that churches generally appeal separately (1) for the financial support of the local congregation and parish and (2) for that of its benevolences and missions. Thus, in the current methods of financial solicitation, separate pledges are generally taken for these two classes of objects. The distinction between the two is consequently to be carried out in the accounting.

It is equally important to know where the church gets its money. It may come, and usually does come, from current sources; that is to say, from sources contributing within the year (through pledged subscriptions, collections, pew rents, gifts, etc.); or it may consist of income from previously accumulated capital made productive in the form of interest-bearing investments or in some profitable business. The distinction between current income and capital income is therefore also to be carried out.

On the expenditure side, one wants to know: (1) the financial outgo connected with the current expenditure (a) of the local parish, and (b) of the objects to which benevolences are contributed; and, on the other hand, to know (2) what is saved out of annual receipts and set aside by way of additions to permanent capital either in the form of endowments, permanent property, or sundry forms of working capital.

The major categories of accounting being thus determined, the items chosen for specific report are those that most completely summarize under a few heads the financial transactions that most need to be discriminated in the practical understanding of the church. On the side of receipts for the account of local parish expenses, eight such items should be included, as shown for an actual case in the table on page 41. The items shown in the table under the head of expenditures on current parish account attempt to summarize the church's business in terms giving the maximum insight into the situation as practically viewed. Religious workers' salaries will take the largest single fraction of the current budget. General administrative expenses, cost of music and publicity are self-explanatory items that are commonly distinguished. The item "general operating expense and upkeep of property" includes a large number of expenditures that churches commonly show in detail, such as replacements and repairs, fuel, light, water, insurance, taxes, etc. In the thought of this study it is not important to a general view of the church to know the exact amount of any of these accounts. What is important is the ratio, say between salaries and operating expenses, music and publicity; also the ratio between general expenditures undertaken for the sake of the church as a whole and those of separate organizations. The separately reported expenses of the subsidiaries represented nineteen different organizations in the case of the sample church. It is to be noted that they all have a share in the benefits of all general and administrative expenses, and in the expenses incident to upkeep and operation of property and of the church's publicity. It is not easy to apportion the benefits of these expenditures among the subsidiaries; but it is clear that their actual cost is much greater than the net sum to which they are charged.[3]

On the side of capital account, all the likely items of expenditure should be provided for. Thus a church may increase its equity in its permanent property by paying indebtedness on property, it may invest in new property or business, or make permanent improvements on old property; or start or add to endowment. The use of these categories of accounting is shown in the following table:

[3] For detailed forms by means of which it attempted to work out the actual cost of religious education in a church, see Athearn, *The Indiana Survey of Religious Education* (New York: Doran, 1924), Vol. II, pp. 509-13.

TABLE VIII

TABLE —FINANCIAL ACCOUNTING, UNION METHODIST EPIS-
COPAL CHURCH, ST. LOUIS, CONFERENCE YEAR, 1924-25

RECEIPTS

Items		*Amounts*	
Balance from previous year			$ 2,826
Total from current sources		$38,522	
For local parish from	$24,914		
1. Individual pledges	$11,891		
2. Loose collections	4,727		
3. Pew rentals	0		
4. Commercial transactions (Dormitory fees)	3,440		
5. Raised by subsidiary organizations	2,953		
6. Subsidies (from denomination)	1,878		
7. Special gifts	0		
8. Miscellaneous	25		
For benevolence account	13,608		
Total from capital account		7,062	
1. Interest-bearing investments	3,386		
2. Sale of property	3,676		
3. Income-producing business	0		
Total Receipts—Current year			45,584
Total available for expenditure			$48,410

EXPENDITURES

Expenditures on current account		41,552	
On local current account	29,164		
1. Salaries (religious workers)	11,732		
2. General administrative expenses	405		
3. Music (including salaries)	2,524		
4. General operation and upkeep of property (including Janitors' salaries)	7,230		
5. Expenses of departments and subsidiaries (19 organizations)	5,309		
6. Publicity	1,038		
7. Miscellaneous	926		
On benevolence account	12,388		
Additions to capital account (from above receipts)		3,450	
1. Increase of endowment	0		
2. Permanent property (non-income producing)	3,450		
3. Increase of investment (in income-producing business)	0		
Total Expenditures			45,002
Unexpended balance			$3,408

9. *Public Services*

An investigation of public services comparable in a semi-intensive study with that of other phases of the church is frankly impossible. The means of making even competent judgments are, at present, beyond formulation; for, in spite of all endeavors to establish canons of preaching or of officiating in public worship, there is no more actual agreement among ecclesiastical experts on these aspects of the church than there is among book reviewers on books, or among dramatic critics on plays.

And obviously no ready means exist of gauging the effectiveness of the service in its moral and spiritual results.

Method of Recording Impressions of Public Services

The study is therefore held to the concrete externals of public services; and no attempt is made to reduce its observations on these aspects to a precise schedule. An outline for a systematic memorandum of observations, however, should be filled out; and this should be supplemented by an examination of announcements of public services in the church calendar and by other descriptive data.

The best observers will not be hardened attendants at the particular church of the study; but strangers who will be sensitive to new impressions and free from local preconceptions. The observers should attend at least two of each of the major services. The audience should be counted and the approximate age- and sex-distribution of the congregation carefully estimated where exact count on these points is lacking. The observers should be seated, if possible, where they can face all or part of the audience. It will be well to have the ushers make a careful count of the audience on the same Sundays so that counts may be compared. (1) The prevailing tone of the period before the actual opening of service, and the conduct of the gathering audience, should be studied; also (2) the order and content of the broad items of the service, (3) the degree to which the ritual elements of the service are present or emphasized, (4) the place and character of the music, and (5) the manner and tone of the preaching. In further investigation of pulpit work, a digest of a year's sermon announcements should be made, the character and frequency of special services and the character of the habitual topics being noted; also the use of discussion methods, of visual devices or other unusual features. With these data in hand, the pastor should discuss with his associates in the study his own conception of the character and significance of his preaching. He should also furnish a classified digest of a year's sermons, showing what proportion of the whole was given to specified themes, issues, or methods of psychological approach.

The existence and character of separate services for children, or of the recognition of children in the regular public service, also afford special points for observation.

How to record the results of such observations of public services may be best suggested by a summary of the independent notes of two observers on the same services of a Methodist church. The morning service on the Sunday studied was attended by about 350 people. The points noted were: the relatively equal proportions of the two sexes, the large numbers of young adults, the quiet order-liness of the period before the opening service, but the absence of set form of devotion and of the specifically liturgical mood.

Both observers noted the smart vestments of the choir (consisting of fourteen voices) and the good style of the processional.

The order of service was more than usually elaborate, including musical responses and a recessional as well as the processional; a prayer read by the congregation at the conclusion of the invocation, followed by a Te Deum rendered as a hymn. One of the services attended included the celebration of the communion in an impressive and dignified manner with organ accompaniment throughout. The leading musicians appeared to be of more than average talent, and the music was acceptably performed.

Judged by the sermon heard, the pastor's characteristic preaching is topical and his presentation moderately oratorical, in the mood of forceful and interesting popular appeal. One of the sermons heard was entitled, "Selling the Gospel." The theme was developed in the terms of commercial salesmanship. "The house" for which the Christian representative works is of undoubted integrity and strength. "The goods" are trustworthy. "The samples" (profess-ing Christians) are too often inadequate and ought to be better. "Honest representation" is all that is necessary to sell the goods. Lies and exaggeration are unnecessary.

The departing congregation spent a rather unusual amount of time in a general exchange of sociability to which the broad lobby and parlors opening on either side particularly lend themselves. The pastor stood at the door to greet the people and other members of the staff were actively engaged in sociability.

The evening service was attended by about 220 persons, as high as 40 per cent. being young people, mostly young adults. The par-ticular features were: a "popular hymn service" at the beginning, and special musical numbers, on one evening presented by a church glee club of sixteen men, and on the other, by the pastor as soloist.

The midweek service is part of a varied church-night program. Following a dinner (attended by forty-seven persons on the night of the study) there are group meetings consisting, on the sample occa-sion, of the glee club, the choir, and a mission-study class attended by forty-three persons. These are followed at eight o'clock by the devotional hour attended, on the night of the study, by sixty-seven persons, including twenty-one men, twelve adolescents, and six children. The meeting was in charge of the Epworth League cabinet and presided over by the assistant pastor.

Such a method of directed observation by impartial observers is a perfectly respectable preliminary to scientific investigation when the methods peculiar to science are inapplicable because appropriate ways of regarding the facts and methodology for studying them quantitatively have not yet been invented.

10. *Religious Education*

The method of studying religious education in a single church has been more fully developed in other published reports of research than almost any other topic.[4] Most of the authoritative studies, however, have gone much further than is necessary in a semi-intensive investigation.

They furnish adequate models in case a church worker wishes to expand the consideration of this topic into a separate intensive investigation. In the present study, one of the chief problems is to avoid too great detail. No effort should be made to reach the more technical aspects of the subject, such as the contents of the curriculum, the elements of the program of worship or of service. Religious education is to be studied by means of a schedule that shall summarize the major aspects of the Sunday school revealed by existing current records, supplemented by data concerning other organizations of the church included in, or closely related to, the religious education program; also, by a condensed statement of the general policy of conducting religious education, of its place in the church, and of its broader relationships. A schedule suitable for these purposes is presented on pages 46-50 and should be consulted at this point.

The terms and abbreviations used in this schedule will be intelligible to any one familiar with Sunday-school work; and the form should present no difficulty in its application to an individual church. If, however, it is to be used in the comparative study of a group of churches, every term must be carefully defined in advance.

Method of Filling out the Schedule; Summarizing of Results

The method of filling out the schedule is sufficiently indicated by the form used. Explanatory notes should be added when necessary to make any entry clear. Thus, in Table IX, on page 45, it is noted that, of a total cradle roll of 158 infants, only 17 constitute an attending Sunday-school department.

The table illustrates, in brief form for summarizing, the basic quantitative data regarding the Sunday school. In the example cited, a Sunday school of 750 members is accounted for.

4 Athearn, *The Indiana Survey of Religious Education* (New York: Doran, 1924), Vol. II, especially Pt. V; Vol. III, pp. 24-80.

TABLE IX

TABLE   —SUMMARY OF SUNDAY-SCHOOL STATISTICS

DEPARTMENT	PUPILS		TEACHERS	
	Age	Enrollment	Male	Female
Total		549	16	30
Cradle Roll	Under 4	17 *	0	3
Beginners	4– 5	32	0	3
Primary	6– 8	49	0	7
Junior	9–11	53	2	6
Intermediate	12–14	57	4	3
Senior	15–17	66	4	3
Young people	18–21	80	3	2
Adults	21 and over	195	3	3

Summary:

Grand Total, 750. Pupils attending departments, 549; officers, 14; teachers, 46. Average attendance, 67 per cent. of enrollment of attending departments.

Approximate Age-distribution (attending departments):

	Number	Per Cent.
Children	208	38
Adolescents	146	27
Adults	195	35

* Total Cradle Roll, 158.

The number and age-limits of the departments, and the definition of child, adolescent and adult, will vary, of course, with the usage of the particular church or denomination. What these terms mean should be made plain.

If the church maintains a branch Sunday school, say for Chinese, or if it is responsible for the Sunday-school work in connection with some community house or denominational social enterprise, a separate schedule had better be filled out for these enterprises and total figures arrived at by addition.

Again, the statistics of supplementary agencies of religious education should be combined with those of the Sunday school, so as to account for all the facts. These agencies are commonly (1) character-building organizations for group activity (e.g., Scouts and Camp Fire girls); (2) organizations for devotional expression and service (e.g., Epworth Leagues); (3) organizations for missionary education and giving; and (4) organized young people's Sunday-school classes carrying on regular week-day programs. There may also be Saturday Craft Schools, or other forms of week-day religious instruction, and the summer Daily Vacation Bible Schools.

Schedule VII, as shown for the Sunday school, should be used in modified form for these later activities.

Schedule VII

SCHEDULE —RELIGIOUS EDUCATION

Church.................., Denomination.................., City.................., Date..................

Sunday School..................

Enrollment: Total .... M. .... F. Average Attendance: Total .... M. .... F.

Age-distribution of Pupils

Under 3		3-4-5		6-7-8		9-10-11		12-13-14		15-16-17		18-19-20		21 & over	
M.	F.	M.	F.	M.	F.	M.	F.	M.	F.	M.	F.	M.	F.	M.	F.

Cradle Roll

Grand Total

Home Department

Departments, Classes, Rooms, Curriculum

Name of Department	Ages of Pupils in Department	Number Pupils Enrolled	Average Attendance	Teachers		Special Superin-tendent?	Special Depart-mental Rooms?	Number Individual Class-rooms	Courses of Study			
				M.	F.				Lesson Helps		Special Courses	
									Name	Grade	Name	Text

Officers, No. .... (List)

Pupils between ages 3-21

46

Organized Classes and Other Organizations Regarded as Connected with Sunday School

Name of Organization	Ages Included	Regular Members		Number Meetings		Leader		Purpose and Program
		M.	F.	Week Day	Sunday	S.S. Officer	S.S. Teacher	
Total								

Other Organizations Regarded as Having Religious Education Program (Not Part of S. S.)

Name of Organization	Ages Included	Regular Members		Number Meetings		Leader		Purpose and Program
		M.	F.	Week Day	Sunday	S.S. Officer	S.S. Teacher	
Total								

47

SCHEDULE VII (*Cont.*)

SCHEDULE —RELIGIOUS EDUCATION (*Cont.*)

Church.................., Denomination.................., City.................., Date..................

Grading				Promotion				
By Age	Scholarship	Public School	Natural Grouping	By Examination	Other Mental Tests	Charting Pupil Rating	Personal Interviews	Other

Sessions

Length..................; Time: a.m.................., p.m...................; Division: Worship—Number Minutes..................; Classes—Number Minutes..................; Other—Number Minutes..................

Space		Lighting		Seating
Number Square Feet Floor Space per Pupil		Number Rooms Lighted..................	Rooms Inadequately	Number Classes Sitting at Desks or Tables
Rooms Used for Sunday School Purposes			Number Unsuitable Rooms.................. Why?..................	

Staff

Teaching Preparation						Supervision			
Number with General				Number with Special		Kinds			
Not Elementary	Not High School	Normal School or College	Now in Training Classes	Normal School or College	Training School	Reports Made	Conferences Held	Class Visiting	Other

Tests for selection?

Standards agreed on?

Training Methods and Facilities

Teachers' Meeting		Parochial	Denominational	Community	(Number Sessions per Week and Number Weeks in Session)	Reference Library	Number Volumes
Frequency	Training Course?						

Annual Sunday School Exhibit or other

Equipment

Stereopticon?

Other Illustrative Material? (List)

Administration and Control

Name of Executive Officer	Name of Superintendent	Director Religious Education	How Appointed	Reports to Whom?				What Professional Preparation Has He?
				Minister	Church Board or Meeting	Sunday School Board or Cabinet	Entire School	

49

Schedule VII (*Cont.*)

SCHEDULE —RELIGIOUS EDUCATION (*Cont.*)

Church............................, Denomination............................, City............................, Date............................

Religious Education in the Home. Is there any stated meeting of parents and teachers together?............................
For how many weeks and how frequently?............................ Any regularly organized Parent-Teachers' Association?
Have you a family altar league or other systematic effort to foster worship at home?

Coöperation with Other Religious and Social Agencies of Community. Name the agencies to which a collection has been given within a year.

Which Sunday school has promoted or advocated by announcement or notice?

Describe how:

Neighborhood Service. List and describe activities carried on or occasions celebrated by the Sunday school during the year primarily for the sake of the neighborhood and not for the church or itself.

Data Carried Forward

When a topically conducted research gets part way into the actual processes, data already secured in the investigation of other topics should be brought forward. This is natural, since topics stand for different ways of observing the same sets of facts, not for a wholly different content.

In the case of the religious education investigation, the relation of Sunday-school pupils to the church, on the one hand, and to other subsidiary organizations, on the other, has already been included in the general study of the church's constituents.[5]

One knows how many of the pupils were also church-members; and how many are also members of various subsidiary organizations; and how many are members of Sunday school, church and subsidiaries, all three. This shows the degree of integration between the agencies of religious education and the other major phases of the church.

Values

Certain of the values of such a going-over of religious education in the local church are obvious. Omissions of vital activities are brought to light. Does the Sunday school maintain a monthly teachers' meeting? Has it a small teachers' reference library? Again, comparison with denominational standards of religious education is facilitated. Perhaps two-thirds of the Sunday-school teachers have been prepared in an approved teachers' training school in which a few pupils are enrolled at the time of the study. How does this compare with denominational standard requirements? The ultimate responsibility for Sunday-school interests is vested in the Sunday-school board of the church. Is this the right arrangement?

Of greater value still, such a study compels the church to identify the total group of activities that it conceives of educationally. It may wish to departmentalize them. By such an arrangement, administrative unification is attained in a field usually divided among many, perhaps an unnecessarily large number of, distinct organizations with ostensibly separate interests. On the other hand, departmentalization has dangers almost equal to its possible advantages. One strong reason for making the study of religious education part of a comprehensive study of the church, even though it is thereby limited in detail, is that the church is thus compelled to view the subject in relations, as part of and not sundered from the total on-going life of the institution.

11. *Growth and Conservation of Membership*

Churches grow by winning new members and not losing too many old ones. No other quantitative data are so universally kept by

5 See p. 17.

churches as statistics of their gains and losses. The sources of gains are commonly recorded (as by letter of transfer from some other church, or on first confession of faith) as are the occasions of losses (as by death, discipline, or transfer by letter). Ministers generally have some consciousness of other recurrent factors related to losses and gains of which no statistical record is kept. It will be sufficient for a semi-intensive study of the subject to pick out and make a statistical statement of the frequency of the more important of these factors.

Religious and Community Antecedents and Status of Church Recruits

A new member of a particular church may or may not have previously been a member of some other church. If he has been, the other church may or may not have been one of the same denomination. His status in the community has not been always the same. He may have been a well-established resident with plenty of social ties, or a stranger needing to get socially established and finding in the church rewarding companionship as well as religious satisfaction. He may have been already attached to the church in some relation subordinate to membership—by attendance on services, or enrollment in the Sunday school, or belonging to some subsidiary organization; or he may have had nothing to do with the church before uniting with it. He may have lived in the vicinity of the church or remote from it.

It is evident that in dealing with these different types of recruits, a church exhibits different levels of capacity to grow. Upon the church-member (especially one of its own denomination) it has a potential hold that it does not have on those who are not members of any church. The adherent who has already been brought into the Sunday school or club is in the half-way house toward membership. The stranger trying to establish himself socially has more active need of the church than the comfortable, settled "old timer." The neighbor is ordinarily more accessible than the distant person. Bringing in established and remote people not previously church-members is evidence of aggressive evangelism. Drawing upon one's own reservoir of Sunday-school and club members testifies to the success of cultural and nurturing processes. A live church in normal circumstances should be able to recruit somewhat proportionately in all areas. How far a given church is doing so, may be ascertained by a study of cases, and a count according to classes of recruits above distinguished.

Method

In carrying out this study, the first requisite is a schedule on which may be indicated by a check-mark the religious antecedents, previous

Schedule VIII

SCHEDULE —RELIGIOUS ANTECEDENTS, PREVIOUS RELATION TO CHURCH AND COMMUNITY, AND DISTANCE OF RESIDENCE OF MEMBERS RECEIVED FROM..............TO..............

Name of New Member	Status		Address	Distance from Church			Resident in Community		Previously Related to Church by			Not Previously Related to Church	Received by			
	Adherent Family	Detached Individual		Near	Average	Far	More than 1 Year	Less than 1 Year	Church Attendance	Sunday-school Enrollment	Membership in Subsidiary		Transfer or Letter		Confession of Faith	
													From same Denomination	From other Denomination	Previously Protestant	Not Previously Protestant
Total																

relation to church and community, and distance of residence, of a sufficient number of new members to show how the church's growth is conditioned. Seventy-five or more cases are desirable. If the church has not received as many new members as this during the last year, carry the study back a year and a half or two years.

The form of the schedule is shown on page 53.

Fill in the dates in the title of the schedule, to show what period the study covered; and put check-marks in the proper columns after the name and address of each new member. The member's residence should be checked as "near," "average distance," or "far," with respect to the church building. The meaning of these terms will have to be determined for the particular church with reference to the facts of its parish distribution as discovered in a previous section.[6]

On the basis of these facts, decide what distance is comprehended under near or far. Notes showing the contributing influences in turning the new member to the church should be entered on the back of the card. Was it in connection with trouble or bereavement?

TABLE X

TABLE —SUMMARY OF MEMBERS RECEIVED FROM
..............................TO..............................

ANTECEDENTS	RESIDENCE RELATIVE TO CHURCH			
			Average	
	Total	*Near*	*Distance*	*Far*
Total				
Church-members (received by transfer of letters)				
From same denomination				
Resident in community more than one year				
Previously related to church				
Not previously related				
Not resident in community more than one year				
From other denominations				
Resident in community more than one year				
Previously related to church				
Not previously related				
Not resident in community more than one year				
Not Church-members (received on confession of faith)				
Resident in community more than one year				
Previously related to church				
Not previously related				
Not resident in community more than one year				

6 See p. 19.

Did he marry into a church family? Or were there other family influences, such as a child in Sunday school?

Interpretation and Summary

The following example shows how the result of such a study of church recruiting may be briefly stated, together with some of the obvious inferences to be drawn from the facts in the particular case:

> During the church year preceding the study, the Blank Methodist Church received 180 new members. Nearly 60 per cent. came by letter from other churches, of whom one-fifth were non-Methodists. Of the 40 per cent. coming by profession of faith, about one-fourth were advanced from preparatory membership, while well over a third (counting these preparatory members) had been in previous definite relation to the church, chiefly through enrollment in the Sunday school. This left nearly two-thirds of those coming by profession of faith without previously established relation with the church. These persons were won somewhat directly from the ranks of the non-adherent population in general. In all (including accessions by letter) about one-fourth of those received during the year had been already somewhat assimilated to the church by one or another subsidiary relation; not a very high proportion.

> Of the total 180 new members of the year, about 60 per cent. had been resident in the community for at least a year. Of those received on profession of faith, however, nearly one-half were newcomers. These facts reflect the large element of new population in the areas on which the church draws.

> Of the 180 new members, 56 per cent. came from less than an average distance and 44 per cent. from a more than average distance, as estimated by the church officials. This shows that the present scattered parish is the result of widespread recruiting and not merely of the removal of members who were received from near-by residence and later shifted to a greater distance. Newcomers to the community, whether uniting by letter or on confession, were chiefly won from the immediate vicinity of the church. This illustrates the greater influence of proximity upon the stranger. Over two-thirds, however, of old residents who brought letters lived at some distance from the church. Does this reflect a deliberate cultivation, in this case of remote people in the more desirable residential areas of the city?

> Summarized, the chief sources of accessions for the year studied were:

Sources	New Members		Tendency as to Distance of Residence
	Number	*Per Cent.*	
Old residents by letter	49	27	Far
Newcomers by letter	37	21	Near
Sunday-school pupils	23	13	More near than far
Old residents on confession	23	13	More near than far
Newcomers on confession	20	11	Near
All others	28	15	——

> This shows that the church had a variety of resources and that it was able to draw somewhat proportionately upon all.

When these schedules have been filled out and the entries counted and tabulated, the church will have gained new insight into the nature of its recruiting processes. The preceding form will serve as a tally-sheet, and also as the outline of a table for summarizing the major facts. Separate schedules should be made for recruits from adherent families and also for detached individuals, and the totals should be combined into one table.

With respect to losses of members, it will be sufficient in a semi-intensive study to make a statement of the facts, using the conventional categories, viz., lost by death, by transfer, by discipline, or by the dropping of the name from the roll. In the case of transfer, the statement should distinguish transfers to other churches within the community from transfers outside the community; and in the former case should note whether it accompanied a change in the member's place of residence. With respect to dropping names from the roll, it would be significant to classify the circumstances believed to justify the church in such action in each case; but this is a different field, perhaps beyond the proper bounds of a limited study.

12. *Current Church Life*

Studying a church topic by topic fails to reveal the vital relationships of the different phases of its life as an on-going process from week to week. There should be devised, therefore, in a semi-intensive study, methods of summarizing the course of a year's work, and of noting the more distinctive features as they fall into a true perspective viewed as part of the church's current history.

An exceptionally active church may express itself in a total of seven or eight different meetings on Sunday and an average of two or three gatherings per day during the week. But the number and character of its activities reflect the seasons and seasonal habits, such as the taking of vacations. They are largely focussed upon, and find their more colorful accents in connection with, the memorials and celebrations of the Christian year, now made to include the national holidays. Such turning points block out recurrent epochs within the single year, together with important special circumstances and events. These furnish headlines for the church's institutional story.

Seasonal Aspects of Current Church Life

An example will serve to show the largely seasonal characteristics of modern church life. The pastor returns from his vacation on the last Sunday in August. A "loose ends" campaign is immediately announced, designed to get the church into its stride for the full operations of the active season. An important special event of the early fall is the entertainment of the annual conference of the denomination. Labor Sunday is celebrated with a special sermon.

In the fall, the special seasonal stress of church announcements relates, first, to finances, with the definition of the objectives of the church for the year. The opening of the junior church services is announced. There is a call for additional choir members and for pupils for special Sunday-school classes. In the fall also, extra speakers are brought on for a series of consecutive Sunday evenings, including denominational leaders on their annual rounds, representatives of special missionary interests, and one or two popular entertainers. After the holidays comes the Lenten preparatory class and campaign of personal evangelism. Holy Week is observed, and great emphasis is placed on the post-Easter reception of members. Spring brings a recurrence of financial effort in the "loyalty and tithing" campaign. Along with the regular course of meetings of the subsidiary organizations come frequent extra social events taking their form from the seasons; pageants, parties, outings, etc.

Means of studying the church from this viewpoint are found in its printed weekly bulletins, in its printed publicity for special events, its minute books and press notices. Most churches will have kept more or less complete files, or will have assembled this material, as the basis of routine annual reports.

In dealing with this material, it should be systematically digested from the records of several successive weeks. An outline suitable for this purpose is presented below.

OUTLINE FOR ANNUAL DIGEST OF CHURCH BULLETINS AND OTHER CURRENT ANNOUNCEMENTS

(1) Special Major Services or Anniversaries
    Church
    Sunday school
    Subsidiary organizations
        (Attendance, themes, speakers, other features)
(2) Minor Occasions Specially Announced
    Church officers
    Men's and boys' organizations
    Women's and girls' organizations
    Mixed organizations and informal groups
    Others
(3) Other Events Announced
    Community
        Other churches or religious organizations
        Other constructive agencies
    Denominational events
(4) "Causes" advocated (denominational, inter-denominational, non-denominational.)
    City
    National
    Foreign
(5) Other types of recurring announcements

The actual process of making the digest is to rule large sheets of paper into spaces for each week of the year and with the above topics as column headings. Entries are then made for each week in which anything significant occurs under any topic. Part of the data falling under these heads simply concerns the time, place, and external forms of events; other parts reveal interests, that is to say ideas, offered to the attention, or appeals to conscience.

In the final literary summary of the digest that completes this phase of the study, recurrent events may be recorded by count; for example, ten special speakers in the pulpit for the year; eight weeks of mission study; two weeks of evangelistic meetings. Interests will have to be treated analytically and interpretatively. Previous phases of the study that have covered a year's time may be drawn upon, as for example, the classified count of annual attendance on all organizations and activities (pp. 27-28) and the annual financial showing (p. 38).

The result will be a sort of annals, more scientific than the ordinary annual church report because compiled more systematically, expressed more accurately, and free from sentimentality and mere honorific attitudes; in a word, de-bunked. Such records, accumulated through the years, would have great value as historical materials, and would also afford a vital summary of the topical investigations of a semi-intensive study at any given time.

13. *Community Relations*

Organized churches are naturally in contact with, and have relations with, other constructive agencies of the community. In this way, they project themselves into the general social life and enlarge the sphere of their own service. This expression of the church through its institutional extensions and allies is in addition to the community values embodied in the individual lives of its members.

A comprehensive study of the local church must take account of these organized relations. Ordinarily no formal records of them are kept; and in a semi-intensive study the creating of the data by consulting in detail the very numerous sources of information involved will not be justified.

Method

A fairly simple method of treating the matter involves the following steps: List all institutions and organized constructive agencies of the community with which the church might be expected to have coöperative relationships. These should be classified under such heads as the following: religious agencies (denominational, interdenominational, non-denominational); general civic agencies; social service agencies (for care of needy families, for care and protection of children, homes for adults, health agencies including hospitals, agencies for relief and education of defectives, corrective agencies,

agencies of character education, recreational agencies, all other social agencies).

The lists of these agencies, together with the names of their paid staffs, officers and boards of directors, may generally be secured from Councils of Social Agencies or the Community Chest organization of the city.[7]

These lists should then be checked against a list of the church's membership; and a classified list should be prepared of all church-members who are officially related to any constructive community agency. In case lists of the directorates of such agencies do not exist, a questionnaire may be sent to the church-membership and the returns tabulated on the questions involved. Five questions may then be answered with respect to the church's relation to each agency on the list: (1) Has the church contributed to this organization in money or goods within a year? This will be shown by the financial study already made.

(2) Has it been represented by members on the paid staff or board of directors?

(3) Has it appointed official representatives to the administrative board of the organization? (Most social agencies are self-governing corporations that choose their own directors on such grounds as availability, personal interest, community influence and wealth. A relatively smaller number have other organizations as constituent members; and these organizations appoint official representatives to constitute their boards of direction. Questions (2) and (3) are answered by the processes described just above.)

(4) Has the church had practical coöperative relations with the agency; and, if so, what?

(5) Has it advocated the work of the agency in its pulpit or printed publicity? Questions (4) and (5) may be answered from the examination of the year's records as described in the last section.

The tabulation of results from this inquiry may be made according to the following form, which quantitatively summarizes the relationships of the church to the community.

The results of this study should be written up interpretatively, so as to show what kinds of social interests the church stresses, and particularly the kinds of coöperation it affords the community agencies.

In passing judgment upon facts of this kind in the case of any church, it is important to consider (1) how far the church's own

---

[7] The preparation of such a list raises the somewhat complicated problem of what constitutes a social agency. The problem is sometimes especially difficult with relation to social work conducted under church auspices. The degree to which such work is admitted as constructive social effort by councils of social agencies and the Community Chest machinery is of vital importance. Not infrequently certain departments of local churches are recognized and receive community subsidies on the grounds of effective social work. If, however, the existing lists are biased against social work within the church or under its auspices, they must be correspondingly supplemented.

TABLE XI

TABLE —RELATIONS OF CHURCH WITH RELIGIOUS, CIVIC AND SOCIAL AGENCIES OF COMMUNITY

NUMBER OF RELATIONSHIPS REPORTED BY THE CHURCH WITHIN LAST YEAR

CLASSIFIED LIST OF AGENCIES WITH WHICH CHURCH HAS RELATIONS*	Financial (Collections given)	Board Members	Official Delegates	Practical Coöperation (Specify)	Publicity Promotion	Total
Religious						
Denominational						
Non-denominational						
Interdenominational						
Public and Civic						
Social						
a.						
b.						
c. etc.,						

* Write in the names of particular agencies under the appropriate headings in this column.

program includes the conduct of "community service," and to what extent such work constitutes a first call on the church's service through personal work and gifts; and (2) how far the denomination to which the church belongs is maintaining in the community a varied group of social agencies that constitute a second claim on the church; finally, how much margin the church has of personnel and of wealth that are available for the more general field of constructive community work. It is fairly obvious that the churches that are doing least along these lines, either on their own account or through their denominations, are the more free to project themselves into the community through other agencies.

The first of the above questions may be directly answered from the study of the church's program in a previous section; the second requires a special study of denominational relationships.

14. *Denominational Relations*

Within a merely semi-intensive study of the single local church, no room will be found for the securing of any first-hand data for the other churches of the same denomination, nor for the denominational overhead agencies that constitute its ecclesiastical partners. Obviously, however, a church's denominational relationships are an important aspect to which at least a limited amount of attention must be given.

At this point a new element enters the study; namely, some consideration of standards of church life. In no previous topic has it been assumed that any particular condition ought to pertain. The single church has been considered in itself alone. No evaluating comparisons have been instituted and no external norms set up.

But denominations undertake, in greater or less degree, to tell churches how to conduct themselves. Moreover they make specific demands, in fulfilling which the churches prove themselves good and loyal. These standards, implied or expressed, should be in mind in the study of denominational relationships.

The points of view necessary to be considered may be roughly stated as (1) what the church gives to the denomination; (2) what it gets from the denomination; and (3) the comparative amount of give and take.

Data bearing on these points may, in the main, be found in the previous studies. (1) A statement of what the church gives to the denominational agencies locally in money, leadership, advocacy and coöperation may be brought over from the last section. (2) Financial contributions may be analyzed in detail from the source material of the financial section. Numerous pertinent aspects of the financial data may easily be expanded; as, for example, the number of givers and the amount of per capita giving to denominational objects classified as to kind. (3) The coöperation of the church in denominational projects may have further numerical statement; as, for example, the number of subscribers to denominational journals; or the number and ratio of participants in training projects denominationally promoted, such as school courses for the training of teachers and the study of missions.

All these studies should be combined into a statement of what the church has done for the denomination during the year.

What the denomination has done for the church may be summarized under the following questions, answers to which may be compiled from data organized under preceding sections, or directly from church records:

(1) How many new members has the denomination transferred to the church by letter?

(2) What financial aid had it given the church in grants and loans?

(3) What rallies, union meetings, etc., has the denomination conducted in the benefits of which the local church has participated?

(4) What supervision has it given the church?

These questions should be given quantitative answer. How many visits, for example, did the church have from supervisory officers; how long were these visits; how many communications did the church receive from such officers and on what subjects? A carefully objective appraisal should also be made of the value of these supervisory services.

In denominational yearbooks and minutes, presumably some light has already been thrown upon the relations of the churches of a denomination to one another. The most important point at which to supplement this is that of parish distribution. In the study of a single church one cannot survey the parishes of all the rest. When one has studied one's own parish, the results may, however, be sent to other churches showing how many members there are in each district; and one may ask the other churches to reciprocate by telling how many members they have. This helps to round out the statement of denominational relationships by giving it a geographical aspect.

If the denomination has set up a pattern of church organization, or has ordained particular objectives in any phase of the church that has been studied, or if it has specified what is proper in church relationships, the degree to which the church's performance meets the standard should finally be stated. The reasonableness and validity of these standards may then be discussed, and the degree of the church's actual success measured as candidly as possible. This is as far as a semi-intensive study can properly go.[8]

8 More intensive methods of studying groups of churches, which are applicable to denominational groups, are shown in chap. v.

SUMMARY AND CONCLUSIONS

After such an extensive and varied process of discovering facts as has been outlined in the foregoing semi-intensive study, the results have to be brought together in summary form. This may be done under the several topics already discussed; or the whole may be re-cast into some more effective literary mold. But some method of summation is necessary in order that the mind may grasp the results as a whole.

The results must also be brought together, from the standpoint of their significance, into a set of conclusions supposed to be drawn from them. As a matter of fact, conclusions are never drawn purely from a given body of data, but rather from the application to data of some set of working presuppositions and theories. As a result of this contact a fusion takes place between the two. A conclusion is thus the product of a process of assimilation now dominated by the traits of the new evidence, and again by those of the old.

In summarizing and drawing conclusions from any study of church data, two different viewpoints are almost always involved: (a) that of practical interest—the realization of the objective which the church had in mind in making the study; (b) that of science. Research is rarely attempted purely from scientific motives. Generally it is hoped and believed in advance that the facts will back some particular project or view of what the church ought to do.

The scientific viewpoint is more nearly detached from particular interests. The desire is, in a scientific study, to understand the Church through the particular case; and hence to put the facts discovered upon the broadest possible background of general significance. But it should be frankly admitted that both viewpoints are limited. If the first is determined by the nature of the object which it is hoped to accomplish, the second is at least partially determined by some theory implicitly held if not explicitly announced. This leads to some hypothesis as to what, in the phenomena under consideration, is significant with respect to the Christian Church. Both the practical objectives and the theoretical assumptions should be admitted and kept in the light, so that they may not be confused with the narrow body of inference directly drawn from the data.

APPLICATION TO THE PRESENT STUDY

As was announced at the outset, in connection with the basic plan, the factual examination of the church is to be concluded, in the present study, by a summary derived from a special point of view; namely, that of the adaptation of the church as an institution. This involves a hypothesis, viz., that any church as it stands is the result, to a greater or lesser degree, of the influence of external environment upon its fortunes; and the ultimate interest in the present case is assumed to be to discover how and in what degree the church corresponds to the situation in which it exists. This implies the belief that, consciously or unconsciously, any institution must show something of adaptation; and that the relationships of old and new elements in its external program will reveal how old and new attitudes have met and adjusted themselves. This particular hypothesis is assumed strictly for methodological ends, to show how any study reaches conclusions with reference to a previously accepted point of view. The contrary hypothesis; namely, that all churches resist environment and that adjustment is but partial, would have illustrated the point just as well. In that case the summary would have been made in terms of conservatism and persistence instead of those of modification and change.

ENVIRONMENTAL CHANGE AFFECTING THE CHURCH

Since change is to furnish the clue to the present summary, the first step is to pick out from this history the major crises from which epoch-making innovations have arisen. In the case of the church used illustratively,[9] the major crisis was found in removal to a new site. After some years of uncertainty and decline, the church pronounced its old environment impossible; so much so that it abandoned an expensive property on which it had spent largely for remodeling. For another church the decision not to remove may have been equally momentous and epoch-making.

Following the account of the great historic changes—whatever they are—in the church's fortunes, the summary must identify the series of pressures that the church now feels, the stings of circumstance that compel it to action, the uncertainties that "keep it guessing." Here one will look for the explanation of minor adaptations, for the little causes of change that may accumulate into great ones. Thus, though in making its change, Church X succeeded in large measure in keeping its former character, its hold on large numbers of children and adolescents, its predominant family constituency and its almost compact parish, it by no means escaped problems. In the decade following relocation, changes within the new environment were increasingly radical. The area of deteriorated housing occupied by transient populations living in rooming and light-housekeeping quarters rapidly increased. On the other hand, the skyrocketing of land values checked the permanent occupancy by Negroes and foreigners of the area immediately adjacent to the growing center; so that the prospects of the general district were radically improved. A new type of housing represented by apartment hotels, and the

9 See p. 10.

erection of a cluster of great buildings housing social institutions, accompanied the development and improvement of the commercial and recreational center.

Under the hypothesis, the summary of a study of a church in such a situation would generalize the influence of these changes upon the facts as discovered especially in the sections on Parish or Environment.

SPECIFIC INSTITUTIONAL CHANGES

The next step, accordingly, is to record all the specific institutional changes in the church which the previous study has discovered. The example presents a church that met dual change (first, of location, and, second, change within the new environment) (1) by a working program including a number of unusual features. It shifted emphasis away from that of a traditional church until a fifth of the total program, as measured by attendance, represented week-day activities, and nearly a fourth, activities other than the formal services of church and Sunday school. (2) By adding numerous additional organizations to the six standard subsidiaries of its denomination, the church heaped up a total of nineteen separately organized groups within itself. (3) It enlarged the professional staff until it included four specialized workers in addition to the minister, a director of religious education and a girls' worker being the most distinctive. (4) It made no structural changes in its second-hand plant, but supplemented it by acquiring a large adjoining residence which it used as a young men's dormitory and as supplemental space for more general church purposes. (5) It gave its public services a more popular tone, including a considerable variety of "features," and established its ability to attract numerous strangers and transients from the vicinity, as well as to win an increasingly city-wide constituency of more established people. (6) It doubled its expenditures. (7) It established more specific relations with its own denomination to get help in effecting some of these changes.

A similar inventory of changes apparently adaptive in character would be made by any church summarizing a self-study under the same hypothesis.

GENERIC ADAPTATIONS

The next step is to generalize in terms of some more inclusive category. In all this modification of institutional life, what was the church trying to do? For what rôle was it preparing in making these changes?

In the illustrative case, alternatives were definitely before the church when it made its decision to remove. Its neighbors, with hardly an exception, had taken themselves to the new residential districts. This church, however, moved to the very heart of the secondary commercial and recreational center of the city, knowing that it would there have to adjust itself radically to meet the changes in immediate surroundings. In brief, it undertook the part of a down-town church.

In some such generalized way, any study of a church's adaptation would seek to compress the meaning of what happened into a single inclusive statement. But, as the result of changes subsequent to removal, the above statement in the case of Church X has to be revised. The ambition has gradually emerged to achieve the character of the great central church of its denomination and to erect on its valuable central site a skyscraper building. This would constitute a cathedral for the whole communion to which the church belongs, and would include income-producing business and office space, the cost running into millions.

Plans conceived on a smaller scale have all been scrapped, and the church more or less marks time while waiting for means to attain its greater objective.

In brief, the church is now preparing to become a very new, special and commanding down-town church of a pioneer type infrequently found.

For any parallel case study, the conclusion must similarly tell and explain not merely what has happened, but what the church wants to have happen in the future.

MODIFICATION OF FUNDAMENTAL THINKING

The next step is to see whether any change in the church's fundamental thinking has accompanied or followed the shifting of its immediate objectives and its accepted rôles.

Why does Church X want a skyscraper building? And what will it do with one if it gets it?

The church has assumed, without discussion, that having such a building will not involve the loss of its earlier local constituency—the following that moved with the church to the new site.

Experience proves, however, that any church adapting itself radically is sure to fall into situations in which immediate objectives conflict. Church X wants a skyscraper building; it also wants to retain its old clientele. But if the two conflict in actual test, which shall be subordinated?

It is the weighing of conflicting claims, the thinking over and over of the implications of immediate objectives, that sometimes leads to the redefinition of ultimate objectives, sets the church to serving God and the city from a new standpoint, and finally even leads to the revision of creed and code.

If the concluding processes of a study lead to any such results in a given case, this will constitute by far the most important discovery possible. Otherwise the conclusion will simply have to point out that one side of the church's mind looks in one direction, the other in a contrary direction; no revision of basic thinking having occurred to comprehend and unify the different points of view. This will probably have to be the more frequent conclusion from any honest study.

THE CHURCH'S PRACTICAL SUCCESS

Somewhere in the conclusion of a study must come a reasoned statement of the degree of a church's success or failure as the result of, or in spite of, its efforts at adaptation.

If a church has received from its denomination, or elsewhere, authoritative criteria of success, it needs only to compare itself with them. They are the scale. It remains to take the measurements. No satisfactorily standarized means of rating a city church have come to notice, consequently it will be well to fall back on the common sense tests of institutional success in numbers and resources.

From these a simple statement may easily be made with the objective data of the study as its evidence. The following summary of the success of Church X will serve as a rough model:

Judging success by standards deducible from the church's behavior and recognized objectives, one notes the considerable actual growth of numbers, the notable capacity for assimilation of newcomers, the ability to recruit from a wide range, the church's proven accessibility to strangers while the strong hold on its older constituency is maintained. The church shows very notable success with young people. It has worked over into its character as a city-wide enterprise with constantly increasing prestige. Its public services are fairly well attended and adapted to the situation, and its local ministries, though not highly intensified, have distinct character and value.

On the other hand, the church staff is not very adequate as to size, nor fully effective as to personnel. The plant is not well adapted to the work in hand, nor in harmony with the character of the site. While the acquirement of exceedingly valuable new property in exchange for old has been carried out as a highly successful transaction, the problem of really suitable and adequate improvements for so strategic a site, looms before the church rather exigently. The church has lost considerable financial strength by death, and its future prospects in this line present some difficulties.

The church has distinctly cluttered internal organization which greatly needs simplification. It is stronger in denominational and interdenominational relationships than in its general community standing. The active and intimate participation of its members in a varied current church life makes a pleasant impression; but how to staff the church for an enlarged work, and how to relate the work of the staff to the development and organizing of a sufficient force of volunteers, present many unsolved problems.

The trend of the situation as a whole, including both the environment and the church in its present degree of adaptation, seems to lead to something like this: Until the environmental situation has settled a little more, the church must maintain a policy of tentativeness and an experimental mood. It is not in position to risk all on the glory of some great adventure while the situation remains clouded. It is developing two or three somewhat separate constituencies whose points of view are not fully unified, any more than their subsidiary activities are. Might not the church most wisely intensify its efforts to reintegrate the elements of which it is composed and the activities which they are carrying out, so that it will be as nearly as possible of one mind when the opportunity for external advance comes? Meanwhile its obvious duty is to study the situation continuously and earnestly and to be guided at all times by the greatest possible knowledge of the facts.

THE FINAL STEPS

The summary of a study will presumably be made, and the tentative conclusions drawn from it, by the minister or church leaders who have carried on the processes of factual investigation. These persons, who constitute the natural advisors of the church, will doubtless want to follow the study with a series of suggestions showing its bearing upon the practical problems of the church. These furnish the culmination of the investigation in its utilitarian aspect. But the reaching of conclusions in this sense is clearly the province, not of the surveyors, but of those in whose behalf the surveyors acted in making the study.

The final steps in the semi-intensive study accordingly include referring the data to the group under whose auspices the study was made; that is to say, in such a case as the one under consideration, to the church as a whole or as represented by its officers. Before announcing the conclusions, it is obvious wisdom to put the facts before those most concerned. The facts should be thoroughly discussed and the conclusions drawn from them submitted to criticism, so that the person announcing the conclusions will not need to take purely individual responsibility for them.

This step, moreover, is not to be thought of as a mere diplomatic concession to a group of people who have in some measure to pass upon a body of facts without clearly understanding them. A fair attempt by a responsible group to approach and discuss the facts in a constructive spirit, however limited the understanding of the members of the group may be, will make a contribution to the thinking even of the leaders who have spent so long a time upon the study. The responsible authorities should then decide what to do in the light of the study; but this takes them beyond the limits of the study itself.

From the standpoint of scientific interest, this process of group thinking is regarded as having a certain creative significance; that is to say, it constitutes an essential step in the process of ascertaining truth; processes of research and of thinking with reference to practical action being ultimately indistinguishable.

SCHEME OF STUDY

(Chapters I and II)

(It is assumed that the semi-intensive study of a single church
will be conducted by the church.)

PLANNING THE STUDY

1. Reach preliminary decision as to scope and contents.
2. Make outline of survey by topics.
3. Plan requirements in time, money and workers.
4. Supply working facilities and assemble data.
5. Devise method of checking progress.

MAKING THE STUDY

PRELIMINARY

1. List all church's organizations and activities.
2. Classify each under outline of survey.
3. Determine historical epochs of church's life.
4. Organize historical data according to these epochs.
5. Write brief historical sketch.

CONTEMPORARY FACTUAL STUDY

I. Members and Constituents

1. Combine lists of constituents into a single list.
2. Provide schedules for entering constituents' relations.
3. Fill out schedules for all constituents.
4. Discriminate classes of adherents not formally expressed on the
   schedule.
5. Tabulate according to columns of schedule.
6. Consider whether constituents have proper relation to church.

II. Parish

1. Tabulate location of constituents' homes from schedules.
2. Make parish map.
3. Make series of maps for different constituencies.
4. Make summary table showing parish distribution.
5. Consider causes of variation in distribution.

III. Environment

1. Decide how far to carry environmental study.
2. Consult existing sources of information.
3. Take notes and transcribe data to maps.
4. Write summary of the church's social background.
5. Consider bearings of data on church policies.

IV. Organization and Activities

1. Inventory all organizations and stated activities.
2. Define "regular" organizations and other necessary terms.
3. Fill out schedule of attendance.
4. Check estimates of attendance for reliability.
5. Classify and calculate general distribution of attendance.
6. Calculate distribution according to age and sex.
7. Consider balance and proportion of church's program.

V. *The Ministry*

1. Collect personnel records of church staff.
2. Summarize personnel records.
3. Have work records kept by staff. (See chapter iii, B.)
4. Calculate time spent in different kinds of work.
5. Consider accuracy of designations applied to workers.

VI. *Staff Organization and Relationships*

1. Fill out schedules for workers' relations to lay boards.
2. Fill out schedules for workers' relations to subsidiaries.
3. Fill out schedules for workers' relations to one another.
4. Tabulate according to columns of schedules.
5. Consider whether staff relations are satisfactory.

VII. *Plant*

1. Get "Standards for City Church Plants."
2. Have three judges score the church plant.
3. Consider and explain differences between standard and allotted score.
4. Criticize the standard from church's standpoint.

VIII. *Finances*

1. Assemble financial summaries of all church organizations.
2. Discover shortcomings of the data.
3. Determine categories for accounting.
4. Construct a financial summary.
5. Consider ratio of items of income and of expense to one another.

IX. *Public Services*

1. Devise a method of systematic recording of impressions.
2. Attend sample services and take notes.
3. Write summary of impressions.
4. Make practical suggestions for improvement.

X. *Religious Education*

1. Determine proportions of religious education study.
2. Provide and fill out schedule for Sunday school.
3. Define terms used in schedule.
4. Provide and fill out schedule for supplementary agencies.
5. Bring forward Sunday-school data included under previous topics.
6. Compare results with denominational standards.
7. Consider the place of religious education in the church's organization.

XI. *Growth and Conservation of Membership*

1. Provide schedule showing religious antecedents of new church members.
2. Define terms used in schedule.
3. Analyze and interpret results.
4. Study losses of membership by similar processes.

XII. *Current Church Life*

1. Make a digest of weekly church bulletins and for a year.
2. Calculate frequency of recurrent but irregular activities.
3. Write systematic annals for a year.

XIII. Community Relations

1. Classify and list all community agencies with which church might have relations.
2. Discover how many of the church's members are related to each.
3. Discover what direct relations the church has had to any.
4. Summarize the findings.
5. Consider whether these relationships are adequate.

XIV. Denominational Relations

1. Bring over from previous sections organized data concerning what the church contributes to the denomination.
2. Summarize denominational financial contributions and their distribution among objects.
3. Summarize what the denomination has done for the church.
4. Gather collateral evidence as to the relations with other churches of the same denomination.
5. Estimate degree to which the church fulfills denominational requirements.

SUMMARY AND CONCLUSIONS

I. Summary of Historical and Factual Data

1. Summarize total factual study of the church.
2. Interpret results from standpoint of the church's practical interests.

II. Generalization from Special Viewpoint of Scientific Hypothesis

1. Examine major crises of the church in the light of the hypothesis of the study.
2. Summarize minor adaptations.
3. Inventory specific institutional changes.
4. Generalize from these instances the apparent causes of change.
5. Note changes in the church's thinking consequent upon changes in experience.
6. Estimate the degree of the church's practical success.
7. Refer conclusions for group criticism.

SUGGESTIONS FOR SUPPLEMENTAL RESEARCH

1. List and suggest general methodology for studying important aspects of the local church that are omitted in chapters i and ii, and for which data are reasonably obtainable.
2. Keep a careful time-accounting with every process of an actual church survey and estimate cost of the current salary per hour of the surveyors.
3. Make a more extensive historical sketch of the church for publication, organizing the treatment around epochs scientifically determined.
4. See chapter iii A for more intensive study of members and constituents.
5. Map and calculate parish distribution by districts (determined as directed in chapters vi and vii) as well as by distance and directions.
6. Make a more accurate study of the church's environment by methods shown in chapter vii.

7. Study internal church organizations in terms of particular organizations as well as of types of organizations.
8. See chapter iii for a more intensive study of the minister and staff at work.
9. Make an organization chart showing relation between all staff members and lay boards and officials.
10. Carry out in full detail the use of the "Standards for City Church Plants."
11. Devise and improve summary of church finances for regular use.
12. Record impressions of competent judges of public services over a considerable period of time.
13. Conduct a more intensive survey of religious education.
14. Devise a practical, permanent record of the social and religious antecedents of new members.
15. Devise a practical, permanent form for summarizing a church's annual reports.
16. Devise a method of recording and summarizing all community service rendered by church organizations.
17. Formulate all important things which the denomination requires or expects of the church during a given year, and devise means of accurately measuring the degree to which the church fulfills them.
18. From the standpoint of their sociological significance, criticize descriptions and interpretations of churches found in denominational literature.

BIBLIOGRAPHY AND REFERENCES

Bailey and Hewitt, *Pastor's Manual of Survey and Program* (New York: Methodist Book Concern, 1921).
A loose-leaf book intended as a laboratory guide for instruction in church administration. Designed for rural churches but largely applicable to city churches as well.
Douglass, *The Church in the Changing City* (New York: Doran, 1927).
Sixteen case studies made substantially by the methods developed in this chapter, with an introduction.
Douglass, *The Springfield Church Survey* (New York: Doran, 1926).
Materials for case studies of most of the churches of the city may be located by means of the Index. These include brief formal studies of sixteen churches.
Douglass, *1,000 City Churches* (New York: Doran, 1926).
Includes thirty-one case studies.

CHAPTER III

INTENSIVE TOPICAL STUDIES

Instead of making an all-round study of itself, a church may wish to investigate some particular phase of its life or work that seems to need immediate attention: perhaps something that may be going wrong, or that ought to be lined up to accord with new experience or insight. This type of study may be made independently, or may be inserted as more intensified treatment of one or more topics within a general study; and, of course, it may be applied to groups of churches as well as to a single church.

Methods of research appropriate to intensive topical studies are illustrated in this chapter by two examples. The first is a comprehensive analysis and statement of the relationships of a church's members and constituents; the second, an intensive study of a church's staff at work.

Both examples differ from the semi-intensive treatment of the same topics in that they analyze more minutely the phenomena with which they deal, and submit the data to more elaborate statistical processes. The first example differs from the second with respect to the sources of its data and the balance between elements in its procedure. Thus, the first is concerned with existing data and their interpretation. It starts with various church records, completes and systematizes them, puts them together in new ways, as a consequence of which it is possible to draw novel conclusions. The second creates the data that are to be studied. It starts by inducing the members of a church staff to keep records of their daily duties which they have not previously kept. It then proceeds to examine the data thus secured. In handling data in a study of the first kind, after preliminary analysis and definition, statistical use is made of classifications already established. In the second kind of study it is necessary to devise distinctly novel classifications; and it is only secondarily that it becomes statistical. The two kinds of studies thus cover a considerable range of methodological issues likely to arise.

But any one of the topics covered in the last chapter might have been chosen with equal justice to illustrate intensive treatment, or may actually be chosen from time to time as particular interests come to the fore in connection with first-hand studies of particular churches. The comprehensive content and balanced interests presented in an all-round semi-intensive study permit its plan to be arrived at by logical analysis primarily. In studies of the present type the particular purpose much more completely dictates the plan. The method then follows directly from the nature of the available data.

A—A TOPICAL STUDY OF A CHURCH'S MEMBERS AND CONSTITUENTS

A comprehensive study of a church's members and constituents should start with existing church records whose characteristics must be understood. Most ministers will assert that they have records enough and in such shape as to yield a good working knowledge of their constituencies. But an attempt to use the church records as a basis for scientific research quickly proves a number of characteristic shortcomings: (1) The lists as currently kept are rarely entirely up to date. It is simply the normal situation that a considerable number of names are in an equivocal position, either because the addresses have been lost or because the church does not really know whether the person listed should still be counted as a member, or as an adherent, or not counted at all. To some extent this situation is inherent in the transiency and mobility of city populations.

(2) But the church's records of members and constituents, even when highly accurate, are rarely coördinated. The church list is in one office and one file, the Sunday-school list in another office and another file; while frequently the only lists of members of various subsidiary organizations are in the hands of the different secretaries, and are not kept according to any uniform or well-defined standards of membership or connection. The indistinct circle of remoter adherents falling outside the several formal memberships may not be regularly listed at all.

In view of the unprecise character of the minister's knowledge of his constituency, he is likely to fall back upon some such epigram as that one-third of the church consists of adherents who come without calling, one-third of adherents who come when they are called, and one-third of adherents who will not come in any circumstances.

In place of this kind of smart inaccuracy there was substituted, in the semi-intensive study of members and constituents described in chapter two, a complete listing, and an elementary statistical analysis, of all persons attached to the church in any recognizable way, either near or remote. In the present intensive study, an attempt is made to provide a method of adequate accountancy with respect to these, the church's human materials. The statistical processes are carried enough further to investigate successive aspects of the subject relative to other aspects, in order to discover the permanent inner characteristics of the constituency under investigation.

MEANS OF STUDYING MEMBERS AND CONSTITUENTS

As is shown in chapter ii, the study of members and constituents requires the creation of a comprehensive card index showing the facts about all probable relations between the constituent and the church. The schedule-card devised for this purpose is shown on page 14 and is followed by directions for filling it out. This card should also be used in the present study. It covers the age, sex, and family status of each constituent, and all the ways in which the constituent is definitely connected with the church. When the card is fully made out, it includes in succeeding columns a complete church-membership list, a complete Sunday-school enrollment, and the entire membership of every internal organization of the church.

Refinement of Definition

An intensive study is justified in drawing somewhat finer distinctions than a semi-intensive one does.

Thus, the majority of constituents of the average church belong to families that show a sort of group adherence in the sense that the family includes several of the church's members or adherents. But exactly what constitutes an adherent family? Is it simply a family that has more than an individual, say two or more persons, related to the church; or must there be an adherent *head* to constitute an adherent family? The latter definition has been somewhat arbitrarily adopted; namely, that an adherent family is one in which one or more adults, functioning as heads of the family, are adherent to the church, *along with* one or more other adults or children. Adherents not members of such family groups are denominated detached individuals. Even two or more Sunday-school pupils from a single family are put in this category unless one of the heads of the family is also an adherent. This distinction is dictated by the desire to find out how far the solidarity of the family group carries over into the church in whole or in part.

Similar refinements of definition should be made as found necessary in any intensive study.

The study of occupation presents greater difficulties. The last U. S. Census classified the gainfully employed into five hundred seventy-two different occupational groups compiled from over twenty thousand occupational designations. This shows that there are many kinds of jobs; that the same one often has many different names; and that merely to record the answer to the question, "What is your occupation?", would give nothing of scientific accuracy.

What is needed is, first, a brief and comprehensive classification of the great types of occupational activity to which all these jobs belong. This the Census furnishes under nine heads. The second great need is an indication of the status of the worker within the general occupation. There is a great gulf between a railroad president and an engine wiper, though both are engaged in transportation. Such an index is furnished by the subdivision of the Census occupations in the following list, which should be the basis of the occupational questionnaire.[1]

The questionnaire should ask specifically: "Under which of the following classes does your occupation fall?" (Check answer.) "What is your particular work called?"

TABLE XII

TABLE —OCCUPATION AND SOCIAL-ECONOMIC STATUS

I. Agriculture, forestry and animal husbandry
    a. Proprietors, officials, managers
    b. Semi-skilled workers
    c. Laborers
II. Extraction of minerals
    a. Proprietors, officials, managers
    b. Semi-skilled workers
    c. Laborers
III. Manufacturing and mechanical industries
    a. Proprietors, officials, managers
    b. Skilled workers
    c. Semi-skilled workers
    d. Laborers
IV. Transportation
    a. Proprietors, officials, managers
    b. Clerks
    c. Skilled workers
    d. Semi-skilled workers
    e. Laborers
V. Trade
    a. Proprietors, officials, managers
    b. Clerks
    c. Semi-skilled workers
    d. Laborers
VI. Public service
    a. Officials, etc.*
    b. Laborers
VII. Professional service
    a. Professional persons
    b. Semi-skilled workers
VIII. Domestic and personal service
    a. Proprietors, officials, managers
    b. Semi-skilled workers
    c. Servants
IX. Clerks

* Includes semi-official employees.

In entering the returns from the questionnaire upon the schedule card as a permanent record, the number of the occupational class (Ia, IIb, etc.) should be entered in column three, together with the particular designation as reported.

[1] Adapted from Fry, *American Villagers* (New York: Doran, 1926), p. 89.

PROCEDURE IN THE STUDY

Additional Data on Nativity, Early Environment and Occupation

Nativity, early environment and occupation are covered by columns two and three of the schedule card. In the semi-intensive study of church constituencies they were omitted, because church records rarely include them. But it is assumed that in an intensive study these additional data will be secured by means of a questionnaire mailed to the church's entire constituency. Delinquents in answering questionnaires will generally respond to one or more follow-up letters, or may be questioned in personal interviews. Failure to respond in any way should ordinarily constitute cause for removing the delinquent's name from the constituency list.

The returns may then be tabulated on a form corresponding to the questionnaire; and the number and per cent. of constituents belonging to each occupational class on each level may be calculated, together with the number in each particular occupation that it seems important to distinguish.

Column two covers two items, both of which are assumed to be indices of still more significant facts—the place of birth generally (not always) tells a man's race, language and broader national habits and viewpoint.

The questionnaire covering these points may be in the following form:

Questionnaire for Church Constituents as to Nativity

Were you born in the U. S. ...., foreign country............? (Check which.)
If a foreign country, which?............................... (Write present name of country.)

The answers to this questionnaire should be tabulated; and the number and per cent. of native- and foreign-born constituents, and of foreign-born constituents by country of nativity, should be calculated.

The subdivision in column two under the heading U. S., is intended to answer the question (which should be used in the questionnaire), "Was your early bringing-up in the city or in a rural environment?" The number and per cent. of each of the two classes found in this way, should be calculated. The assumption is, of course, that the hold-over of rural traits in the second case may distinguish the part of the city's population that came by immigration from those who were city-born.

Both early environment and occupation may then be calculated for the different age- and sex-classes shown in column one, and according to the family status of the worker.

Intensive Editorial Processes

An intensive study implies that besides the ability to take time to collect additional data, it is also possible to work over existing data

77

more carefully. The most important of secondary processes to which the data one has gathered must be subjected, is that of editing for clearness and uniformity. This process can frequently save otherwise unusable data. Thus, in a St. Louis church, the original entry on the schedules was, in two instances, such that the sex of the person whose name was entered could not be determined. The *number* of cases of this sort being *negligible,* they were disposed of by calling *one* case male and the other female. This is good statistical practice. Age, however, in the case cited, presented a more serious problem. No age was given in column one of the schedule for nearly one-fourth of the minor adherents. (Age-data are not accurately kept by most churches, at least not for entire constituency.) It was therefore necessary in these cases to *derive age-data* from other sources. One of these sources was the grade of such minors as were enrolled in Sunday school, as determined by Sunday-school records. The *school* being *closely graded* on a basis of age, it was possible to supply approximate age-classification nearly approaching accuracy for a large fraction of the missing cases.

The schedule-card itself also, in Columns six to fifteen, *involved* a broad *age-classification.* Thus, while one could not be sure that no adults just over twenty-one remained in the young people's organizations, or that no backward young people continued in boys' and girls' clubs, the subsidiaries to which the constituent belonged afforded secondary age-information, and furnished a check upon the relatively few cases not determined either by the schedule or by the Sunday-school enrollment cards. These processes furnished virtually complete age-material for the classification of minors as either adolescents or children, which was the closest classification carried out in tabulation. Editing thus saved the data. But the necessity of resorting to approximations, of course, made it *impossible to use the data with the same assurance,* or to carry them *into the same detail,* as could have been done if they had been entirely accurate originally. This distinction is of general importance in statistical work.

TABULATION AND STATISTICS

The further series of statistical tables that will naturally be drawn from upon the membership and adherence cards, have already been indicated in chapter ii. They are based on the following nine primary categories or ways of regarding adherence; namely, with respect to: (1) determinate adherence as distinguished from indeterminate adherence; (2) family status (adherence by family groups as distinguished from adherence of detached individuals); (3) age; (4) sex; (5) manner of adherence; (6) number of adherents' connections with church; (7) number and nature of connections of most intimately related adherents; (8) regular church attendance; (9) pledged support. Theoretically it is possible to start with the total constituency classified under any one of the heads and to subclassify it from all the other standpoints singly or in any logically possible combination. But subdivision of the constituency on all the measurable items covered by the schedule would give a series of six hundred seventy-two subclasses. Practically, as always, the cost of statistical comparison dictates that it be limited to those points at which it is most fruitful for interpretation. Comparison of differences among constituents, adherent families, and detached individuals; between male and female constituents; and between old and young; are important enough to be carried throughout the series. The resulting tables are too extensive to be presented in entirety; but the following sufficiently illustrate the general principles of tabulating and using the data.

(1) *Constituents by Age and Sex*

The first count and tabulation may summarize the family status, age and sex of all constituents. (1) Make a table in the following form:

TABLE XIII

TABLE —CONSTITUENTS BY FAMILY STATUS, AGE AND SEX

			CONSTITUENTS' FAMILY STATUS					
			BELONG TO FAMILY GROUPS			DETACHED INDIVIDUALS		
AGE	TOTAL							
	Male	*Female*	*Total*	*Male*	*Female*	*Total*	*Male*	*Female*
ALL AGES								
Adults (21 and over)								
Adolescents (15–20)								
Children (5–14)								
Infants (under 5)								

Church X, for example, has forty-three males to every fifty-seven females in its total constituency; but there are striking differences among the constituent classes with respect to sex-distribution. Minors from adherent families show almost equal numbers of male and female constituents; and female minors among individual adherents exceed male minors by only 4 per cent.

The total sex-discrepancy, consequently, lies almost entirely with the adult group. But with adults drawn from adherent families, the discrepancy is just about the average. Among detached adults, however, there are thirty-one men to sixty-nine women. This fixes the chief source of the total excess of female constituents in the detached adult group. The result is the discovery that nearly two-thirds of the constituents not connected with adherent families are female.

While, therefore, one knows that the characteristic of the church constituency as a whole is that it contains nine members from family groups to six detached individuals, or seven males to nine females, one can also tell in exactly what proportion the different elements of the constituency contribute to the total, how much each varies from the total, and in brief, what are, or may be, some of the causes of the variation.

(2) *Comparison with Other Pertinent Data*

An intensive study will naturally go outside its own data when other immediately comparable data are available. It will be natural, for example, to see how the sex-distribution and age-distribution of the church's constituency differ from those of the general population of the city or district from which the constituency is drawn. For large cities, the age-distribution of population is given in total and by wards in the U. S. Census, so that the distribution according to various broad age-groups can be calculated. Thus for the ages indicated in the following table, the distribution of the population of St. Louis is 72 per cent. adult, 11 per cent. adolescent and 17 per cent. child. That of a certain St. Louis church is shown in a parallel column, with the result that one sees the church to be deficient in adults and strong in children.

TABLE XIV

TABLE —CONSTITUENTS OF THE UNION METHODIST CHURCH BY AGE COMPARED WITH THE CORRESPONDING POPULATION OF ST. LOUIS

Age	Per Cent. Distribution Union Methodist Church	St. Louis
Total	100	100
Adults (21 and over)	65	72
Adolescents (15–20)	10	11
Children (5–14)	25	17

In normal populations the sexes almost exactly balance each other, so that any discrepancy of female over male in a church constituency shows the one-sidedness of the appeal of organized religion. In small areas of a city, however, like wards and enumeration districts, the general population may show very great differences in sex-distribution as well as in age-distribution; as, for example, a great excess of single men in lodging-house districts, or of young children in certain suburbs. Comparison on this basis shows how much the church's variation from a true cross-sectional distribution as to age or sex exceeds the variation, itself abnormal, of a limited population with which the church may have to do.

80

(3) Manner of Adherence

The next point in the study of the church's constituency relates to manner of adherence.

When the schedule-card is filled out for all the subsidiary organizations of a church, it may involve twenty or thirty different determinate ways of belonging to the church or some of its organizations. The combination of ways arising from so many organizations and relationships manifestly results in classes too numerous to handle. Consequently some method of generalization with respect to manner of adherence will have to be adopted.

TABLE XV

TABLE —RELATIONSHIP OF CONSTITUENTS TO THE CHURCH BY FAMILY STATUS

RELATIONSHIP	CLASSES		
	FAMILY STATUS		
	Total No.	Family Group No.	Individual No.
Total constituency	1,590	921	669
Total			
Members of church	885	581	304
Members of Sunday school	625	338	287
Members of subsidiaries	571	360	211
Exclusive Relationships			
Members of church only	523	313	210
Members of Sunday school only	316	121	195
Members of subsidiaries only	201	98	103
Overlapping Relationships			
Overlap of church and Sunday school	94	67	27
Overlap of church, Sunday school and subsidiaries	113	89	24
Overlap of church and subsidiaries	155	112	43
Overlap of Sunday school and subsidiaries	102	61	41
Indeterminate Adherents			
Related through family only	60	60	0
No specified connection	26	0	26

It will be accepted that the church commonly expresses itself in three major fields of activity; namely, its worship and public services, its Sunday school, and its subsidiary organizations and activities. The study therefore proceeds to classify the manner of the constituents' relationships to the church from these controlling standpoints under seven categories, three exclusive and four overlapping, as shown in the preceding table. The sum of exclusive and overlapping memberships of church, Sunday school, and subsidiary organizations, respectively, gave their totals as shown at the beginning of the table. The table that presents an actual case illustratively also accounts separately for determinate constituents and for those listed by name only.

Graphic representation of the manner of adherence may be made in the form shown in Chart IV. In the illustrative case the 1,504 determinate constituents tend to fall into three major groups; namely, church-members only, Sunday-school pupils only, and subsidiary members only. These are joined together by rather narrow overlapping memberships and have as their nucleus a small fraction (8

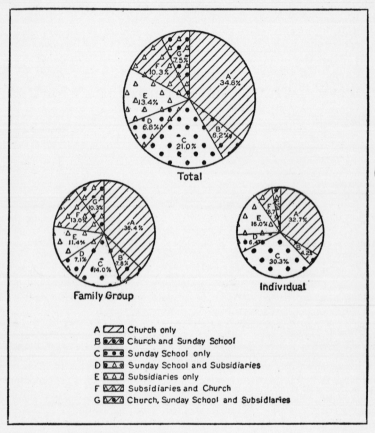

CHART IV—RELATIONSHIPS OF ADHERENTS TO A CHURCH, OVERLAPPING AND EXCLUSIVE.

per cent.) of adherents related by triple overlapping membership in church, Sunday school, and subsidiary.

The next study of manner of adherence is with reference to family status. In the illustrative case, it appears (in the preceding table) that overlapping membership is relatively much more frequent with adherents coming from adherent families, and that such adherents furnish a particularly large proportion of triply related constituents. Detached individuals, on the contrary, furnish a larger proportion of constituents who belong to the Sunday school only, or to the subsidiaries only. Similar comparisons should be made for any church studied intensively.

When manner of adherence is studied from the standpoint of age, the adult and minor groups may show very different tendencies. Adults account for a disproportionate fraction of the overlapping memberships in the sample case, except those in Sunday school and subsidiaries and those who belong to the church only. Minors, on the contrary, as would be expected, supply a disproportionate number of constituents who belong to the Sunday school or the subsidiaries only. But the proportions would vary from church to church.

Manner of adherence studied with respect to sex, shows in the sample case that male and female minors tend to belong to the church

TABLE XVI

TABLE —NUMBER OF ADHERENTS' CONNECTIONS WITH THE CHURCH, BY FAMILY STATUS AND BY AGE-GROUPS

NUMBER OF CONNECTIONS				AGE-GROUP				
	TOTAL			ADULTS			MINORS		
	Total	Family Group	Individual	Total	Family Group	Individual	Total	Family Group	Individual
Total	1,590	921	669	1,029	648	381	561	273	288
Reported	1,517	868	649	968	601	367	549	267	282
One	859	415	444	471	249	222	388	166	222
Two	350	219	131	265	170	95	85	49	36
Three	187	141	46	143	112	31	44	29	15
Four	90	69	21	70	55	15	20	14	6
Five	23	17	6	14	11	3	9	6	3
Six	5	4	1	3	2	1	2	2	0
Seven or more	3	3	0	2	2	0	1	1	0
Not reported	73	53	20	61	47	14	12	6	6

in about the same ways; but that in the adult group, the excess of females is much greater in the Sunday school and in the subsidiaries than in the church, and especially in the overlapping memberships of church and Sunday school, and of church, Sunday school and subsidiaries.

Similar calculations for any church being intensively studied would show what classes of adherents account for the generic phenomena of adherence, and in what proportion.

(4) *Number of Connections*

A rough measurement of the closeness or remoteness of the adherents' relation to the church is implied in the distinction between overlapping and one-connection adherence. This should be supplemented by a direct measurement of closeness or remoteness of relation of adherents, by counting the exact number of their connections;

and for this purpose making a pledge of financial support should be counted as a connection, as also should membership in church, Sunday school or subsidiary. The form of tabulating, and the results of this count in the sample case, appear in the table on page 83.

In the sample case, well over half of the total number of constituents have but one determinate relationship with the church. Con-

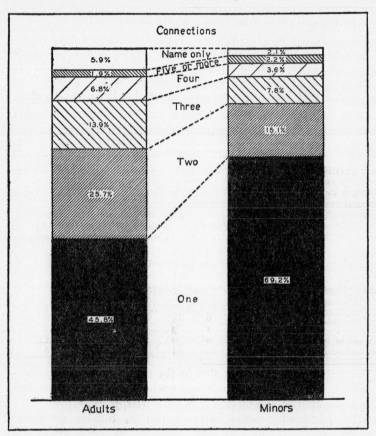

stituents belonging to adherent families show a considerably greater tendency to numerous connections than do detached individuals.

Just under one-half of the adult constituents are "oncers"; but this is the case with 70 per cent. of minor constituents. Adults, especially those belonging to adherent families, show a greater tendency to numerous connections all the way up the scale. A sex tendency relative to closeness of connection with the church has already been hinted at in the study of manner of adherence. Consequently, in order to economize labor, comparison on the basis of sex need not be made directly on this point. The general picture produced by this process corresponds to the one previously discovered. Even when financial support of the church is added to attendance and participation, the majority of adherents have only one attachment. This would be found true in all churches; but the proportion of those with more attachments might vary greatly.

(5) *Constituents with Numerous and Intimate Relations*

It obviously will be advantageous to study the exceptional group of very closely connected constituents. These may be defined as persons who attend church regularly, are members of the Sunday school and have two or more other stated connections with the church.

A count, and a form of classification, for these constituents are shown in the following table. In the sample case they were limited to one hundred and eight persons, or about 7 per cent. of the total constituency.

TABLE XVII

TABLE —CHURCH ATTENDANTS WHO ARE SUNDAY-SCHOOL MEMBERS AND HAVE TWO OR MORE STATED CONNECTIONS, BY AGE AND SEX

Age-Group	Total	Male	Female
Total ages	108	39	69
Attend church, belong to Sunday school, and two other connections	53	20	33
Attend church, belong to Sunday school, and three other connections	39	14	25
Attend church, belong to Sunday school, and four or more other connections	16	5	11

(Subdivide in the same form for adults, adolescents and children)

In the sample case, almost exactly one-half of the one hundred and eight closely connected adherents have only two connections in addition to church attendance and Sunday-school enrollment, while about one-third have three, and nearly one-sixth four or more.

Nearly two-thirds of these ultra faithful constituents are women whose preponderance is somewhat greater in the adult group than in the minor group.

Again, such calculations locate degrees of adherence with particular groups of constituents. Checking back against the preceding study of manner of adherence, it is obvious that close relationship should be looked for among the constituents who belong to church and subsidiaries, to Sunday school and subsidiaries, or to all three. It will interest one to calculate the per cent. of each of these classes who have as high as five or more connections with the church (that is to say, who attend, belong to the Sunday school, and either pledge or belong to a second or third subsidiary).

In the sample case, the following results were found:

Manner of Adherence	Per Cent. with Five or More Connections
Members of church and subsidiaries	4
Members of Sunday school and subsidiaries	5
Members of church, Sunday school and subsidiaries	19

This further demonstrates the extremely large number of church relationships that are entered upon by a small fraction of constituents. This fraction, however, will vary significantly from church to church.

(6) *Regular Attendants*

What proportion of the total constituency of the church can be reported as regular attendants at public services? This question involves a definition of regular attendant, such as one who attends at least one service per Sunday for thirty-six or forty Sundays in the year (or a smaller fraction in churches that hold no summer services).

A form for comparing attendants with total constituents according to manner of adherence is shown in the following table.

TABLE XVIII

TABLE —REGULAR ATTENDANTS, BY TYPE OF RELATION TO CHURCH AND BY CONSTITUENT CLASSES

Type of Relationship	Total Constituents	Regular Attendants
All classes		
Member of church only		
Member of church and Sunday school		
Member of church, Sunday school and subsidiaries		
Member of church and subsidiaries		
Member of Sunday school only		
Member of subsidiaries only		
Member of Sunday school and subsidiaries		
Related through family only		
No specified connection		

This table should be filled out separately for constituents from family groups and for detached individuals. Similar tables may be made classifying attendants with respect to age or sex.

As might have been expected, regular attendants, in the sample case, come much more frequently from adherent families than from detached individuals. Only 14 per cent. of all non-family constituents attend church regularly. And this group consists largely of children. More significant is the fact that of church-members themselves, only one-fifth attend regularly. Constituents of this class can have no substitute interest; if they do not attend, they are in no actively participant relation with the church at all, because they belong to none of its organizations. Almost none who are members

86

of the Sunday school only, or of the subsidiaries only, attend. That is to say, in this case at least, public congregations are not strengthened by these minor organizations, save for the few members who are in dual or triple membership. On the other hand, well toward one-half of those who are members of both church and Sunday school, over half the members of church and subsidiaries, and 70 per cent. of those with triply overlapping membership in church, Sunday school and subsidiaries, are regular attendants. This shows how strongly regular attendance is associated with closeness of connection. It is not a substitute for some other relation, but a consistent supplement to the already numerous relations of the most faithful constituents. Other churches would be likely to find similar conditions, but with variations.

(7) *Pledged Contributors*

Only one-fourth of the total constituency of the sample church, and about 41 per cent. of the total church-membership make a specific pledge of financial support. The proportion is 30 per cent. with constituents from adherent families and 19 per cent. for detached individuals. The proportion of non-members of church who pledge is negligible.

These proportions should be calculated for any church intensively studied, and should be tabulated in the same form as attendance has been.

(8) *Logical and Practical Outcome*

The study of a church's constituency may be carried along these lines into any convenient detail. It should stop at the point where statistical analysis no longer yields anything of significant weight.

What general gains in the understanding of the church can fairly be credited to the more intensive processes just illustrated, as compared with those on the semi-intensive level of study? Besides great completeness and accuracy of description, what intensification really amounts to scientifically is this: It locates with one or another subdivision of the constituency phenomena that are first observed as pertaining to the constituency as a whole. The varied qualities of the group are thus traced to their sources in parts of the group, and insofar the characteristics of the group are explained.

The church is then in a position to act with precision. If it knows anything that can be done to effect desired change, it knows where and toward whom to direct its efforts.

B—The Church Staff at Work

A natural subject for intensive study in a staffed church is the work of the staff over a period of time; and a considerable number of churches have been found engaged in such studies. Their results show what specific duties in the church have come to be performed by paid workers; how much work there is of each sort; and how the work is distributed among the members of the staff. These constitute grounds for the consideration of the assignment of duties; and a basis for supervisory methods which, according to common knowledge, are frequently very inexact at present.

A method of making such a study of a staff at work is set forth in the following section.

PLAN OF THE STUDY

Delimitation of Field

Who constitute the church staff? Shall the understanding be that the staff includes only religious workers and their immediate assistants, and excludes sextons and musicians; or that it includes all paid workers?

Should not the worker's leisure be studied as well as his work? Clearly, leisure has important bearings upon work; and the church is rightly interested in it. Since, however, the worker is presumably not accountable to the church for the expenditure of his leisure time, it may be better to limit the study to duty-time only. At any rate, decisions must be made at the outset as to who and what are to be investigated.

Basic Plan

What shall be the ways of regarding the minister and his staff at work? Workers have already received designations roughly indicating what sorts of work they do. But there is no standard terminology. One does not really know from a worker's title what his specific duties are. It is therefore natural to attempt more exact classification according to the kind of duties performed. Again, one member of the staff works a short day or week, others long ones. The amount of time spent in duty furnishes a second common-sense ground of classification. One may count the number of kinds of duties and record the length of time each takes. These measurements may then be used to read exact meanings into popular distinctions. Thus, a certain minister acquires the reputation of being "bookish." How much time spent on reading for sermons or in cultural pursuits should be held to justify this designation? Or, fraternal gossip says, "X is a good pastor but not much of a preacher." In such a case, it may perhaps be shown that he spends distinctly more time on pastoral work, and less on homiletical preparation, than the average.

In short, the doing of duties, because it is capable of being observed, classified and measured, is the most profitable aspect from which to study the work of the staff. On the other hand, purposes,

88

feelings experienced while doing the work, and results, cannot be directly observed, nor satisfactorily classified, nor measured. One would like to investigate these doubtless more important things; but they are ruled out for lack of available method in a study no more extensive than the one now in mind.

Means of Observation

The fundamental means of observing the staff at work is a work-record.

If the church worker's duties all consisted in applying labor-power to material objects, as is the case when the janitor cleans the floor or arranges the chairs in an assembly room, one might follow him through the week with a motion-picture machine and, by analysis and comparison, determine the effectiveness of his every motion. Since, however, most of the time the outward aspect of what he does has to be explained, one might better delegate a reporter to accompany him, to observe and record all his doings, and to explain them in the light of intelligent questioning. The best substitute for this is to let the worker be his own observer, reporter and interpreter, by means of a systematic work-record.

For what period of time shall the work of the staff be studied? Obviously, an hour, a day, or a week furnish samples of work that goes on for months or years. But an hour or a day cannot include enough pieces of work to represent all the kinds that come within any given worker's experience. Can a week do so? Possibly, if it is a thoroughly representative week—especially since most church workers follow something of a fixed routine from Sunday to Sunday. But since the church work is to a considerable degree seasonal, the sample would be more adequate if a representative week were taken from each of the four seasons.[2]

The Work-Record

A form of work-record devised from the points of view just explained, is here illustrated. On this form every worker of the church studied, accounts for all working hours during which he is on duty for at least a week, as a Minneapolis minister did in the example on page 90.

The data specifically called for by the schedule are: (1) a description of the particular work in which each worker was engaged throughout every duty-period of the day for seven days; (2) the number of minutes devoted to the performance of each separate duty for this period; (3) a designating term indicating the category or classification to which the worker thinks each particular duty belongs (as, for example, "pastoral," "homiletical," "secretarial," "janitorial"); (4) supplemental explanatory notes are invited in

2 For further discussion of the principles of sampling, see pp. 106 f.

SCHEDULE IX

WORK-RECORD SCHEDULE

(Worker's Name) .... (Street & Number) .... (City) .... (Church) ....

Full-Time Worker? .... (Yes or No) .... Part-Time Worker? .... (Time Employed Weekly) .... Position ....

1 *Time of Day*	2 *Specific Work Done*	3 *Time Consumed (Minutes)*	4 *Worker's Classification of This Work*	5 *Purpose or Problem Involved*	6 *Circumstances* (Persons, place, facilities and transportation involved)
a.m.					
8:00	Read Life of Lincoln in sermon preparation	30	Homiletical	For Lincoln's Birthday memorial sermon	
8:30	Conference with assistant pastor	20	Administrative	Arrange for calls in Sixth Ward	Regular daily conference—church secretary present
9:00	Conference on finance with chairman of trustees	25	Administrative	Preliminary to proposing Every-Member Canvass at next Trustees meeting	At his office in bank
p.m.					
2:30	Call on sick child	15	Pastoral		With visiting nurse
3:00	Interview with secretary of Council of Churches	45	Administrative	To improve relations of churches in community service	As member of Comity Commission
7:45	Arranged chairs and helped move piano	10	Janitorial		Janitor late and room not in order
8:00	Conducted prayer meeting	60	Homiletical	To produce mood suitable to the day	Special Lenten address—75 per cent.
9:00	Chatted with people socially after meeting	10	Pastoral	To develop social spirit in parish	Two strangers present

Total Hours on Duty..........

Day's Summary: Date .... Day .... Month .... Year .... Time Used in Travel .... Miles Covered ....

columns five and six of the schedule to throw light on the larger situation of which each particular duty was a part. It will be observed that only column three in the sample schedule directly calls for quantitative data; the other columns all call for qualitative data intended as aids in the more exact determination of kinds of duties.

Detailed directions for filling out the schedule should be appended to it, as follows:

Directions:

Column (1) divides the day into half-hour periods and is merely a scale over against which you are asked to write an exact description of the particular duty of which a record is being made.

Column (2). In this column please describe the work you were engaged upon at the time stated. Kindly be as specific as possible. For example, do not enter "Bible Study" but "Studied Bible in sermon preparation" or "Studied Bible for prayer meeting address."

Column (3). Enter as accurately as possible the number of minutes devoted to the performance of this work. When duties overlap, enter the major one, and explain the situation under Remarks.

Column (4). Immediately after making an entry in Columns (2) and (3), enter in Column (4) the kind of duty you have just performed, according to the classification which follows these directions. If no one of the fourteen classes fits, classify the item as "Other Classes," and write in the designation that you think ought to be applied to the duty in question.

Columns (5) and (6) afford an opportunity to throw light on the situation that led to the doing of the particular work recorded, and to state what you were trying to prepare for or to accomplish. For example, questions that may be answered here are: Who aided you? Who was there? Where was this particular duty performed? (What travel, if any, did it involve?) What problems were you trying to solve?

Classification of Duties

The duties of the entire week are to be classified under the fifteen categories enumerated below. (This classification was derived from the examination of about five hundred work schedules.) It is simply a working arrangement intended to systematize the statement of the week's work in terms drawn from practical administrative experience; not a closely logical scheme.

The particular definitions adopted for the classes of duties enumerated below are as follows:

Ministerial:—Things done by ordained clergymen by virtue of their office or by non-ordained persons exercising the offices of the minister, and not ordinarily by laymen, such as:
    Conduct of formal public services (including
      sermon delivery)
    Solemnizing marriages
    Conducting funerals
    Celebrating sacraments and ordinances
Homiletical:—Preparation and composition of material for public discourse for the pulpit or other occasions in connection with formal religious services, for other public discourse to audiences

91

in religious or related fields; or literary composition in which the minister addresses his public from the same point of view that he adopts in the pulpit and in the same field.

Pedagogical:—Teaching or direction of study of classes or groups and direct preparation for the same. (Does not include educational administration, which classifies under *homiletical* duties.)

Pastoral and Fraternal:—Face-to-face, or other, intimate personal and social relations and services conducted with view to influencing the lives or securing the welfare of individuals, families or other small and informal groups. (Such relations with fellow ministers and professional church workers are classed as "fraternal.")

Administrative:—The conduct of the church, local, denominational or interdenominational, as an organization—its business, as related to the government, finance, property, internal organization, meetings, publicity, etc., its records and all regular routine processes other than those previously classified.

Civic:—Duties performed by the worker in the community or larger area as representative of the attitude and interests of the church or of his particular organization, but outside his own parish and individual church auspices and usually in coöperation with laymen and in movements under lay initiative and control.

Clerical Duties:—Duties like those of secretary, stenographer and general office worker.

Attendance at Meetings on which attendance is expected of one in the worker's position—but which he does not conduct, and for which he is not directly responsible.

Preparation and Delivery of Formal Discourse other than under homiletical, e.g., lectures, papers, articles for publication, etc.

Specific Professional Work of Any Technically Trained Specialist when performed by himself directly; for example, that of nurses, librarians, play directors, or when performed by another in place of a trained specialist.

Leadership of Systematized Group Activity—especially that of leaders of boys' and girls', or other work following a set program other than that of the class or school session.

Duties involved in the *Maintenance of Social Position* required by the worker's position;—courtesies, social entertainment and attendance on functions which are the worker's obligation.

Duties involved in the *Maintenance of Essential Tools or Facilities* of the job; such as the upkeep of an automobile used professionally, or incidental janitorial functions.

General Cultural Pursuits:—Time spent in serious study, or attention to cultural interests, that reacts immediately upon the quality of the worker's services.

Other Classes:—Classify here all duty items that will not go under any of the previous fourteen categories.

Method of Handling the Data

The record of a week's work performed by a church staff of any considerable size is almost certain to contain several hundred separate duty-items, each classified by the worker who performed it, according to the foregoing categories.

The first step in handling the record is to edit it for consistency.

Many times the sum of the time spent on the reported items will not equal the total work-time claimed for the day. Only time accounted for in detail should be admitted; but the amount of the discrepancy between time accounted for and time claimed should be recorded, to make it possible to see whether it is characteristic of all the records.

Editing must also consider the consistency of column four with columns two, five, and six. A duty may mistakenly have been classified as administrative when the explanatory data clearly prove that it was pastoral. In this case the editor will correct the classification. If inability to classify with reasonable accuracy appears to have been characteristic of a worker, his schedule may have to be omitted from consideration in this respect.

The actual use of this schedule proves, however, that the workers' discrimination is usually significant even when not entirely accurate. The pastoral intent, for example, of sociability as expressed in the minister's greeting of the congregation at the church door, or his dropping in on social events, is nearly always recognized; and the mixture of pastoral and administrative motives in most business calls is made clear. One worker reported participation in a basketball game as "recreational-pastoral" work. Apparently he felt that, while the form of his activity was that of a sport, the purpose was to gain helpful influence over the other participants. In all such cases the effort in classification should be to try to penetrate beyond the letter of the entry to the motive; the item reported above was allowed to stand as pastoral work. Thus, also, a minister who had to deal with a case of bootlegging on the part of one of his church officers reported it as a "pastoral" duty; and the classification was accepted on the ground that his mind was evidently more concerned with the individual problem involved than with the administrative or disciplinary aspects of the case. The distinction between homiletical reading immediately related to the preparation of the sermon of the particular week, and general reading that might have incidental or future homiletical value, is found to be somewhat more difficult of classification. Workers frequently point out their uncertainty at this point. Nevertheless, in a very large proportion of cases, the worker will be able to tell whether or not sermonic preparation, at the time or later, was the dominant motive of his reading.

A final editorial problem has to do with items included in the work-record when it may be doubted whether the worker was on duty at all. The schedule has been generous in providing for conscience to be the guide in the matter. It assumes that a worker may be engaging in cultural pursuits, or in social activities necessary for the maintenance of his position, or in keeping up the necessary facilities of his office, and still be at work; but only the minister editing the work-records of his associates, or the church officers examining those of the whole staff, can decide whether the particular employing church will admit as work the particular activities claimed under these heads for the length of time claimed. Editing at this point becomes virtually a supervisory decision as to what constitutes work in a given position.

Tabulation and Summary

These editorial steps being completed, the individual work-records may be directly summarized as to duration and kind of duties in the following form; and the combined work of the staff may be similarly summarized in parallel columns, and totaled.

HOW ONE PASTOR SPENT HIS WEEK AND DIVIDED HIS WORK

CLASSIFICATION OF DUTIES	TIME SPENT (Minutes)	PER CENT. DISTRIBUTION
A. *Ministerial*	885	19.4
Sunday services	195	4.3
Midweek services	60	1.3
Weddings	165	3.6
Funerals	465	10.2
B. *Homiletical*	1,165	25.5
Preparatory study	240	5.3
Undifferentiated sermon preparation	925	20.2
C. *Pedagogical*	75	1.6
Teaching Sunday-school class	75	1.6
D. *Pastoral and Fraternal*	900	19.7
Conferences, etc.	195	4.3
Calls	510	11.1
Correspondence	30	0.7
Sociability after services	60	1.3
At social functions	90	2.0
Kindnesses—"good turns"	15	0.3
E. *Administrative*	735	16.1
Conferences staff members	120	2.6
Other conferences	180	3.9
Correspondence, reading letters	75	1.6
Correspondence, writing letters	105	2.3
Keeping records	180	3.9
Attendance, deacons' meeting	30	0.7
Attendance at church club session	45	1.0
F. *Civic*	315	6.9
Participation in meeting	165	3.6
Making address	150	3.3
G. *Maintenance of Social Position*	180	3.9
Entertainment of church dignitary	180	3.9
H. *Maintenance of Necessary Facilities of the Parish*	0	0
I. *General Cultural*	315	6.9
Reading	315	6.9
Total	4,570	100.0

76 hrs., 10 min.

STUDY OF THE TABULATED DATA

(1) *Length of Work Period*

The length of the work-week, or of the average day (either on a basis of five and a half or seven days a week), can then be calculated for all full-time and part-time workers separately, and for the entire staff. The number of days and half days off should be noted in this connection.

This calculation will probably show a striking contrast between the length of the work-week of clerical workers observing fixed office hours, and of principal workers (pastor, department heads, and deaconess) working without fixed hours. The latter, besides working more hours on the average, are likely, in addition, to be on duty on Sunday, while the secretarial workers are not.

The work-days should next be classified as to length, for each worker and the entire staff, according to the grouping shown in the following example:

Class	Duration of Duty-time	Number of Days
Short days	7 hours or less	
Medium days	7–10 hours	
Long days	Over 10 hours	

Each member of the staff should now be classified according as his average day is short, medium, or long.

(2) Work Rhythm

The rhythm of the work-week should next be studied. This will require the keeping of a supplementary record of the length of the work-day for each day during a number of weeks. As every one knows, the world's holiday is the climax of the minister's work-week. But do other members of the staff have ordinary week-ends? The tendency with respect to duration of duty-time on each of the days of the week may be studied for the staff as a whole by means of a table like the following:

DAY	DURATION OF DUTY-TIME		
	No. Days Reported	Times Longest	Times Medium	Times Shortest
Sunday				
Monday, etc.				

This table will help to reveal the time-framework within which the duties of the church workers fall. It will tell, for example, when workers who have Sunday duty take their relaxation; whether "Blue Monday" is actually observed as a holiday; and whether the minister loafs the forepart of the week and has to crowd himself at the end.

(3) Variety of Duties

The tabulation, in parallel columns, of classified statements of the week's work for an entire staff, enables one directly to read off the number of kinds of duties that fall to each member. The work of some is varied; of others, monotonous. Thus, in a certain church the director of religious education showed the widest range of duties;

the directors of pastoral and physical activities followed; and next came the deaconess. In contrast with these workers, the pastor concentrated on only four kinds of duties. The church secretary also had four kinds of duties, minor administrative duties and bits of essentially pastoral work falling to her in addition to strictly clerical work. The subordinate clerical workers, however, had but one kind of duty; they never got outside that single limited field. The staff as a whole performed eleven of the possible fourteen kinds of duties; but in the sample week, no one of its members engaged in the technical conduct of group activity (such as scoutmastership or club leadership), no one had to do any janitorial work, and no one attended a social function primarily to save his face or because his position demanded it.

(4) *Kinds of Duties*

The same tabulation enables one to note what kinds of duties each worker has, as well as how many, and how far any two or more have the same kinds. Obviously the different kinds of duties are not equally applicable to each member of the staff. Thus in a staff of nine workers, six did work in some degree pastoral, administrative, and clerical. Next in frequency was attendance at meetings for which the worker had no direct responsibility, which occurred in four cases (and which may have included partial indirect pastoral or administrative functioning); while cultural pursuits within admitted duty-time were engaged in by the four major male workers, but by none of the women workers. Presumably keeping up professionally was regarded as essential to the job in one case; and as additional to it in the other.

Ministerial functions and homiletical preparation naturally fell only to the three ordained ministers. Only the director of religious education and the deaconess did any teaching, while the single civic duty of the week fell to the director of pastoral activities.

Such an analysis enables one to assign generically similar work to different levels of responsibility; or else to raise the problem of further specialization so that the same persons may not have so many kinds. It also enables one to trace the unintentional gravitation of duties into inappropriate hands; or into the hands of those for whom the work was not intended; and it enables one to understand the actual nature of positions that have come to have their present characters through evolution rather than by deliberate creation.

(5) *Time-emphasis on Classes of Duties*

Next comes the problem of the relative amount of time required for each class (or subclass) of duties, both for individual workers and for the staff as a whole. Percentages should be calculated, and the actual compared with the desired division.

The following terms may be adapted to express the proportion of work-time spent upon a given duty:

Proportion of Time Occupied by Duty	Term Adapted to Express This Fact
Over 50 per cent.	Predominant Duty
25–49 " "	Primary Duty
10–24 " "	Secondary Duty
4–9 " "	Tertiary Duty
Less than 4 per cent.	Residual Duty

(6) *Types of Workers*

Each worker's duties should be classified in these terms. A worker whose record shows that only one duty is primary or predominant may be provisionally characterized by this fact, as belonging to a *simple* type; for example, the minister as typically a pastor or an executive. In case of two primary duties, the worker may be designated as belonging to a *mixed* type; for example, the homiletical-executive or cultural-homiletical. (Only in rare cases will as many as three primary duties be found.)

The study of the distribution of the worker's time evidently throws light upon two things: first, the demands of the position; second, the emphasis that the worker himself puts upon his job by reason of temperament or preference.

Of course, the habitual trend of the emphasis of each worker cannot be fairly determined from a single week. Nevertheless the single week's record may be valuable as a challenge even when it is not conclusive evidence. For example, a pastor spent twenty-nine hours of a week of sixty-nine duty-hours on homiletical preparation. This identified him with the preaching type of the ministry, pastoral functions occupying a strongly secondary place. But he insisted most vehemently that he was essentially an administrator. It was apparent evidence of a smoothly running system of departmentalized activity that he should have had to give only eleven hours of the sample week to administration. In the same church, the work of the director of religious education was more exclusively administrative than that of any other worker, with incidental pastoral functions. The deaconess was primarily a pastoral visitor, with secondary work as teacher; while the church secretary had absorbed limited administrative and pastoral functions in addition to clerical ones. The director of physical activities spent most of his time in the actual conduct, or coaching, of games; but with administrative duties as athletic director constituting a strong secondary element in his work. Classification according to the tendencies thus revealed may at least stand till corrected by better evidence.

Another obvious item for investigation is the cost of each worker's work per hour. The workers are paid different salaries; their work also varies in duration. Do the large salaries go with longer hours (vacations considered); and how do actual rates per hour compare? This should be calculated.

The time spent in transportation to or between duties is included in the time allowed for the duty to which it pertains. But the schedule also isolates the total of transportation time. The ratio of this item to total duty-time should be calculated; and the workers should be compared on this point.

(7) Supplemental Schedules

Since the workers of a large staff differ greatly with respect to the amount of movement from place to place involved in their work, and also with respect to the degree in which their work involves or directly affects other people, schedules supplementary to the work-record may well be added to cover these points. In effect they add additional columns to the work-record and require the worker to report where he was, and with or for whom he was working, at every duty-period for a week.

By noting the habitual differences in the records of staff workers and calculating the amount of time each worker spends in each type of place and in each type of contact with persons, one objectively distinguishes between the office worker fixed at the desk and the pastoral worker going out into the highways; between the solitary worker dealing with ideas, and the administrator dealing with men; and is able to measure the gradations from one to the other type. Then, when new workers are engaged, their qualifications may be more exactly matched with the requirements of the job.

(8) Use of Facilities

Still another useful supplemental record may be made of the frequency of the worker's use of given facilities. Make a check-list of all the professional tools, apparatus, and equipment that the church or its workers possess; and have each worker check the list whenever a given tool is used during a week. The results will throw light upon the adequacy of the equipment and the resourcefulness of the individual in using what is already provided.

PRACTICAL VALUES OF THE STUDY

The study of the church staff thus obviously raises important problems for the responsible administrator which it is not the business of a methodological discussion to solve. One is the distribution of the total time of the staff between classes of duties. In Church X, clerical work represented by four workers took nearly twice as much time as either of the two next most extensive functions; namely, the pastoral and the administrative. These, in turn, took twice as much time as homiletical preparation; and homiletical preparation took twice as much time as the performance of all ministerial functions. The time given by the director of physical activities to the conduct of games was more than that spent by all three of the ordained ministers in the conduct of religious services. The case doubtless shows the very great importance of records and long-range methods of communication, and of recreational activities, in the modern city church. Any church making such a study will have to decide whether the distribution of total time satisfactorily fulfills its purpose and ideals; also whether the duties are properly distributed among the members of the staff.[3]

SCHEME OF STUDY

(Chapter III)

(It is assumed [A] that an investigation conducted by a church relative to its own constituency will be based upon existing records supplemented by questionnaires.)

PROCEDURE

1. Bring together all the church's membership and constituency lists and records.
2. Correct lists to date.
3. Provide a schedule consolidating upon one card all the church's records relative to each family group and individual constituent.
4. Define all terms indicating manner of constituent's adherence to the church.
5. Devise classification of constituents' occupations.
6. Devise and secure filling out of questionnaires on nativity and environmental antecedents.
7. Edit returns from schedules and questionnaires.
8. Calculate family status of constituents.
9. Calculate age and sex of constituents.
10. Compare age-distribution of constituents with that of corresponding population.
11. Calculate the number and per cent. distribution of constituents according to nativity, occupation and environmental antecedents.
12. Calculate manner of adherence of constituents.
13. Calculate number of constituent's connections with church.

[3] The application to groups of churches of this method of studying the staff at work would involve the carrying out of all the processes illustrated for all the representatives of each kind of position; for example, all ministers, all assistant pastors, all secretaries, etc. Many additional comparisons as between members of these homogeneous classes would be appropriate which are not between members of a single staff representing, in the main, different types of positions in the church.

Any one of the topics suggested for semi-intensive treatment in chap. ii may, on occasion, need to be investigated on the intensive scale just illustrated for the study of church constituencies and church staffs. Suggestions for thus expanding some of them are found at the end of chap. ii, pp. 71 f.

14. Calculate the manner of adherence of constituents most closely related to the church.
15. Calculate number and per cent. of regular attendants according to manner of adherence.
16. Calculate number and per cent. of pledged contributors according to manner of adherence.
17. Plan a method of organizing the church (1) so as to increase the closeness of the average constituent's relations to it; and (2) so as to distribute responsibility more equitably and overcome its harmful concentration in the hands of a small minority.

(It is assumed [B] that a study of the church staff at work will be conducted by the church itself.)

PROCEDURE

1. Decide who are to be recognized as belonging to the staff.
2. Determine the measurable aspects of the staff's work for investigation.
3. Provide a work-record showing particular duties, their time of occurrence, duration, classification and circumstances; and have staff-members keep account of their work for a week.
4. Edit the records.
5. Summarize as to kinds of work and total and distribution of work-time, for each worker and for the entire staff.
6. Calculate the average length of the work-day and its variations for different kinds of work.
7. Calculate the variety of duties performed by each worker and by the staff as a whole.
8. Calculate the characteristic amount and per cent. of work-time spent upon the several classes of duties by each worker and by the staff as a whole.
9. Discriminate types of workers on the basis of time-emphasis on various classes of duties.
10. Calculate the cost of each worker's services per hour of work.
11. Study the time involved in transportation.
12. Have staff-members keep supplemental records for a week showing where each item of work was done, and with or for whom.
13. Record and calculate the frequency with which each item of apparatus or equipment is used by each worker for a week.
14. Criticize the amount and distribution of the staff's services in the light of the church's ideals and purposes.
15. Consider whether the staff's conditions of labor and remuneration are equitable and satisfactory.

SUGGESTIONS FOR SUPPLEMENTAL RESEARCH

(A)

1. Correlate nativity, occupation and environmental antecedents of constituents with their manner of adherence and closeness of connection with the church.
2. Calculate what proportions of the constituency belong to neighborhoods in common; i.e., live in the same districts, use the same local schools, stores, recreational facilities, etc.

3. Calculate whether and how far distance of residence from the church influences closeness of connection with any given age-group of constituents.
4. Calculate whether and how far distance of residence influences regularity of attendance and pledged contributions.

(B)

1. Analyze and classify the particular skills required by each member of the staff in the performance of his week's duties.
2. How far do different levels of intelligence on the part of those worked for, and of responsibility on the part of the workers, distinguish items of work taking identical external form: for example, (1) how is a sermon to children different from a sermon to adults; (2) how is the administrative work of an assistant minister different from that of a minister?
3. Plan the better supervision of a staff in the light of the study of its work.
4. Plan the further education of staff-members in light of the requirements of their work.
5. Show what aspects of the work of a staff are not revealed by the method of investigation discussed in the text.

BIBLIOGRAPHY AND REFERENCES

(A)

Bailey and Hewitt, *Pastor's Manual of Survey and Program* (New York: Methodist Book Concern, 1921), pp. 38-45.

Douglass, *The Springfield Church Survey* (New York: Doran, 1926), p. 211 f.

Douglass, *The Church in the Changing City* (New York: Doran, 1927). Each case study has a section on members and constituents.

(B)

Douglass, *1,000 City Churches* (New York: Doran, 1926), pp. 212-215 and 330-332.

Taylor, *Survey of Standards for Women Workers* (New York: Women's Auxiliary to the National Council, Protestant Episcopal Church, 1923).

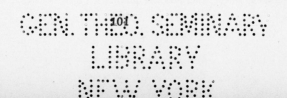

CHAPTER IV

The Study of Religious Population

Of first-hand research undertaken by the local church, one of the most frequently occurring types is the study of religious population.

Such a study is going on incidentally all the time in connection with the pastoral work of the average church. As the minister makes his rounds he gradually extends his knowledge of the parish. Strangers are located and adherents are listed territorially. One learns from the neighbors the religious proclivities of the people in the next house. The motive of all this is the desire of the church to extend itself through its regular processes of securing members.

But the city is so large and complicated, population changes are so rapid, and so many adherents keep dropping out of sight, that there is strong motive for more comprehensive study of the religious relationships of people of entire areas. Many gaps exist in the piece-meal knowledge of the parish, and people who ought to be in relation with the church are frequently missed.

Consequently a church frequently undertakes a house-to-house canvass of some area it feels responsible for in order, if possible, to secure knowledge of the general religious affinities of the population, and the particular affiliations of the individual residents, thereby to discover who are valid prospects for the church's own cultivation. A study of this kind in a city presents so great a task that it is often undertaken by groups of churches. It will here be assumed, however, that such a house-to-house religious census is to be taken by a single church. How then is the church to go about it; and what supplemental methods will be necessary to reach the fullest understanding of the data secured by such a census?

Planning the Study

THE AREA TO BE CANVASSED

The first step is obviously that of determining the area to be surveyed. Naturally it will be the church's parish in whole or in part. But just what is the church's parish? It is not, one may assume, the whole area of the community where it has any adherents, but that part where its adherents are numerous enough to imply that the church has some especial responsibility for it, or within which it seems profitable to make efforts to attract and cultivate people re-

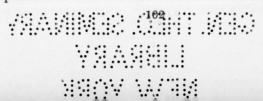

ligiously. If a campaign for members is the object of the household census, it will be wise not to cover a larger area than can be followed up; while, if the object is a discovery of the religious complexion of a part of the parish that is not well understood, say, because of rapid change of population, it will not be necessary to cover other areas at the same time. Other principles of territorial limitation may be involved in the particular purpose of a given household census.

In Case Z, which will be used illustratively, the area chosen for study consisted of thirty-four blocks, ten of them east and twenty-four west of the church building. The length of the area of the survey was nearly twice its breadth. The excess of the western sector over the eastern reflected the elongation of the parish in a westerly direction, while the narrowness of the area revealed that the parish tended to be confined between major thoroughfares on the north and south. At any rate, the church felt that this block of territory, constituting its near-in parish, was the area most in need of investigation by the method.

Subdivisions

The second step toward a household census is the subdivision of the area to be studied. This grows out of the same problems that are presented in a political, or in any general, census. These problems are, first, administrative. If the parish is not already satisfactorily districted, it will be necessary to divide up any considerable area into units to be assigned to teams of canvassers, each of which teams will be under the charge of a lieutenant responsible for carrying out an assigned part of the total survey.

Secondarily, however, the subdivision of an area is related to the interpretation of the data after they have been secured. A religious canvass will, if possible, use the same territorial units that have been used by other studies. For example, in Case Z, a recent extensive economic study had revealed that the twenty-four blocks west of the church represented much higher rental average than the ten blocks east. The church fortunately was able to arrange its data to show whether it was succeeding better, or whether it had left more people uncultivated, in the higher or the lower rent areas.

This case also illustrates the scientific requirement that areas covered by the subdivisions should be as homogeneous as possible, so that, before attempting comparisons, one may know that like is being compared with like.[1]

[1] The United States Census gives an elaborate analysis of population for wards of cities of 100,000 inhabitants and over. If the area surveyed substantially corresponds to a city ward, these data throw important light on the general characteristics of the people who are being studied religiously in the household census. These data are originally gathered by small enumeration precincts of a few blocks each. A good many cities have secured these data from the Bureau of the Census. In case they are available in any given city, they afford an exceedingly important background for the study of religious population. For an example of such a utilization of the census data, see p. 109.

HOW TO STUDY THE CITY CHURCH

ORGANIZATION AND ADMINISTRATION OF THE CENSUS

The area of the religious census having been determined, the series of steps relating to its practical organization and administration must be taken. Because it may be helpful in the assigning of work to the canvassers, and in the directing of that work, as much information of certain kinds as it is possible to get should be secured in advance. It is particularly necessary to discover about how many families live in each block or enumeration precinct, so as to apportion the work. For this purpose the addresses in city directories should be counted block by block, or the poll-books of enrolled voters secured. People change their addresses so rapidly in cities that no list of names derived from a book will be up to date; and it ordinarily confuses the canvasser to look for a given family and be unable to locate it. It is better therefore to be able to say to a team of canvassers: "There are ten families in six houses on the end of this block, or about fourteen families in this apartment house. The number may have changed by some one moving, or by the doubling up of families in the same apartment. You are to find and get information from *whoever is there;* but we take these means of determining that you know in advance within these rather narrow limits, with what your canvass will have to deal."

A routing for each team from the church to the place of canvass, with a suggested method of transportation, will be serviceable to canvassers who have to work in parts of the city with which they are unfamiliar. The entire work must be so organized that every family in the area canvassed will be reached smoothly and without duplication within the time and by the number of canvassers available.

It is easier to control a canvass, and to create enthusiasm and morale on the part of the canvassing force, if the work is done simultaneously, say, within a single Sunday afternoon. A team of two canvassers, with a reasonable schedule-card, can ordinarily cover eight or ten families within a three-hour period; and, on the likelihood that some may be away, such a team may even be given a maximum of twelve family addresses.

THE SCHEDULE

What constitutes a proper schedule-card? In other words, what information does the religious census seek, and what are the questions that have to be asked family by family as the canvassers go from house to house? A reasonable schedule-card must confine itself to the amount of information that can ordinarily be secured by strangers presenting themselves at one's door and asking what are bound to seem somewhat intimate questions. The card used in the Interchurch survey of St. Louis was a simplification of the official Interchurch

World Movement card, intended for inexperienced canvassers; and it proved fairly successful in their hands. The card was similar in form to the one shown on page 108.

Besides getting the family relationships of all members of every family, and the ages of children under twenty-one years, this card asks five questions that reveal the religious status of the persons canvassed: namely, whether they claim allegiance to any faith; whether they belong to any particular denominational church; whether they attend though they do not belong; whether they prefer any particular denominational church though they neither belong nor attend; and whether or not they are enrolled in Sunday school. The card is made out by entering a check-mark for every question answered by "yes," a zero for every question answered by "no," and the letters "n.i." (no information) for cases where information cannot be secured.

The low proportion of cases in St. Louis in which information was refused, and the tabulability of most of the returns, indicate that a schedule of the degree of complexity illustrated will work in an ordinary canvass. On the other hand, the returns on more complicated cards have generally proved so incomplete that the tabulable material did not greatly exceed that on the sample card.[2]

SECURING AND TRAINING CANVASSERS

The plan of the canvass and the schedule to be used being determined, the next step is to develop a corps of canvassers. A church will naturally look to its own congregation, and will find itself limited to fairly active persons of some experience in contacts with people. Intimate knowledge of the area to be surveyed is, of course, an obvious advantage. Employed young people make good canvassers; but children should not be used.

MAKING THE STUDY

The canvassers should have their assignments of territory clearly and definitely made, and should be drilled in the technique of obtaining the information included in the schedule-card. One of the best ways of giving such training is to conduct a series of dramatizations in which some of the canvassers represent the families being called on, and the others the canvassers themselves. The method of introducing oneself to the family, of stating the object of the call, and of getting the items of information one by one, can then be drawn out inductively; and the entire group present can contribute to the criticism and discussion. Courtesy, simple and businesslike statement of what is wanted, tact and sympathy in asking the questions, per-

[2] A sample of a schedule suitable for more experienced canvassers in a more leisurely study is shown on p. 108.

sistence in getting the information when it is slow in coming, as well as the need to stop when the bounds of courtesy and reason have been reached, are the chief points to be considered. As previously indicated, the majority of people of all faiths and of none will cheerfully tell the bare facts of their religious predilections; and Protestants will almost always give the additional facts requested to a canvasser of their own faith. It is easier and, on the whole, more practical in a Protestant canvass not to ask how frequently one of another faith attends church, or whether his children attend Sunday school. When this has been attempted, the data generally have been so indefinite as to be untabulable.

With proper selection and assignment of territory and the organization of the survey under a general director and teams with their own lieutenants each covering a limited area, with a reasonable schedule and a body of canvassers trained in one or two institute periods, the census will be successfully carried out with about the rapidity previously indicated: namely, two canvassers going together can handle an average of from eight to ten families (with a possible extension to twelve contiguous addresses to allow margin for people not at home) in about three hours' actual canvassing time.

The results from all canvassers should immediately be returned to the central church office on the day of the canvass so that the returns can be checked up promptly.

THE STUDY OF RELIGIOUS POPULATIONS BY SAMPLE

A comprehensive canvass intended to cover every family in a given area is the only method of studying religious population that yields an actual "prospect list" for the church to cultivate pastorally. If, however, the object of the investigation is to understand the religious complexion of an area, say, with reference to the desirability of starting a new church, or to the development of the service program of an old church with a view to adaptation to the community, a better method of conducting the census is probably that of sampling.

With a proper guarding of the character of the sample, the scientific results may be broader and fully as accurate as those of the attempted 100 per cent. canvass. A sample of from one-tenth to one-fifth of the population will be sufficient. The quality of a carload of wheat may be judged from a handful if it is certain that the qualities of the whole are present in the limited quantity and that they are there disposed according to their proportion throughout the whole.[3] This principle of sampling applied to such a social phenomenon as population requires that the samples of population be chosen from socially homogeneous areas within the total area under investigation. This principle has already been presented as the proper basis for the subdividing of any area to be studied. Blocks including people of

[3] Chaddock, *Principles of Statistics* (Boston, Houghton Mifflin Co., 1925), p. 382.

like nationality, wealth, etc., should be grouped together and a sample taken separately from each. Some of the criteria of homogeneity will be manifest to any one generally familiar with the area. Others will have to depend upon precise measurement arrived at in previous studies, such, of course, as various official censuses. In the case of Church Z already cited, ten blocks east of the church were known from previous economic studies, to be poorer than the twenty-four blocks west of it. Therefore the church properly subdivided the territory so it could study the two sides separately. On both sides, two- or four-family houses were the prevailing type of residence, with a few one-family houses, some apartments over retail stores, and an occasional apartment house. In areas of more mixed housing, it would obviously be necessary only to take, as a religious sample of population, every fifth or tenth family in each block. An adequate sample would require that the same proportion be taken from each type of housing within each block.

In an area of more complex social character, it will be necessary in planning the canvass to consult social workers or other authorities who have a scientific knowledge of the community in detail; also, perhaps, to take something of a reconnaissance cross-sectional canvass. That is to say, before making even the sample canvass one might have to go to every tenth or fifth family along a number of streets of different characters so as to find out just where one type of population ends and another begins. If by these means the representative character of the sample is assured in terms of small areas, the proportions, say, of Catholics, Protestants and Jews, may be very accurately estimated for the area as a whole by the combination of the separately secured results.

The advantage of the sampling method is that, for an equal expenditure of time and effort, experienced canvassers can be hired who can handle a more complicated schedule-card and bring it back more accurately filled out. The time required to secure, organize and train volunteer canvassers, and to use the great mass of somewhat inaccurate data which they bring back, will frequently be better expended under this alternative. The sampling canvass carried out by hired canvassers can be more leisurely, the canvassers can be sent back to secure information missed on the first rounds; and in general they can be held to more exacting standards in their work than volunteers can.

A sample schedule-card suited for use by paid canvassers or by the professional members of church staffs in ordinary parish work is presented on page 108.

So elaborate a schedule is definitely not recommended for volunteers. As used in volunteer hands in the Springfield Survey, only fourteen of the twenty-nine questions covered by the schedule were answered with sufficient accuracy to permit of the results being tabulated.

SCHEDULE X

FAMILY NAME _____

WHITE ☐ NEGRO ☐ OTHER ☐ (Check Race)

ADDRESS No ____ STREET

DISTRICT No ____
WARD No ____

	ADULTS 21 YEARS OF AGE AND OVER — NAMES (1)	WHERE BORN U.S. CITY (2)	RURAL (3)	OTHER COUNTRY (Give Name) (4)	LANGUAGE OF MOTHER (5)	FAITH CATHOLIC (6)	HEBREW (7)	PROTESTANT (8)	OTHERS (9)	NO PREFERENCE (10)	NAME OF CHURCH AND DENOMINATION OR SYNAGOGUE MEMBER OF (11)	YOU PREFER (12)	ANY FAITH NOT MEMBER (13)	FREQUENCY OF CHURCH ATTENDANCE — ATTENDED LAST MONTH (14)	LAST YEAR (15)	NEVER (16)	DO YOU ATTEND S.S.? YES (17)	NO (18)	ANY CONNECTION WITH OTHER ACTIVITIES OF ANY CHURCH? KIND? (19)
A	FATHER																		
B	MOTHER																		
C	OTHERS M																		
D																			
E	F																		
F																			
	CHILDREN UNDER 21 BOYS GIRLS AGE																		
G																			
H																			
I																			
J																			
K																			

HOUSEHOLD CARD   DATE ____   NAME OF VISITOR ____

Springfield Social and Religious Survey 1922

108

Besides the fact that it covers more items of information, the chief differences in principle between this schedule and the one previously presented are: (1) that the more inclusive schedule furnishes data that enable one to classify population by language of mother, as well as by country of birth, in determining race as related to nationality. The reason for this will be apparent to any one who has attempted to use the population data of the United States Census. These data are entirely blind with respect to persons born in countries inhabited by mixed races. Thus the majority of immigrants reported as born in Russia are actually Jews. The language of the mother, in addition to the country of nativity, really is needed to fix the population type.

(2) In the fuller schedule, frequency of attendance at church is asked for rather than the bare "yes" or "no" answer.

(3) Connection with the church through activities other than attendance at church and Sunday school is also added.

METHOD OF HANDLING AND UTILIZING RETURNS

Whether the household religious census is by total or by sample, the method of handling the data for utilization will be the same. The principles of tabulation and statistical organization of any data secured by the method of filling out schedules are discussed elsewhere,[4] and only their particular application to the household census need be mentioned here.

Check on Completeness

After the census canvass has been made, the first step is to determine its degree of completeness with reference to total population, if that is known, or to the estimated number of families, if accurate knowledge was not secured in advance of the canvass. In the example from the St. Louis Survey presented below, the population by age-groups was accurately known for small districts on the basis of the 1920 Census, the canvass having followed within two years.

District (*Carondelet*)

Number of blocks in which household information was secured	130
Households visited	2,094
Households for which information was secured	
Number	1,820
Per cent. of households covered	86.9
Population	
Total estimated 1920	37,879
Estimated 13 years of age and over	27,652
Estimated under 24 years of age	18,561
Individuals for whom information was secured	
13 years of age and over	5,496
Per cent. of estimated 13 years and over	19.9
Under 24 years of age	2,414
Per cent. of estimated under 24 years of age	13.0

4 See pp. 16 f.

In the case cited, information called for by the schedule was received from 86.9 per cent. of the households visited; but the total population reached by the canvass was only 19.9 per cent. of all persons thirteen years of age and over, and 13.0 per cent. of those under twenty-four years old. In other words, though the canvass was undertaken on the 100 per cent. basis, it turned out to be merely a large sample, the validity of which was dependent upon its representative character; that is to say, its proper distribution through the subdivisions of the district according to which the canvass was taken. In this particular case, there was no adequate method of checking back to determine the validity of the sample, since the canvass was not projected on the sampling basis. Hence the results, as an interpretation of the religious relations of the 37,879 people of the district, had only limited validity; and estimates were actually resorted to to correct them. This illustrates the diminished usefulness of a canvass projected on so large a scale that the complete task of carrying it out is beyond the power of the persons engaged in the work.

Sorting Schedules and Tabulating Returns for Immediate Use

In a household religious census undertaken as a basis for a campaign for church-members, it is highly probable that the zeal to use the information will not last so long as the slow statistical processes necessary to interpret it are likely to take. Hence it is important to get the first practical values out of the data promptly. The schedule-cards should be thrown as quickly as possible so as to segregate the following data: names and addresses of (1) persons preferring the church making the canvass; (2) persons preferring the denomination of the church making the canvass; (3) Protestants with no church preference; (4) persons with no faith; (5) children conveniently located with respect to the church and out of Sunday school. There will be some question of the propriety of cultivating unchurched Protestant children of the vicinity whose parents prefer some other denomination; each church will settle this for itself. In the large, the classes above named represent the prospects revealed by the canvass in somewhat the order of practical hopefulness of getting results from them. The names of these persons should be drawn off in duplicate lists, so that the original cards are free for statistical use. The immediate uses of a household religious census may be illustrated from the Springfield Church Survey. Immediately after the canvass, the cards were assembled in the central office. Sixteen churches, including some of the largest in the city, drew off lists of membership prospects which were effectively used, as was proved by subsequent testimonies, samples of which follow:

"Our church had out one hundred and one canvassers and visited 1,078 families, 244 of whom were not at home, but 834 furnished information."

"Immediately after the assembling of the 3,000 cards returned for the Forest Park District, the church put a force of fifteen on the examination of the cards, borrowing five typewriters in addition to those already belonging to its office.

"They found 360 cards of people preferring the Baptist denomination, or having no preference though Protestant; and of these, 155 families were selected as being live prospects and the church is beginning immediately to cultivate them."

"After numerous calls the pastor reported that he believed that from 50 to 75 per cent. of the persons covered by these cards would come permanently upon his calling list as in some measure constituents of the parish. He stated that he was finding three classes of persons as the result of the canvass:

1. Those who had just come to town.
2. Those who had fallen out of churchgoing habits but still regarded themselves as connected with the churches; and
3. Those who had been for many years out of touch with the church but who were in many cases recoverable as the result of cultivation." [5]

STATISTICAL STUDY

The most obvious statistical result of the household religious census is to get a count, by total area canvassed and by subdivision, of the faith and denomination of every family and individual from whom information was secured. For administrative and pastoral reasons, the summary of results should be made by blocks or such subdivisions as may be used for later follow-up work. For scientific reasons it should be by subdivisions representing homogeneous territory. The summary of results of the canvass of thirty-four blocks by Church Z may serve as a suitable example.

Criticism of the Method of Tabulation

In the case mentioned, 28 per cent. of the families canvassed yielded no information, and the canvassers did not go back to secure it. If these cases were equally distributed throughout the population, the ratios secured by the incomplete canvass would hold for the whole population. If those failing to answer were chiefly Catholics and Jews, the results would be highly unreliable. In view of the very small number of Negroes in the district, the ignoring of the four cases found was practically legitimate. The inclusion of vacant property under "number of families canvassed" was, however, not legitimate. Vacant property, if enumerated at all, should have been subtracted before the data were summarized by families.

In the table, the 71 per cent. of the families of the areas, who gave information, are classified according to faith; and, within the

[5] Douglass, *The Springfield Church Survey*, p. 391.

TABLE XIX

FIRST SUMMARY OF HOUSEHOLD RELIGIOUS CANVASS, CASE Z

DENOMINATION	NUMBER OF FAMILIES BY DIRECTION					PER CENT.	
	Northwest	*Southwest*	*Southeast*	*Northeast*	*Total*	*By Church*	*By Faith*
Presbyterian					159	23.0	
Church Z	22½	47½	13½	10½	94		
Other churches	19½	25	11½	9	65		
Episcopal	14	24	5	8½	51½	7.5	
Methodist Episcopal	24	50	21	14½	109½	15.9	
Baptist	21	25	19	29	94	13.6	
Congregational	26	19½	17½	10½	73½	10.6	
Christian Science	17	20½	9	8½	55	8.0	
Christian	16	20½	9½	8½	54½	7.9	
Lutheran	12½	7	13	6	38½	5.6	
Evangelical	2½	4½	5	2	14	2.1	
Divine Humanity	1	0	0	0	1		
Ch. of Christ Carmelite	0	0	1	0	1		
Reformed Church	0	0	0	1	1		
Intern'l Bible Student	0	0	1	0	1		
Latter Day Saints	1	0	0	0	1		
Truth Center	0	0	1	1	2		
Missionary Alliance	1	0	0	1	2		
Unitarian	3½	1½	0	0	5	1.0	
Ethical Culture Soc.	2	0	0	0	2		
Spiritualist	0	½	1	1	2½		
Divine Metaphysics	0	1	0	0	1		
Adventist	0	0	0	½	½		
Nazarene	0	0	0	2	2		
Pilgrim Holiness	0	0	0	1	1		
Church of Christ	0	0	0	1	1		
Protestant preference —no church	2	9½	0	5	16½	2.3	
Total Protestant	185½	256	128	120½	690		48.6
Roman Catholic	149	139	69½	51½	409		28.8
Jewish	34	55½	22	117	228½		16.1
No Church —no preference	23	40½	20	10	93½		6.5
Total	391½	491	239½	299	1,421		100.0
No information	181	201	47	120	549		
Refused information	12	14	1	8	35		
Vacant property	10	20	6	12	48		
No response to bell	159	167	37	99	462		
Negro family	0	0	3	1	4		
Total families (55 families divided)					1,970		

Protestant group, by denomination. The division of Presbyterians between the church making the canvass and other Presbyterian churches is also indicated. This is a good illustration of subdividing that part of the data for which subdivision is important. The device of accounting for families divided as to denomination or faith by a fractional score is also a good one.

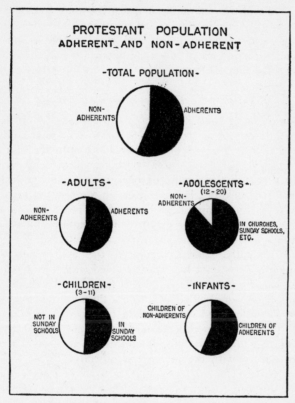

CHART VI—PROTESTANT ADHERENTS AND NON-ADHERENTS IN SPRINGFIELD BY AGE-GROUPS.

But this tabulation gives only the bare fact of religious connection and not the manner or degree of connection. The sample schedule-card indicates three relationships with the church: namely, by membership, by church attendance, or by preference without membership or attendance. There should evidently be a second tabulation making those distinctions, say, by denominations. Similarly, persons under twenty-four years of age who are in and out of Sunday school should be tabulated. The correlation of information as to faith and denomination with age-data could also be carried out. Where a household religious census is made part of an intensive study of a local church, the checking of data secured from religious populations over against that secured from church records is obviously important. Thus, the age-distribution, manner of adherence, and the composition of the constituency according as it is composed of adherent families or of detached individuals, should be worked out from the census schedules in tables corresponding with those used in the intensive study of the church constituency on corresponding points.[6]

Additional tables based on the items of the more complete schedule should be worked out in similar fashion when that schedule is used. Thus, the ratios between urban and rural nativity, and between native- and foreign-born, throw very important light upon the characteristics of denominations.

Testing the Results by Facts Independently Known

The completeness of the household canvass made by Case Z was easily verified on the basis of an elaborate economic study of the same area made a few months earlier. Sometimes a church itself has previously covered the same territory within a relatively short time. In this case the results of one canvass will naturally check the other. It is possible, however, that in the securing of confirmatory results, a church may have been merely repeating some permanent bias. Thus, in both the extensive household canvasses made by the St. Louis and the Springfield surveys, a testing of the results by facts independently known convinced the statisticians of these projects that a Protestant bias was involved which rendered some of the statistical results untenable. With no purpose to omit any one, Protestant canvassers had simply been a little more enterprising and persistent in finding and securing data from people who might yield prospects for their own churches than they had been in getting the same data from others. This illustrates the danger in mixing the campaign motive with the attempt at objective discovery of facts. The only remedy in such an event is to devise some method of systematic correction of the bias. Such a remedy was employed in both of the surveys cited. The method of making such correction, and of supplementing data derived from household canvasses with other data in church studies of religious population by other methods, is discussed in chapter vi.[7]

INTERPRETATION

The validity of the results of a religious census being established (or corrections of their bias satisfactorily made), the approach to the interpretation of the data will be determined by the utilization that the church desires to make of it. Thus, besides the cultivation

6 See p. 80.
7 See pp. 163 ff.

of persons discovered as immediate church prospects, the church may use such a measurement and analysis of religious population simply to challenge the attitudes of its constituents. It may convict them of harboring marked feelings of social distance from others who are their immediate neighbors geographically, and may raise the question of practical religious fraternity between its constituents and these others.

Or it may go on and devise practical methods of community co-operation which the church may foster in harmony with religious bodies of the other faiths. With other denominations of the same faith, this may well take the form of still more extensive religious canvasses suitable as a basis for united evangelistic campaigns or forms of joint social work.

Finally, the church may see in the religious analysis of adjacent population a basis for the discussion of its service program, and may get an insight into the possible unmet needs of classes or groups that may prove amenable to its cultivation in new ways if not in the ones already existing.

CULTIVATION OF AREA ACCORDING TO NEED

In case the church is willing to bring itself to such precise policies in its evangelistic effort, it may well carry the study further to the point of calculating the relative religious standing of the several sub-divisions of the surveyed area.

Methods of deriving approximately accurate population figures from census data for small areas are presented in other connections.[8] If undertaken for every house in a given area, the house-to-house religious canvass itself constitutes a census of population. Its results should be checked against census data when these are available. And, when the degree of completeness of the canvass is known, fairly reliable estimates of the population remaining uncanvassed may be arrived at.

When the population of the parish subdivisions has been arrived at in any of these ways, calculate the distribution of population according to faith from the schedule-cards for each district. All who claim allegiance to any faith, together with such of their children as are too young for active adherence, may be regarded as its historic constituency. Naturally those who are related to some particular church and denomination in a determinate way constitute its active adherents. Active adherence, however, is limited by age, say, five years and upward, as the possible limits of Sunday-school enroll-ment; or thirteen years and upward as the possible limits of church-membership. Decide which limits to use in calculation. Calculate for each district the number of active adherents, as shown by sec-

[8] See pp. 163-165.

tion (4) of the schedule, and the ratio of active adherents to historic constituents.

Active adherence in three ways is recorded on the schedule-card, viz.: by belonging, attending, or preferring some particular church or denomination. Calculate for each district the number of active adherents who are related in each of these ways, and the ratio of each to the total.

For each district, calculate for each faith and denomination the number and per cent. of historic constituents under twenty-one years of age who are enrolled in Sunday school; also those who are in Sunday school and are also church-members; and those who are neither.

RANK OF SURVEY DISTRICTS
BY NINE RELIGIOUS CRITERIA

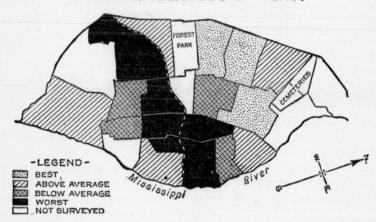

CHART VII—PROTESTANT RELIGIOUS GEOGRAPHY OF ST. LOUIS.

The table on page 117 suggests a form that may be modified to fit the several contents just described.

This series of calculations makes it possible to compare the several parish districts with respect to a group of criteria that fairly reflect the relative excellence of their religious situations from any given standpoint, say, that of orthodox Protestantism. The criteria are as follows:

Criteria of Excellence in Organized Religion

1. A large ratio of adherents to some faith relative to total population.
2. Many Protestants relative to adherents to other faiths.
3. Few belonging to irregular or non-evangelical Protestant denominations.
4. A normal ratio between classes of active adherents, i.e., not far from the average.

116

TABLE XX

TABLE —NUMBER AND DISTRIBUTION OF PROTESTANT ADHERENTS (13 YEARS OF AGE AND OVER) ACCORDING TO KIND OF ADHERENCE

DISTRICTS	TOTAL		SPECIFIED PROTESTANT DENOMINATIONS										
			ADVENTIST		BAPTIST		CONGREGATIONAL		DISCIPLES OF CHRIST		OTHERS	
	No.	%	No.	%	No.	%	No.	%	No.	%	No.	%
All Districts												
Members												
Attend												
Prefer												
1. Members												
Attend												
Prefer												
2. Members												
Attend												
Prefer												

117

5. A high ratio of attending adherents in contrast with merely preferring ones.
6. Large Sunday-school enrollment relative to religious constituencies of between five and twenty-one years of age.
7. A proper proportion both of children and adolescents in Sunday school.
8. A high proportion of adolescents belonging both to church and Sunday school.
9. Few adolescents belonging to neither.

Rank the parish districts according to these criteria separately calculated, and calculate their rank according to their combined weight by the method given on page 173. Classify the parish districts in four groups according to religious quality by the grouping shown on page 174.

Direct the church's evangelistic and pastoral effort to equalizing religious opportunity in the area now most deficient.

SCHEME OF STUDY

(Chapter IV)

(It is assumed that the church will conduct the house-to-house religious census.)

PLANNING THE STUDY

1. Determine area to be surveyed.
2. Subdivide area.
3. Plan organization and administration.
4. Determine time of canvass.
5. Provide schedules.
6. Secure and train canvassers.

ALTERNATIVE PLAN BY SAMPLING METHOD

1. Determine whether sampling method will serve ends sought.
2. Determine size of sample.
3. Assure homogeneity of units for sampling.
4. Make reconnaissance canvass.
5. Secure semi-expert canvassers.
6. Provide more elaborate schedule.

MAKING THE STUDY

1. Carry out the household canvass.
2. Check on completeness.
3. Tabulate returns for immediate use.
4. Tabulate by race, faith, and denomination.
5. Tabulate by manner of adherence.
6. Tabulate by age and Sunday-school relationship.
7. Tabulate by nativity and antecedents.
8. Test results for bias and make systematic correction.

9. Calculate relative religious standing of parish subdivisions.
10. Rank subdivisions according to standing.
11. Devise practical methods of utilizing results.

SUGGESTIONS FOR SUPPLEMENTAL RESEARCH

1. Study the physical, economic, social and institutional structure of the parish area by methods set forth in chapter vii, as a background for the study of religious population.
2. Subdivide parish using elaborated method shown in chapter vi, as basis for census.
3. In case of survey by sample, with elaborated schedule, use data as to nativity and language of mother as means of determining racial neighborhoods; and tabulate religious data according to these neighborhoods as well as by larger subdivisions.
4. Study the religious composition of families as shown by the schedule-cards, and especially families showing mixed religious allegiance.
5. Compare families showing mixed religious allegiance with others with respect to race, nativity of parents and language of home.
6. Compare churched and unchurched population of Protestant origins with respect to race, nativity and language of home.
7. Compare denominations with respect to race, nativity and language of home.
8. Compare denominations with respect to sex-distribution of constituencies.
9. Compare denominations with respect to rural and urban antecedents of constituencies.
10. Make a careful sampling census of population omitted in the original canvass, to see whether the latter had bias, and if so, how much.
11. In view of the religious situation as disclosed by the canvass make an appraisal of the division of responsibility between faiths, denominations and individual churches within the area canvassed.
12. Devise methods of practical coöperation among the religious forces.

BIBLIOGRAPHY AND REFERENCES

Douglass, *The St. Louis Church Survey* (New York: Doran, 1924), p. 83 ff.; chapter vi and appendix vi.
Douglass, *The Springfield Church Survey* (New York: Doran, 1926), chapter iv and appendix iv.

PART II: HOW TO STUDY GROUPS OF CHURCHES

CHAPTER V

Limited Surveys of Groups of Churches

This chapter opens a second major division of the book: namely, that relating to the study of groups of churches.

The first section had in mind the pastor or officers of a single church studying their own institution more or less intensively, or investigating the population in its territorial field. But individual churches belong to larger groups. These groups may be classified according to their nature as territorial (that is to say, composed of all the churches in a given area), ecclesiastical (that is to say, united by the fact of belonging to the same denominational jurisdiction), or fortuitous (as when a random sample is selected to stand for some larger group). The circumstances that cause certain churches to be considered as a group may thus demand a study of their common interests as related to a common territory, or from the standpoint of denominational objectives and progress; or a chance group regarded as typical may be studied to throw light on actual groups that have a permanent unity.

These classifications reflect recurrent situations in which actual requests for help in making surveys have been received by the Institute of Social and Religious Research.

Classified still further, according to time, the study of groups of churches may be either historical or contemporaneous. In the first case it will be concerned with church records from one period to another; in the second, with the varied aspects of church life as it is observed at a given time.

Again, classified according to method, studies of groups of churches may be limited to conventional categories or regularly recorded ways of regarding churches, or they may be enlarged so as to include novel and more broadly sociological points of view.

In contrast with the study of the single church, the study of groups of churches is based upon the principle of formal comparison. This principle was, of course, implicit in single-case studies. One always tends to compare any newly discovered fact with what one already knows in the same realm. But in the type of studies now being considered, comparison becomes central, continuous and systematic. Such studies are therefore characterized by the use of technical devices that facilitate comparisons and measure likeness and unlikeness.

The researches described in this chapter are limited by the fact that they deal with churches as ecclesiastical institutions only, without considering their community settings. Studies of a broader type, which regard each church in relation to its community setting, and the entire group of churches as constituting an important factor in community life, are described in subsequent chapters.

Specifically, the present chapter illustrates studies of groups of churches from two standpoints: namely, (1) the historical, in which groups of churches of one or more denominations are studied over a period of time by means of conventional categories; and (2) the contemporary, in which similar groups are investigated in their current aspects by the use of somewhat more varied categories.

A—A Limited Historical Study of a Group of Churches

It is assumed that a group of churches, constituted in one of the ways set forth in the introductory paragraphs, has decided to study itself over a period of years; also that the study is to be made by the ecclesiastical authorities of the group or some one acting for them. In case of a self-survey by a denominational group, those making the study will need to observe the practical counsels of chapter i; but no specially devised machinery of survey will have to be set up. In case the churches of the group are not permanently under one jurisdiction and not accustomed to coöperate, the terms of coöperation should be carefully explained and agreed to; and some special research or survey organization will have to be created. Directions for forming an organization of this kind are given in chapter vii.

GENERAL CHARACTERISTICS OF THE DATA

The minor territorial units of the denominations, associations, presbyteries, district conferences, etc., constitute record-keeping groups. The proposal to make such a study presupposes that comparable records have been kept by the group concerned. Their published minutes furnish competent data for the history of the churches in certain of their more formal aspects as social institutions. They go back ultimately to the annual reports of individual churches, as recorded by their local clerks or statisticians and reported to the denomination.

Records of the character just described generally cover such items as: (1) name and location of church; (2) date of establishment; (3) number of members, male and female; (4) losses and gains in membership during the year; (5) Sunday-school enrollment; (6) current local expenditures; (7) benevolent expenditures; (8) amount of salaries paid; (9) value of church property. The study has to accept these predetermined categories, since it is not undertaking to secure any fresh data of its own. They at least make it possible to trace and measure what the churches themselves practically interpret as success or non-success.

SURVEY PROCEDURE

(1) The first step toward an actual survey of the sort indicated is obviously to determine the period to be covered by the study of the records of the group of churches. This period should be long enough to insure that the trend of growth and development shall be clearly established; but short enough to prevent the human interest from thinning out too much. What happened in the remote past stirs no one. Accordingly, it will be well to keep the study within the span of living memory of considerable numbers of people, say, within twenty or twenty-five years. The period chosen should, if possible, correspond with some vital epoch in the evolution of the church group or of the community. On the other hand, certain arbitrary dates need to be considered. The U. S. Census is taken in the first year of each decade and yields important collateral data that help one to understand church history. The intervening special U. S. Census of Religious Bodies brings together a vast amount of data for each denomination and for all religious bodies, by cities and counties as well as states.

In its Table 66, the 1916 Census presents statistical data, classified by denominational groups, for the churches of all cities that had 25,000 population and over in 1910. The data cover the following points: number of churches; number of members, male and female; number of places of worship; value of church property; amount of debt on church property; number and value of parsonages; annual expenditures; number of Sunday schools, and of their officers, teachers and pupils. By comparing the 1906 Census of Religious Bodies on the same points, absolute gains or losses in any of these respects, and changed ratio between any two items reported upon, can be calculated for any city. A similar census was taken in 1926 and its report, when issued, will furnish an important check upon any recent or future study of denominations or Protestant groups of churches in large cities.

If the period which the survey covers corresponds with either of these census periods, numerous comparisons may be made of the relative growth of the churches under consideration and of similar groups in other places.

A recent study, for example (made in 1921), applied the above considerations in the following manner: The period to be covered was fixed as from 1900 on. The reason for the choice of this period was that (1) it covered approximately two United States Census decades in which comparable data regarding the city were available.

125

(2) It covered a definite epoch in the development of the city; namely, that of its most rapid growth, to which new elements of population were the chief contributors. (3) Finally, while many of the individual churches composing the denominations studied were founded after 1890, almost all of them had existed throughout the entire period chosen.

Similar criteria will be helpful in determining the period to be covered by any parallel study. Is the period chosen a significant one? Are there, for the same period, other data that would throw light on the proposed inquiry? Have the phenomena being studied largely remained constant throughout the period, in the sense of having been related to essentially the same component parts all of the time?

(2) The second step is to assemble the data. The principal sources of study are the official publications of the denominations involved for the period chosen. For some denominations these are national yearbooks; for others, the annual minutes or yearbooks of regional ecclesiastical bodies including the group of churches being studied. Files of these books for past years can generally be found in the custody of some local secretary or custodian of historical materials. If not, they are sure to be available at state or district denominational offices.

(3) Next comes the final decision as to the scope and contents of the study. This, however, is largely predetermined by the rigidly fixed character and rather limited scope of the data. There is not much to do but to make the best of the material just as it stands. How many of the items reported upon in the records shall be studied year by year depends partly, however, on such matters as comparability, validity of editing processes in case of gross inaccuracies, cost of transcription and possibly of condensation.

(4) If the group of churches being studied includes all those of a given territory, or if a denomination has changed its forms of accounting, or if the study covers a fortuitous group, the existence of records in identical form cannot be expected. In these cases the persons engaged upon the study face the serious step of making as much of the data comparable as possible. It is necessary to determine how far different terminology stands for identical classes of facts.

While it is obviously much simpler to make use of existing data than to go out and collect them from the books of individual churches, certain disadvantages attach to ready-made data. They were not gathered for the purpose for which they are now being used. One is not always sure in what sense those who furnished the original information understood the language in which it was asked for. Inaccuracies in other people's work cannot be traced so easily as those in one's own. In any case, it may be necessary to recombine and rearrange statistics, particularly the financial ones, for certain denominations. This should be done in conference with the representatives of these bodies, and agreement should be reached as to the meaning of their figures as published.

(5) In extreme cases, the data may have to be modified and made to depart from the exact letter of published statistics. To make such a modification in a body of evidence once adopted as a basis of study, and to do so in one case and not in others, is a momentous procedure, justified only by extraordinary circumstances.

In a Springfield, Mass., survey, for example, it was found that a single church, in revising its membership roll in 1921, had dropped 886 names which had been accumulating during twenty years. This obliterated one-third of the nominal membership of its denomination in that city. But obviously, the lost members had actually been dropping out year by year during the entire twenty-year period in which no revision had taken place. It was only names that were finally removed.

To make it possible to compare the Springfield denominations, and to reach a true understanding of the trend of this particular denomination, this radical reduction of membership was divided equally among the years of the entire twenty-year period. In publishing the statistics, however, both the original figures and the modified figures as well were recorded; so that the results of editing were immediately apparent.

The principle governing any such procedure may be stated as follows: If an investigator knows enough about the nature and source of manifestly incorrect data to use systematic means of modifying them and getting a true understanding of the trends of a period, it is legitimate to do so, provided that he makes perfectly plain what has been done, and that he records the original figures as well as his modification.

(6) After the processes necessary to assure comparability and consistency comes the transcription and tabulation of the data on the major points covered by the record. These are almost sure to include the number of churches and of church-members and Sunday-school pupils; the amounts of current and benevolent expenditures; and the value of church plants for each church of the denominations covered by the study. The mere copying upon tabulation sheets of these data for any considerable group of churches is laborious. For example, twelve days were required to transcribe the twenty-year records of forty-three churches. This process must be completed, however, before any comparative statistical study can begin.

(7) No good purpose is served in following out church history to the last detail. To account for every year in the life of every church on every item of the record, is an expensive and time-consuming process that gives more complicated results than the mind

can easily follow. Some form of statistical condensation will therefore need to be devised as part of the planning of the survey.

For the mere sketching in of an historical background dealing with broad epochs, it would be enough to compare conditions as they stood at dates ten or twenty years apart. The accompanying chart, for example, shows graphically the change in number of churches of four major Springfield denominations between 1900 and 1921. But this is not sufficiently accurate for a study that seeks to explain

TABLE XXI

TABLE —CHURCH-MEMBERSHIP STATISTICS OF MAJOR DE-
NOMINATIONS, SPRINGFIELD, MASS., 1900–1921

SPRINGFIELD POPULATION			CHURCH-MEMBERSHIP				
Year	Number	Period	Baptist	Congregational	Methodist Episcopal	Protestant Episcopal*	Total
1900	62,059	1899–1901	1,985	3,905	2,112	1,220 (1,368)	9,222
1903	68,947	1902–1904	2,083	4,207	2,256	1,503 (1,336)	9,911
1906	76,617	1905–1907	2,360	4,572	2,357	1,606 (1,455)	10,625
1909	85,849	1908–1910	2,420	4,879	2,466	1,860 (1,614)	11,228
1912	94,544	1911–1913	2,540	5,046	2,332	2,154 (1,740)	11,532
1915	102,971	1914–1916	2,740	5,413	3,018	2,415 (1,801)	12,911
1918	118,958	1917–1919	2,906	5,899	3,159	2,611 (1,801)	13,765
1920	129,614	1920	3,016	6,102	3,311	2,746	14,230
1921	134,943	1921	3,572	6,284	3,339	1,930	15,125

* The figures in parenthesis are those resulting after the 886 persons "Lost without Transfer" in 1921 had been distributed over the previous twenty years. They were used in making up the totals.

history. A good compromise may be found in calculating and comparing statistical averages for periods of from three to five years. This is shown for an actual case in the above table in which the data for forty-three churches is summarized by denominational totals for four denominations, and reported in terms of averages by three-year periods. This process condenses the statement of forty-three records into four denominational columns, and of twenty-two years' records into nine periods.

Further reasons for reducing data secured for single years to averages by three-year periods are as follows: In the complete record extreme fluctuations appear from year to year owing to the confusing of occasional and recurrent phenomena within the statistics. For example, the cost of capital investments involved in building opera-

128

tions are repeatedly reported in the same totals as the current opera-tions of churches. Again, churches generally remove members from the roll at irregular intervals rather than regularly from year to year. The use of three-year averages greatly reduces, though it does not entirely remove, the irregularities due to such factors.

In case of the last table, it would have taken nearly two and one-half times as much calculation to work out each point of the record by single years as to do it by three-year averages, and would have involved a corresponding increase in the complexity of tables and charts. These are strong reasons for a reasonable degree of con-densation.

(8) A final step in the planning of a limited historical study of a group of churches is to determine by analysis what appear to be the most fruitful phenomena that statistical records reveal over periods of time, and how they are concretely expressed in church records.

The chief things that may be observed directly are: (a) greater or less degrees of change; (b) consistency of change (whether always in the same direction); and (c) continuity or discontinuity. In typical records, such categories may be applied to the measure-ment of such things as: (1) the rate of increase or decrease in the number of churches or members; (2) the acceleration or diminution of this rate; (3) the ratio of gains to losses or of Sunday-school enrollment to church-membership; (4) changes in ratio from one period to another, and the correlation of the ratio of gains to losses with the rate of net gains; (5) the totals of financial expenditure may also be reduced to rates per member; (6) monetary terms may be converted into units of purchasing power when a change in the value of money was known to have occurred from period to period.

Again, many of the relations thus measured may be compared with those measured for corresponding intervals in other studies. Thus, in the last table, increase in Protestant church-membership is nat-urally correlated with the increase of the total population of Spring-field, and might still more pertinently have been correlated with the increase of the native white population from which Protestants are chiefly drawn. A generalized plan for an actual study of a group of churches, based on typical denominational records, is offered in the following section.

CONTENT AND PROCESSES

1. *Church Organizations*

Count and enter on a tabulation sheet the number of churches of each denomination that existed during each year of the period studied; and calculate the total for the group. In separate columns enter the number of new churches each year and the number of old ones that died or amalgamated with others.

Summarize the results in a table like the following, showing the number of churches by three-year periods, or at the beginning and end of each decade, or for the period as a whole; also the number of new organizations and of lapses.

TABLE XXII

TABLE —CHANGES IN NUMBER OF ORGANIZED CHURCHES,
1900 TO 1922

FAITH	NO. OF CHURCHES		CHURCHES DURING PERIOD	
			Consolidated or Lapsed	New Organizations Started
	1900	1921		
Protestant	40	43	6	9
Congregational	13	10	3	0
Baptist	7	9	2	4
Methodist Episcopal	6	6	1	1
Protestant Episcopal	2	3	0	1
Universalist	2	2	0	0
Other	10	13	0	3
Roman Catholic	7	15	0	8
Greek Catholic	0	2	0	2
Hebrew	2	7	0	5
Total	49	67	6	24

Write a brief narrative showing what particular churches were organized or died—thus accounting for the net gain or loss.

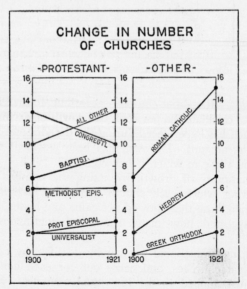

CHART VIII—SLOW DECREASE IN NUMBER OF PROTESTANT CHURCHES IN SPRINGFIELD, CONTRASTED WITH RAPID INCREASE OF NON-PROTESTANT CHURCHES, 1900-1922.

Map the city by districts[1] and show where the new churches and the lapsed ones were located from decade to decade. Correlate this with rate of growth or decline of population, or with the change in character of population in the same districts, deriving the latter data from the U. S. Census for the corresponding decades.[2]

2. Church-membership

The membership of every individual church of the group for the period studied has already been transcribed and calculated by three-

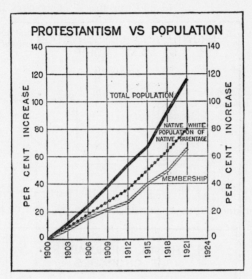

CHART IX—CORRELATION OF CHURCH-MEMBER-
SHIP AND POPULATION GROWTH.

year averages. Rank the churches according to size at the end of each decade; calculate the per cent. of growth or decline in membership that each has experienced during the decade; and note the cases in which the amount of growth has been sufficient to change the ranking, and those in which it has not.

Study continuity of growth by noting the number of three-year periods during which each church gained or lost in membership. Note whether those that showed net gains and losses, gained or lost continuously; and how many showed discontinuous and erratic trends.

Calculate denominational growth by decades, by combining data for individual churches, and carry out for each denomination the processes just applied to the individual churches. Finally do the same thing for the total group, and calculate how much each church

[1] For directions for districting, see pp. 199-201.
[2] See pp. 185-186.

and denomination contributed to the total growth or decline of the group.

A method of graphic representation of changes of phenomena over periods of time has already been illustrated on page 12. This may easily be adapted to show different phenomena. Correlate the total growth of the group in church-membership with that of total population, and with that of native white population of native parentage, deriving the latter figures from the U. S. Census. A suitable form of graphic summary on this point is shown in Chart IX, page 131.

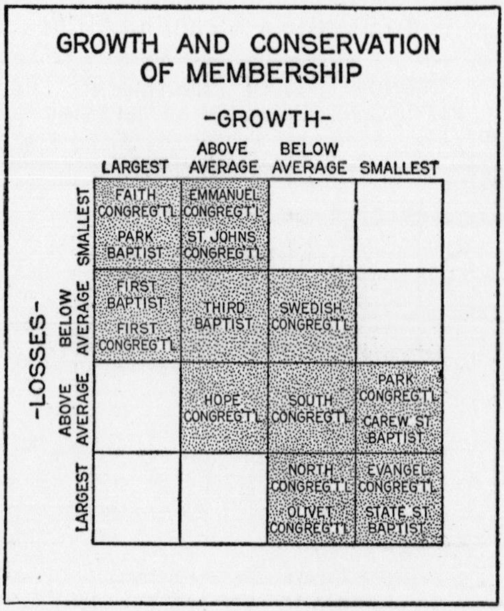

GROWTH AND CONSERVATION OF MEMBERSHIP

CHART X—DEGREE OF NET MEMBERSHIP GROWTH GENERALLY PROPORTIONATE TO DEGREE OF MEMBERSHIP LOSS.

3. *Ratio of Gains to Losses*

Calculate for each church and denomination the ratio of membership gains to membership losses by decades, and rank the churches and denominations accordingly. Note to what extent favorable net growth depends upon a low ratio of losses. The correlation that may be expected between these two factors may be expressed graphically in a chart like the one above. Note whether or not there is a recent tendency toward larger gains and larger losses as contrasted with earlier decades. If so, selective processes are apparently growing more drastic.

If the record includes a statement of the particular occasions of gains and losses in membership, calculate for each church and denomination, the amount and per cent. of each that comes in any specified way; for example, gains by confession or reaffirmation of faith, and by letter; losses by death, letter and discipline or revision of the roll. Note whether the relative influence of any of these factors has changed during any decade of the period being studied.

4. *Special Aspects of Growth*

Calculate the average size of the church, by decades, for the whole group and for the separate denominations. Is the average church growing larger?

Similarly calculate the respective proportions of male and female

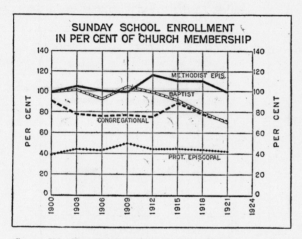

CHART XI—THE SUNDAY SCHOOL NOT GROWING AS FAST AS THE CHURCH IN SPRINGFIELD.

membership. (Sex of members is usually included in church records.) Has there been any substantial change in the ratio of males to females?

5. *Sunday-school Membership*

Each of the processes by which growth in church-membership was studied may be applied to the figures for Sunday-school enrollment and attendance. In addition, the ratio of Sunday-school enrollment to church-membership should be calculated by three-year periods for each church and denomination, and the ratio of the growth of each compared, for similar periods. This will show whether the Sunday school is growing faster or slower than the church.

6. *Current Finances*

Financial data, as well as membership, are assumed to have been transcribed and calculated by three-year averages. Calculate the amount of current expenditures at the end of each decade, for each church and denomination, and for the entire group. Rank the churches and denominations according to these amounts. Calculate for each the per cent. of increase or decrease in current expenditures. Study the continuity of financial gains or losses from period to period, by the use of the same processes as were applied to membership. Calculate the per capita rate of current expenditures relative to membership from period to period for individual churches and denominations, and note the amount and rate of change if any. In view of great fluctuations in the purchasing power of money in recent years, calculate the value of the financial expenditures in terms of the purchasing power of the dollar at the beginning of the period, and by decades, basing the calculations upon the price index

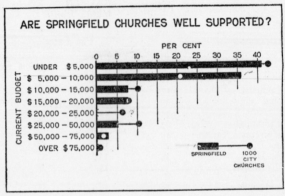

CHART XII—CURRENT EXPENSES OF SPRINGFIELD CHURCHES COMPARED WITH THOSE OF 1,044 CITY CHURCHES.

of the U. S. Bureau of Labor Statistics from year to year, or other competent authority. This will show whether, and how much, church resources went up or down relative to the cost of living.

7. *Benevolences*

The processes used in the study of current finances should be applied to benevolent expenditures also, and the ratio between current expenditures and benevolences calculated and compared. If it has proven possible to put the data of the several denominations relative to the objects of benevolence, into comparable form, it is important to carry out this phase of the study into detail. The results may be tabulated as shown in the form on page 135 used in the St. Louis survey.

8. *Value of Church Property*

Similarly figures showing the value of church property from period to period may be studied for individual churches and denominations. These may be expressed in totals, averages, per cent. of increase or decrease, per capita values, and values relative to current finances. Property valuations, as reported, are, however, less reliable than those of membership or finance; and the fluctuating values of church sites enter so largely with them that the interpretation of the resulting statistics is apt to remain doubtful. The period and location of each new building, or an important addition to church plant, may, however, be studied by the method described for the study of church organizations.[3]

TABLE XXIII

TABLE —PERCENTAGE DISTRIBUTION BY DENOMINATIONS OF AVERAGE ANNUAL BENEVOLENT CONTRIBUTIONS GOING TO SPECIFIED FIELDS OF BENEVOLENCE FOR 1899–1919

DENOMINATIONS	PER CENT.			
	Home Missions	Foreign Missions	Education	Other Benevolences
Baptist	11	20	6	63
Disciples of Christ	17	31	3	49
Congregational	39	14	12	35
Evangelical	11	11	19	59
Methodist Episcopal	23	19	7	51
Methodist Episcopal, South	42	18	4	36
Presbyterian, U. S. A.	28	18	18	36
Presbyterian, U. S.	34	13	33	20
Protestant Episcopal	30	15	7	48
Nine denominations	28	18	11	43

9. *Study of Churches Grouped by Geographical Location*

Because the desire of denominations to trace their growth and to compare it with that of other denominations is so general, it has been arbitrarily assumed that the major classification of the churches whose records are being studied should be denominational. But there is even more scientific warrant for grouping churches according to geographical location, under such categories as central, residential and suburban. Studies of particular cities have proved that sometimes a church's chance of growth is directly proportionate to its remoteness from the area of down-town change and deterioration.[4]

The processes described for the study of membership, at least, should therefore be carried out for churches grouped by location as well as by denomination; but probably for a shorter period of time. Centers expand, residential areas vary, and suburbs are annexed or reach out farther into the county. From the standpoint of these very fluctuative categories, an exact study of changes over a single decade will probably be most revealing.

If the study of groups of churches is a part of a community sur-

3 See p. 131.
4 See pp. 185 ff.

vey, the study of the territorial expansion of the city, and of the social fortunes of its various areas, will throw light upon the phenomena of church growth and decline.[5]

SURVEY OF CHURCH TENDENCIES OVER PERIODS OF TIME

How have the churches and denominations under investigation fared during the decades of the period covered?

A literary summary of the results should now be written, bringing together and interpreting the successive pieces of statistical evidence. Something of the thread upon which they should be strung is suggested by the following questions: Have few or many new churches been organized? Have there been numerous or few lapses and amalgamations of churches? Has the average size of the individual church increased? Is there a tendency to greater gains or greater losses? Has membership growth been relatively slow or fast? Has it approximated that of the white population? Have many churches showed absolute losses of members, and have the churches as a whole showed an excessive ratio of losses to gains? What proportion of persons lost from church-membership lapsed from all known church connections? Were there relatively more male members at the end of the period studied than at the beginning? Has Sunday-school growth been slower or faster than church growth? Were more churches found losing in Sunday-school enrollment than in church-membership? In which of the matters investigated were the denominations alike, and in which were there somewhat different tendencies with respect to church or Sunday-school developments? Has there been an apparent general decline in Sunday-school attendance relative to church-membership? How great have financial gains been absolutely? How great per capita? Have recent official campaigns of the denominations produced a sharp temporary increase, and was this followed by a decrease? Relative to the purchasing power of money, have the churches more than kept up with the existing standards of expenditure? Do benevolent contributions show as large an absolute increase as current expenses and as large a percentage increase as well? In contrast with the major Protestant denominations, how do minor ones show up? Have they organized as many new churches relatively speaking, and have these churches experienced more or less rapid development? Is the numerical ratio of the minor Protestant denominations decreased or increased relative to the total Protestant body?

CHARACTERISTIC LOGICAL PROCESSES

A characteristic cycle of thinking is involved again and again in the historical study of a group of churches as just outlined.

[5] See pp. 175 ff.

One starts with statistical records of individual churches. These one puts together into denominational or geographical totals by a process of synthesizing. The next phase of the cycle breaks up these new totals into component parts different from those with which one started; as when the net gains in the number of churches were resolved into a difference between the number of new churches founded and the old ones lapsed; or when the total denominational figures for losses and gains in church-membership were resolved into classes indicating the occasion of losses and gains.

Finally, both in the summaries as reported and in the supporting tables, data showing the contribution of individual churches to the generalized denominational results, and of the denominations to the total results, were made available and habitually drawn upon for explanation. Some churches gained members throughout the periods studied. Others gained; but not continuously. Still others lost absolutely. But the whole gain ascribed to any denomination was obviously that furnished by its growing churches, and by them only during the periods during which they were growing. Their several contributions are thus kept isolated and measurable. Obviously when one can tell to just how many and to what parts of a thing a quality really belongs that is ascribed to the thing as a whole, one is just so much nearer to the true explanation of the facts. This principle lies at the roots of the method.

VALUE

Studies of records kept over a period of time, along the lines described, will help to tell any group of churches that regard themselves as a unit not only where they stand at any given time, but also which way they are facing, how fast they are moving, and how far they have come. Whether for better or for worse, long-established trends are not easily changed. Nevertheless, when specific causes are located in particular churches, they become susceptible of specific attention and treatment. The chance of being able to control the trend is thus greatly increased.

Ecclesiastical doctors may well pause to take such long-time statistical views periodically. By the method just indicated a study of a group of forty or fifty churches can be made at a probable cost of from $1,000 to $1,500. This would be a highly profitable expenditure, say once in five years, for a large denomination or a church federation.

B—The Contemporaneous Study of a Group of Churches

In contrast with the type of study last illustrated, in which churches were investigated over a period of time, stands a study of present conditions within a group of churches. A method of contemporaneous study of a single church has already been presented in the Semi-intensive Case study of chapter ii. The investigation there outlined would produce an excellent survey if applied to a group of churches, say those of a denomination in one of its minor territorial divisions, or those of a city as a whole.

General Requirements and Larger Characteristics

But in a study in which the data are not found already assembled in printed reports and must be collected, it is not often that two weeks can be given to the field work and two months to the subsequent study of, and reporting on, a single church of the group. The kind of contemporaneous study of groups of churches that will be generally practical must therefore scale down radically in dimensions from the investigation as outlined in chapter ii, even though that study was regarded as only semi-intensive rather than truly intensive. In scaling down, the more time-consuming inquiries will have to be omitted and only those retained that throw the most direct light upon the central purpose of the study.

In scope, therefore, such a study of a group of churches as is now in mind will be strictly limited. But it will go beyond the study of the individual church in that it will make comparisons of case with case possible. This may perhaps be more fruitful of explanations than if the study were to cover a wider range of information. Furthermore, such a study need not be limited to categories conventionally used in published church records, as is necessary in making comparisons over a period of time.

Auspices and Agents

It is assumed that the study is to be made either by the authorities of some minor ecclesiastical unit, such as a denominational association, a city extension society, or a church federation; or else that churches of a group associate themselves temporarily for the specific purpose of making the survey. In the former case, the work may be done through the regular staff, and in connection with the routine processes of recording and appraising the work of the agency. In the latter, special survey machinery may have to be set up. Directions for organizing such machinery are given in chapter vi. But there is a middle ground. The coöperating churches may wish to attempt to make self-surveys primarily through volunteer workers under common administration but without professional leadership.

This is not an impossible plan; but it is one fraught with many difficulties. These include first, all those inherent in the piecemeal work of volunteers: so that the need to set aside a definite amount of time and working force, to insure completion of the task within a given period, becomes especially important.[6] There are the additional difficulties incident to weak organization. A professional survey agency will insist upon definitely assigned authority, binding contracts, and a financial guarantee. Voluntarily associated churches often try to carry through a complicated piece of business with none of these things. A self-survey process may, however, be so valuable a means of educating the participating churches as it is carried on, that these risks should be run; particularly because in a professional survey a long time often elapses between the gathering of data and their final interpretation.

At least a minimum of machinery to make connection between the survey administration and the coöperating churches will be required. Suppose each coöperating church has appointed a survey committee to collect its local data. Students from a neighboring college or theological seminary, or a committee of competent lay volunteers, may then be organized into a seminar group and instructed in methods of the survey and the requirements of usable data. Five or six sessions of this seminar held by the administrative director of the study should enable these workers to assist the churches in preparing and organizing their data.

Finally, one or two field investigators will probably have to make a systematic canvass of the churches to complete the data, and to supplement such as are imperfect. A trained statistician will be necessary to handle much of the data.

Less machinery than this can scarcely do the work; and it is strongly recommended that the more complete form of organization described in chapter vii be employed.

THE PLAN OF THE SURVEY

A schedule outlining the substance of a greatly reduced study, following the same topics as those used in the semi-intensive study in chapter ii, is presented on pages 140-142.

The principles used in cutting the study down to proportions suitable for the present purpose are fairly obvious ones:

(1) Fewer aspects of any topic are studied.

(2) Though going beyond matters formally reported by denominations for groups of churches, the study is limited to the use of data usually available in local church records (like Sunday-school age-data); or to data so accessible that they can easily be given numerical statement (as, for example, attendance at services); or else to the transcription of standard data, like census material.

Even so, what is left will involve an initial tabulation of data on from one hundred to one hundred fifty points for the average church, which implies more work than can be undertaken in some surveys.

[6] See p. 5.

Schedule XI

SCHEDULE —CONTEMPORANEOUS STUDY OF A SINGLE CHURCH

1. *Activities* Which of the following does the church maintain? (Indicate by check-mark.) (See list on page 8 which is to be inserted in the schedule at this point.)

2. *History* Year of organization of church?........Number of members? 1910........1920....Now........

Locations of Church (by streets)

	Dates of Removal
1st	
2nd	
3rd	
4th	

3. *Members and Constituents* Number of members? Male......Female......Families or individuals regularly connected with church through membership.......Attendance.....Sunday-school enrollment......or membership in subsidiary organizations........ Total individual constituency........

4. *Parish* How many members (or adherent families or individuals) live within the following distances of the church?: ½ M, ½–1 M, 1–2 M, 2–3 M, 3–4 M, 4–5 M, over 5 M. [in each of the following directions: N.E, N.W., S.E., S.W.]? Use form of Table III, page 19, indicating clearly whether figures stand for individual members or for constituent's addresses.) How many members (or adherent families or individuals) live in each of the districts shown on an attached map? Enter the number in each district. (Note that map must give clearly the names of streets or other boundary lines dividing the districts.)

5. *Community* How many and what kind of people live in the area from which most of the church's constituents come, and under what conditions do they live? When, as is usually the case, several churches are clustered in a district, the same data will apply to several of them. (Transcribe data from last U. S. Census for wards from which 10% or more of church's constituency comes in the following form. Total the figures and compare with the total for the city or cities.)

What changes in the number, character and status of the population are believed to have occurred since the last census?

6. *Organizations* What and how many subsidiary organizations has the church and how many members has each? (Write in the names of each particular organization under the following classification and enter the number of members.) (See classification on page 26 which is to be inserted in this schedule at this point.)

7. *The Ministry* What kinds of positions are represented by paid workers in this church? (Make classified list.) What are the preparation, experience and pay of the ministry and other paid church workers? (Insert schedule from page 30 at this point.)

8. *Plant* Size of church lot?........Number of rooms?........Materials of which building is constructed?........Architectural style?........Seating capacity of auditorium?........Value of plant?........Additional value parsonage if any?........(Which of the following facilities or equipments has the church? Indicate by check-mark.)

Administration
Church office
Pastor's study
Typewriter
Mimeograph
Addressograph
Card index
Members
Constituents
Church vault

Education
Library
Maps
Blackboards
Stereopticon
"Movie" Machine
Department Assembly rooms
Individual classrooms

Publicity
Letterhead
Bulletin Boards
Inside
Outside
Weekly Calendar
Church Paper
Electric signs
Paid newspaper advertising

Service
Kitchen
Dining room
Toilets (No?)
Drinking Fountains
Fire Protection apparatus
Artificial ventilation
Rooms for women's organizations

Community Service
Gymnasium
Showers
Playground
Stage
Bowling or billiard
Swimming pool
Day Nursery
Kindergarten

9. *Finances* What was the total income of the last church year? Total?.....Current account?.....Benevolent account?.....Property or permanent investment?.....What was the total expenditure of the same period? Total?.....Current account?.....Benevolent account?.....Property or permanent account?.....How many pledged contributors has the church?.....

10. *Attendance at Services* (average) Sunday morning?.....Sunday evening?.....Midweek?.....Are these figures derived from counts or estimates?.....

11. *Religious Education* Sunday school; total enrollment, 1910.....1920.....Now.....Age-distribution of pupils; under 3.....3-5.....6-8.....9-11.....12-14.....15-17.....18-20.....21 and over.....male and female in each age-group. [Sunday-school departments (Name and enrollment, male and female) (1).....(2).....(3).....(4).....(5).....(6).....(7).....] (8) Cradle Roll?.....(9) Home Department?.....Average attendance by departments.....Number of teachers: Total?.....Male?.....Female?.....What lesson system in use?.....Is there week-day religious instruction?.....Days per week and weeks in operation?.....Is there a daily vacation school?.....Weeks in operation?.....

12. *Gains and Losses in Membership* New members received during last church year and last five years: Total.....by letter.....on confession (or reaffirmation) of faith.....others.....? Members lost during same year: by death.....letter.....discipline or revision of roll.....?

13. *Relations with Community.* What community agencies or interests, denominational and non-denominational were supported by contributions during year?.....Cooperated with?.....Advocated?.....

14. *Denominational Relations* How much money was contributed to the denomination last year?.....Were any subsidies received from the denomination?.....How much?.....

TABLE XXIV

TABLE —COMPOSITION AND CHARACTERISTICS OF THE POPULATION IN 1920 IN WARDS MOST NEARLY IDENTICAL WITH CHURCH PARISH, AND OF CITY

	Total	Wards 1	2	3, etc.	Total City
Color or Race and Nativity*					
Total population					
Male					
Female					
Native white					
Native parentage					
Foreign parentage					
Mixed parentage					
Foreign-born white					
Negro					
Indian, Chinese, Japanese and all others					
Illiteracy—Total					
Dwellings and Families					
Dwellings, number					
Families, number					
Home Ownership†					
Total homes					
Homes rented					
Country of Birth of Five Most Numerous Foreign-born Groups (white)					
1.					
2.					
3.					

* *Fourteenth U. S. Census, 1920*, Vol. III, Table 13 under each state.
† *Fourteenth U. S. Census, 1920*, Vol. II, chapter xv, Table 8.

142

In such a case the items bracketed in the schedule, and in the subsequent directions for the survey, may be omitted. It will be wiser to limit the scope of the survey in this way than to endanger its entire value by attempting more than can be carried out.

PROCEDURE IN SECURING AND HANDLING DATA

(1) As in any study, it is first necessary to define the facts concerned. The Protestant church group of a known area is roughly self-defined. But is the area in mind the political city or the metropolitan community including the suburbs? In the latter case, where do the suburbs end? And what is Protestant? In Springfield, Massachusetts, for example, there were seven ecclesiastical institutions assumed to be Christian and neither Roman nor Greek Catholic whose status was locally questionable. It had to be decided whether to include or exclude such cases. Again, what is a church? Is a branch church or mission to be counted as an ecclesiastical unit or not? The study is, by definition, contemporaneous; but when is "now"? Shall the last annual reports of a church (whatever its particular date within a year) be the basis of the data? All these questions are capable of more than one answer, and somewhat arbitrary decision must be made.

Since certain of the topics of investigation go beyond the field in which church usage has conventionalized definitions and classifications, a large number of new problems of analysis are also raised. Shall janitors and musicians be enumerated as members of a church staff? Are associate and assistant pastors to be classified under two heads or only one? What are the stated activities of a church in contrast with its occasional ones? What constitutes one an adherent of a church? The necessity of reaching precise definitions before attempting to put data on such matters into fixed form is self-evident.

(2) Exact definition being reached of all facts to be investigated, and the agency making the study being assumed to have command of the resources and to have completed the practical plan necessary for carrying it out, the next step is the actual securing of the data from their sources in the individual church. By assumption, this will be done either by local church committees that will then send the data in to a central office; or by field workers; or by a combination method. No exact determination of this point is involved in the present directions.

(3) Transcription and editing of data may be involved, under conditions already set forth,[7] and (4) extensive tabulation is, of course, presumed.

When these processes are complete the study of the data as assembled and organized may begin.

[7] See pp. 75 ff.

HOW TO STUDY THE CITY CHURCH

The following directions for the study of the tabulated data are numbered to correspond with the items of the schedule to which they refer.

(1) *Subclassification of Churches by Activities*

The first concern, in the actual study of the data, is with subclassification. As in the case of the historical study of a group of churches, it will be natural to break the total up according to denominational groups, for reasons that may be assumed as obvious. The probable differences between churches in various geographical locations also warrant a subdivision into central, residential and suburban churches, with a separate study of each group on the points covered by data. But there is a third and equally important principle of subclassification: namely, that by similarity of program. The term "church" covers a set of exceedingly varied institutions, and there is little use of attempting to understand the unsorted group except through its like cases. The first item on the schedule, the check-list of organizations and activities, furnishes a means of sorting the churches into groups that are actually doing similar things.

Count the number of items checked against each church and rank the churches accordingly. Even the largest church will rarely include more than forty of the sixty items, so that a natural classification is as follows:

Groups	Number of Organizations and Activities
I	Less than 10
II	10–19
III	20–29
IV	30 and over

The churches in each group are likely to offer something like the same range and types of activities to their constituencies, and to have somewhat similar significance for their communities. Comparisons within these groups should be significant for the practice of the several churches, while comparisons within the whole unsorted group would be blunted by the wide contrasts existing among very different institutions.[8]

The following directions for studying successive items of the schedule are to be understood to imply that so far as time permits, and especially at significant points, the study is to be carried out for denominational and geographical groups and for similar types of churches as just determined, as well as for the total group.

[8] For more refined methods of classification based on the above data, but too elaborate for the present purpose, one may consult Douglass, *1,000 City Churches* (New York: Doran, 1926), p. 646.

(2) History

Classify the churches according to year of organization, by decades. Calculate the average and median age. (The latter is the age of the middle case when the individual cases of the total group are ranked from oldest to youngest.) Note the most frequent age. Classify according to age; for example, calling churches less than twenty-five years old "young"; those between twenty-five and forty-nine years, "middle-aged"; and those over fifty, "old." Are the churches of some denominations younger on the average than those of others? Are the residential and suburban churches younger than those of the center? (Naturally they are younger unless they are themselves churches that were formerly located at the center and have moved out; but how much younger?) Have churches with narrower programs shorter histories on the average than those with broad programs? These questions are answered by comparing the denominational, geographical and type-of-program groups with one another.

The tabulation sheets already prepared show how many members each church had in 1910, 1920 and at the date of the survey. Calculate the amount and rate of growth of each and classify them as churches losing membership, virtually stationary, growing moderately, growing exceptionally. The limits of these classes will have to be arrived at after examination of the data. If average growth turns out to be 15 per cent. for a decade, "losing membership" may be interpreted to mean losing 5 per cent. or more for this period. "Standing still" will then mean not losing or gaining as much as 5 per cent. "Moderate growth" must, of course, include average growth, and may range from 5 to 25 per cent; "exceptional growth" will then be that over 25 per cent. Intervals of this sort, which give exact meanings to popular terms of discrimination, cannot be devised in advance of the determination of the quantitative range and the average of the data; but each term must be assigned an exact statistical meaning before it is attempted to use the data comparatively.

Calculate how many churches are still occupying their original sites; how many moved in each decade; how many have moved once, twice, three times, etc. Tables should be made showing these facts; which may be summarized for the several districts of this city, and which should also be mapped by decades on a chart like Chart XXII. The results of this historical study will be to show comprehensively the origins of the churches, their growth or decline, and their distribution and redistribution in the community. These are important facts to understand comparatively.

(3) *Members and Constituents*

Rank the individual churches according to size on the basis of number of members, constituent families and individuals, or of total individual constituents. Make a table showing the number falling within each size-interval indicated in the following table:

TABLE XXV

TABLE —CHURCHES CLASSIFIED BY SIZE OF MEMBERSHIP AND ATTENDANCE

SCALE	NUMBER OF CHURCHES WITH		
	MEMBERSHIP	ATTENDANCE	
		Sunday Morning Service	Weekly* Aggregate
Under 100	7	14	2
100 to 200	8	10	1
200 to 300	4	9	3
300 to 400	8	3	6
400 to 500	3	1	1
500 to 600	2	1	4
600 to 700	3	1	5
700 to 800	0	1	3
800 to 900	2	0	3
900 to 1,000	1	0	1
1,000 to 1,250	3	1	3
1,250 to 1,500	0	0	2
1,500 to 1,750	2	0	3
1,750 to 2,000	0	0	2
2,000 and over	0	0	2

* At all stated services and activities.

Calculate the average and the median size of the churches; note the size-range and the most frequent size; and calculate the ratio of membership to total constituency by size-groups.

Make parallel columns ranking the churches according to membership-size, constituency-size, and breadth of program as determined by the check-list on page 8; and note how far the rankings agree.

(4) *Parish*

Define parishes with respect to distance in the following terms:

Geographical Type of Parish	*Per Cent. of Members Living Within One Mile*
Compact	75 and over
Medium	50–74
Scattered	25–49
Very scattered	Less than 25

From spot-maps of the several churches, made as directed on page 18, calculate the number of churches in each class. The accompanying diagram affords a convenient means of summarizing parish distribution.

Define parishes with respect to direction in the following terms:

Type of Parish	Per Cent. of Constituents Living in a Single Quadrant
Balanced	Not less than 17 or more than 34
Unbalanced	10 to 16 or 35 to 42
Very unbalanced	9 or less or 43 or more

Calculate the number of balanced, unbalanced and very unbalanced parishes as thus defined.

Attempt to explain the causes of uneven distribution of members in terms of restrictions on account (a) of the occupancy of area by other than residential elements of city life, or of boundaries difficult to cross; (b) attraction of superior conditions; (c) avoidance of undesirable conditions. In this work use the following classification:

Causes of Uneven Distribution	Restriction by Other Occupancy, or Barriers	Attractions	Undesirable Conditions
Physical			
Natural	Body of water, valley or hill	Elevated area	Low or swampy area
Artificial	Business centers	Vicinity of parks	Vicinity of industries
	Railroads		Lack of transit facilities
	Industry	Advantageous traffic facilities	
	Parks		
	Major traffic streets		
Social	Wide differences in poverty or wealth	Well-to-do population	Foreign or Negro quarter
	Difference of race or language	Fashionable direction	Area of slow growth or deterioration
		Advantageous institutions	Poor population

Make a tabulation showing in how many cases each of these factors seems to be involved as a cause of unbalanced parishes. Write up the apparent conclusions as to the character of the church parishes of the group, discussing cases of exceptionally poor and especially advantageous parish distribution.

For the combined constituency of the group, calculate the number and per cent. living at each distance and direction. (For form of summary table, see page 19.) Calculate the total number of church-members and constituents in each district of the city by total and by separate denominations (the districts to be ascertained according to directions in the next section); also calculate the ratio of church-members and constituents to total population. Classify districts as having relatively many, few, or an average number of church adherents. Note whether these results seem to be related to the accessibility and the character of the churches of the districts.

Calculate for the churches of each district of the city the number and per cent. of church-members who come from any given distance; thus:

Distance	Members Coming	
	Number	Per Cent.
½ mile		
½-1 mile		
1-2 miles, etc.		

Summarize by showing how many go far to church (much more than an average distance); how many go much less than an average distance, and how many go about an average distance.

Generalize and try to explain the amount of movement involved in churchgoing, and why some districts are strategic as centers of churchgoing while others with equal numbers of churches are not.

(5) Community Data

On the basis of physical and social barriers as noted in the preceding section, and of local usage, tentatively divide the city (or other area occupied by the church group) into natural districts, for example: down-town; the Heights; North Side; Parkview section; South Side industrial district; river bottom; "main line" suburb, etc. Map these districts.

Draw ward lines (as of the date of the last census) on the same map. Consider how far single wards or groups of wards correspond with the natural districts that have been discovered. From the census data assembled by the schedule, calculate the per cent. of foreigners, Negroes, illiteracy, congestion, home ownership, etc., in each ward, and note which wards are socially similar or different, and which correspond closely or remotely to the average of the whole city.

With the tentative district map, the ward map, and the census data in mind, make new field observations by riding over the city; and as a result of all the information gathered, district it finally into areas as nearly homogeneous as possible with respect to the character and living conditions of the population.

By adding together the census figures for wards most nearly corresponding to each district, get an approximate numerical statement for the district on the points covered by the census; and write a statement of the general characteristics of each district compared with the average characteristics of the city.

Use the district data thus compiled to compare the problems of individual churches or groups of churches. Calculate how many foreigners, Negroes, and illiterates, more or less, live in the vicinity of church A, then of church B, whether housing conditions are more or less congested; and whether more or fewer homes are owned. To the extent that a church draws constituency from its contiguous territory, these are important criteria of its favorable or unfavorable situation.

Complete the study of this topic by writing a conservative statement, as determined by the experience of the churches, of changes that have taken place in the character and quality of each district since the date of the census; also of the effect of these changes upon the fortunes of the churches.

(6) *Organization and Activities*

After classifying and combining the membership of organizations and social activities as called for by the schedule, rank the churches according to number of organizations and activities, and to number of organizations and activities of each class, and find the average, median and most frequent number.

Calculate the number of organizations and activities in each church per one hundred members or one hundred total constituents, and rank and calculate averages, etc., as before. Classify the churches as "highly organized," "moderately organized," and "slightly organized," with reference to the total number of organizations and the number in each class.

Calculate the total membership of all organizations and activities for the group of churches and the total for each class; find the average membership of each class and rank the churches according to their standing above or below the average for each class; for example, with respect to women's organizations, boys' organizations, etc.

(7) *The Ministry*

Make a classified inventory of the paid staff of the group of churches being studied according to types of positions included and sex of worker. The following form may be used for a summary:

TABLE XXVI

TABLE —INVENTORY OF PAID STAFF OF................CHURCHES

TYPE OF POSITION	CHURCHES (Write in Names of Individual Churches at the Heads of Columns)					Total	
	1	*2*	*3*	*4*	*5, etc.*	m	f
Minister	m	m	m	m	m	5	0
Assistant or Associate Minister	m	—	—	—	m	2	0
Director of Religious Education	f	—	m	—	f	1	2
Secretary, etc.	—	—	f	f	f	0	3

149

Total for each type of position by sex. Carry out the list of types of position till all fairly distinct kinds are included; but class together those positions in which essentially the same kind of work is done even when under different designations. In cases where two positions are held by one person, use dual designations; e.g., assistant minister and director of religious education. Make a table showing the number of churches having staffs of a given size, and calculate the average and most frequent size. Note the more prevalent staff combinations.

The schedule covering the education, experience, and pay of the ministry is the same as that used in one section of the semi-intensive study of the same topic,[9] and may be summarized for any group of individuals in the form shown on page 31.

Make a table showing the number of ministers and other paid workers with different degrees of education according to the following categories:

> Less than high-school course
> Not more than high-school course
> College
>   Two or more years but not graduate
>   Graduate
> College and theological seminary
> College and postgraduate work
> Theological seminary without college
> All other

Arrange similar tables covering special education of types of workers other than the minister; also continuation education.

Calculate and compare the average and median length of experience and service of paid workers. Make tables showing the distribution of time covered by different phases of the paid worker's experience, and by his tenure in his present position, and note most frequent length. Since experience may cover forty years and upward while the occupancy of one position rarely exceeds twenty years, different intervals should be used, as follows:

Intervals For

Experience (Years)	*Tenure* (Years)
Under 5	Under 2
10–19	Under 5
20–29	5–9
30–39	10–19
40 and over	20 and over

Rank the churches according to the amount of salary paid each important position, and by the total amount of salaries paid to professional workers.

[9] See p. 30.

Make calculations and comparisons of average and median salaries of each type of worker, and make table showing distribution of salaries, using intervals of $250 for the positions having the smaller average salaries and of $500 or $1,000 for the larger ones. The following table illustrates the method:

TABLE XXVII

TABLE   —DISTRIBUTION OF THE SALARIES OF 42
SPRINGFIELD PASTORS

Salary	Number of Pastors
Under $500	3
Under $1,000	3
$1,000 to $1,999	17
$2,000 to $2,999	9
$3,000 to $3,999	3
$4,000 to $4,999	3
$5,000 to $5,999	3
$6,000 to $6,999	3
$7,000 to $7,999	0
$8,000 and over	1

(8) *Plant*

Rank the churches, calculate average and median size or number; and make tables showing distribution, and exhibiting the most frequent size or number, on the following points relating to plant: size of lot, number of rooms, seating capacity of auditorium, and value of plant and of parsonage.

Note the frequency of occurrence of each kind of building material and each architectural style, and use in a written comment upon the general character of the plant owned by the churches of the group. Under each head of the classification, rank each item of equipment listed in the schedule according to its frequency in the group of churches. Calculate the average, median, and most frequent number of equipment items per church, and add a written statement showing what are the characteristic facilities of the group.

(9) *Finances*

Rank the churches according to total annual financial income, and according to income for current expenses and benevolence separately. Calculate the average and median amount of current and benevolent expenditure, and make tables showing the distribution according to amount and indicating the most frequent amount.

Calculate for each church the amount per capita for pledged contributors, members, or total constituents; rank the churches; calculate the group average, and median per capita, and show the distribution by per capita amounts and the most frequent per capita amount.

(10) *Services*

Rank the churches according to attendance at each of the major services, and show how each stands relative to the average and median attendance of the group. Show the distribution of attendance (by intervals of fifty or one hundred in the case of largely attended services and of ten or twenty-five in the case of smaller ones) and note the most frequent attendance, in tables similar to those used for membership and finance. Calculate the ratio between attendance and size of church-membership or of total constituency.

(11) *Religious Education*

Carry out in the study of Sunday-school enrollment and average attendance the main processes indicated for church-membership on page 146. Calculate and compare the churches with respect to the ratio of attendance to enrollment.

Calculate the age-distribution of Sunday-school pupils for the group as a whole and show how individual churches, denominations or territorial groups, vary from it, using the following broad age-groupings, or others based on the age-classification commonly in vogue in the local schools.

Age-groups

Under 6 (infancy)
6–14 (childhood)
15–20 (adolescence)
21 and over (adulthood)

Compare the age-groups with respect to ratio of attendance to enrollment.

Make a table showing the number of schools that have each a given number of departments, and list departments missing from or added to the standard scheme of departmentalization. A suitable form is illustrated on page 153.

Rank the churches according to number of teachers per one hundred pupils, and ratio of male to female teachers.

List the different lesson systems in use in the churches of the group and count frequency of each.

Count the number and calculate the proportion of churches maintaining daily vacation Bible school and weekday religious education, and the average or median duration of each of these activities.

(12) *Gains and Losses*

Calculate and compare churches according to amount of gains and losses in membership, and the per cent. of gains or losses that have come about in ways specified in the schedule: i.e., gains by confession (or reaffirmation) of faith, letter, etc.; losses by death, letter, dis-

TABLE XXVIII

TABLE —DEPARTMENTAL ORGANIZATION OF SUNDAY SCHOOLS

Number Departments per Sunday School	Number Schools Reporting	Schools with Specified Departments Missing						Schools with Additional Departments (Specify)
		Beginners	*Primary*	*Junior*	*Intermediate*	*Senior*	*Adult*	
7								
6								
5								
4								
3								
2								
1								
Total								

cipline or revision of roll. Also calculate ratio of gains to losses, and compare churches accordingly.

Since these ratios fluctuate greatly in single years they should also be calculated for five years, to make the comparison significant. See directions for study of these data over periods of time, page 132.

(13) *Community Relations*

Make a summary showing with what classes of, and how many, community agencies the church has had relations during this year: by financial support, practical coöperation, or advocacy in the pulpit or other promotional publicity. The facts are to be ascertained by an examination of the church's financial accounts and weekly bulletins for a year. A simplified version of the form given on page 60 may be used; and the results may be summarized for the churches of the group according to the form on page 154.

(14) *Denominational Relations*

Draw off from the financial statements of the individual churches the amounts contributed to and received as subsidies (if any) from their respective denominations. Rank the churches accordingly. Calculate average amount contributed to denomination and average ratio to total expenditures. Calculate per cent. of churches that receive subsidies, average amount, and ratio to total receipts.

A comprehensive church survey has now been outlined both as to topics and as to procedures. It utilizes most of the generally accessible data that can be compiled from records without prolonged processes of translation or fresh observation of the facts. The re-

TABLE XXIX

TABLE —RELATIONS OF CHURCHES TO COMMUNITY
AGENCIES

COMMUNITY AGENCIES		NUMBER OF CHURCHES HAVING RELATIONS	NUMBER OF RELATIONS			
Number	*Type*		*Total*	*Financial Support*	*Practical Coöperation*	*Advocacy*
	Religious					
	Public and Civic					
	Social					
	Family relief					
	Children's Aid					
	Homes for adults					
	Hospitals and health					
	Agencies for defectives					
	Corrective agencies					
	Character education					
	Recreation					
	Employment					
	Other					
	Total					

sults are largely capable of statistical statement and precise measurements. The processes indicated will get one very much farther on in the direction of an interpretation of the churches when they have been applied separately to denominational and territorial groups and to like classes composed of similar churches. The study, having determined the characters of these classes, can then investigate the characteristics of the whole group in terms of the likeness or difference of these homogeneous parts.

The outline and directions are not to be followed slavishly. They are intended rather to stimulate independent thinking, leading to their criticism and modification. The average denominational executive or statistician may get his own basic plan by scaling down more or less drastically from the outline of the case study in chapter ii, and should then be able to adapt the methodologies of the present chapter's study to the investigation of his own group of churches.

CHARACTERISTICS OF THE METHODOLOGY

With respect to logical form, this contemporary study of a group of churches is one in which a knowledge of the characteristics of the whole is reached by a synthesis of qualities known to characterize this or that individual part. It is for some reason practically important to deal with churches of this group as a whole—say, from the standpoint of a city-wide Protestant organization. Consequently it is important to think of them and talk about them, and to promote their interests, as a whole. The characteristics that are read into the group because they are known to exist in the individual cases have been expressed in summary form by averages. The central tendency, or what is true of the group as a whole and more nearly true of each of the churches than any other single statement can be, has thus been discovered. But these group-characteristics can be explained ultimately only as they are referred back to the individual cases from which they are derived, and as the agreement or deviation of the single cases from the group tendency is observed or measured. This summarizing of the facts so as to arrive at group-characteristics, together with their reanalysis so as to explain these characteristics, is the essence of the study as a scientific process.

Since the study lays chief stress on comparisons within a rather small group of churches, considerable value is found in recording quantitative differences that are not measured. Thus the churches are repeatedly ranked; for example, according to size, measured by membership. One can see at a glance which fall in the upper half of the list or the upper quarter, but without waiting to calculate *how much* larger any given church was than any other. Ministers are classified as to whether they have had more or less *than* college education, without going into the question of *how much* more education a theological course afforded.

But, as in all cases when quantitative data are available, measurement of the degree of likeness or difference with respect to some form is the chief vehicle of investigation. Gross measurements arrived at by totaling the columns of tabulation sheets gave, for example, number of churches and members, amount of salaries, etc. But, like all mere aggregations, these totals tell little of practical value. The real understanding of the group of churches begins when one begins to make measured comparisons of one set of facts in terms of another, or in terms of proportions of the whole. How many members are there per church, or dollars of expenditure per member? How large is Sunday-school enrollment relative to church-membership? What proportion of the churches have less than one hundred members, one hundred to two hundred, two hundred to three hundred, etc.? What per cent. of their numbers are children? These measurements of rates, ratio, percentage distribution, and proportion are all ways of measuring one set of facts in terms of another, or of part of the facts in terms of their relations to the whole. The elementary processes used in deriving them are matters covered by general education. Their logical properties and technical methods are discussed in books on statistics, such as are referred to in the Appendix. At least some of the simpler of these books should be read by any one systematically attempting to compare churches by a survey, but their details need not be entered upon here.

EXTENDING THE FIELD OF COMPARISON

In any such study of a group of churches as has been described, there will obviously be a desire to compare results with those of other studies that have been made in the same general field and in which the facts have been classified and stated according to the same method. Thus, in a Springfield study, data relating to the education, experience, tenure and salary of ministers were compared in terms of percentage distribution with similar data secured for St. Louis churches and for a broadly representative sample of 1,044 city churches from many large cities. On items covered by the United States Census of Religious Bodies the Springfield churches as they existed in 1916 were compared with those of other New England cities of similar size, with those of comparable cities of other regions, and with those of large cities of all size-groups throughout the United States. On the basis of these comparisons inferences were drawn, for example, as to whether or not the Springfield ministry was well paid. In other words, a survey director should familiarize himself with the results of similar surveys and note how far they agree with and tend to substantiate his own.

SCIENTIFIC VALIDITY

In general the principle relied upon in reaching conclusions is that facts that fit together, that reënforce one another and make relationships clearer as they accumulate, are provisionally true. Throughout the survey, coincidences of phenomena are therefore to be noted; as for example, the probable facts that churches large in membership are generally large in total program, that down-town churches generally have small attendance at evening service, or that the ratio of losses to gains in equally well-established denominations is approximately the same over similar periods of time. The tabulation and measurement of facts do more than make it possible to formulate true and intelligible individual statements (in the sense that they are statistically valid) about the group of churches. In addition, when these statements are buttressed by related facts, and are proved capable of being explained in terms of the individual units that comprised the group, and especially when they are found congruous with and explanatory of other facts, they become tentatively accepted generalizations, and provisionally established additions to the body of ascertained knowledge.

LIMITED SURVEYS OF GROUPS OF CHURCHES

SCHEME OF STUDY

(Chapter V)

(It is assumed that [A] the limited historical study of a group of churches will be made by ecclesiastical authorities and limited to existing comparable ecclesiastical records.)

PLANNING THE STUDY

1. Determine period to be studied.
2. Assemble the data.
3. Determine scope and content of study.
4. Make data comparable and discard what cannot be compared.
5. Edit data for accuracy.
6. Transcribe and tabulate data.
7. Condense tabulated results.
8. Determine aspects of the recorded phenomena which should be studied.

MAKING THE STUDY

I. Church Organizations

1. Tabulate data for organizations.
2. Map new and lapsed churches.
3. Correlate facts with growth or decline of different types of population.

II. Church-membership

1. Calculate amount and rate of church and denominational growth.
2. Rank churches and denominations accordingly.
3. Note continuity or discontinuity of growth.
4. Correlate facts with growth or decline of different types of population.

III. Ratio of Gains to Losses in Membership

1. Calculate amount and rate of gains and losses in membership and their ratio.
2. Rank churches and denominations accordingly.
3. Correlate gains and losses.
4. Note changes in tendency as to rate of gains or losses.
5. Calculate frequency of the various occasions of gains or losses.

IV. Special Aspects of Growth

1. Calculate changes in average size of churches.
2. Calculate changes in ratio of male to female members.

V. Sunday-school Membership

1. Follow same steps as with church-membership.

VI. Current Finances

1. Calculate amount and rate of increase in current financial expenditures.
2. Rank churches and denominations accordingly.
3. Note continuity or discontinuity of increase.

4. Calculate amount and changes of per capita giving for church support.
5. Translate monetary measures into terms of purchasing power.

VII. Benevolences

1. Use same processes as for current finance.
2. Tabulate and calculate and compare denominations according to objects of benevolence.

VIII. Value of Church Property

1. Calculate amounts, averages, rates of increase and ratios for value of church property.
2. Tabulate dates and locations of new buildings and important additions.

IX. Churches Grouped by Geographical Location

1. Carry out processes called for in sections (II) Church-membership and (III) Ratio of Gains to Losses in Membership, for central, residential and suburban groups, respectively.

X. Literary Summary

1. Write a narrative and exposition of the trend of church history for the period studied.
2. Show what individual churches contributed strikingly to general tendencies.

XI. Conclusion

1. Decide what to do about any tendencies which ought to be changed.

(It is assumed that [B] a limited contemporaneous study of a group of churches will be made by ecclesiastical or Church Federation authorities or as a group self-survey.)

PLANNING THE STUDY

1. Follow the preliminary steps of chapter ii.
2. Make a schedule following the outline of chapter ii, but reduced in scale.
3. Define all terms used or implied.

MAKING THE STUDY

1. Collect data.
2. Transcribe, edit and tabulate data.
3. Classify churches by activities.
4. Classify and compare churches as to age, growth and mobility or permanence.
5. Classify and compare churches as to membership and size of constituencies.
6. Classify and compare churches as to parish distance and direction.
7. Study social quality of various areas of the city from census data.
8. District the city into socially homogeneous areas.
9. Calculate church-members and constituents, and churchgoing, by districts.
10. Calculate and compare churches as to completeness of internal organization and of strength of organization of each type.

11. Classify the paid religious workers of the church being studied.
12. Compare religious workers as to preparation, experience, tenure and pay.
13. Compare church plants, calculating sizes and frequencies of various features.
14. Compare churches financially.
15. Compare churches as to public religious services.
16. Compare churches as to religious education.
17. Compare churches as to gains and losses in membership.
18. Compare churches as to community relations.
19. Compare churches as to denominational relations.
20. Compare results with those of similar studies.
21. Draw conclusions on the basis of the best established findings.

SUGGESTIONS FOR SUPPLEMENTAL RESEARCH

(A)

1. So far as denominational records cover the same points as the U. S. Census of Religious Bodies, compare the changes shown by the Census over a comparable period of time with the findings of the study for the same group of churches (if reported upon); also for similar groups in other cities, noting differences in rates of progress.
2. Critically compare the schedules in current use by the leading denominations in securing annual statistical reports from local churches; if possible organize action looking toward their greater comparability.
3. Go behind the formal statistical data into local church history to find the explanation of unusual trends in the data.
4. Carry out the study of losses and gains of membership over a period of time according to the sources of each: e.g., losses by death, dismissal, etc.
5. Try to explain the unequal rates of growth of denominations. (See Douglass, *St. Louis Church Survey*, p. 200 f.)
6. Try to explain the unequal rates of growth (numerical and financial) of central, residential and suburban churches.

(B)

1. Help any church that desires it, to supplement its self-survey by a more intensive study.
2. Carry out semi-intensively the study of any topic of special immediate importance to the group under survey.
3. Study the memberships, gains and losses, facilities, finances, etc., of the several subsidiary organizations by the methods shown for the church and the Sunday school as wholes.
4. Compare the denominations and the types of churches on all the major topics covered by the schedule. (For model of treatment, see Douglass, *1,000 City Churches*, chapter xi.)

BIBLIOGRAPHY AND REFERENCES

(A)

Census of Religious Bodies, 1916 (Washington: Bureau of the Census, 1919), 2 vols. (Also for 1900 and 1906.)

Carroll, *The Religious Forces of the United States* (New York: Scribner's, 1912).
Compares material of earlier U. S. Religious Censuses.

Douglass, *The St. Louis Church Survey* (New York: Doran, 1924), chapters v-ix.

Douglass, *The Springfield Church Survey* (New York: Doran, 1926), chapter iii.

Year Book of the Churches (New York: Federal Council of the Churches of Christ, Annual).
Includes annual compilation summarizing statistics of all denominations.

(B)

Douglass, *The St. Louis Church Survey* (New York: Doran, 1924), chapters v-ix.

Douglass, *The Springfield Church Survey* (New York: Doran, 1926), chapters v-ix.

CHAPTER VI

STUDYING THE COMMUNITY BACKGROUND

The method of studying the community background of religious institutions is essentially the same whether the study concerns a limited urban community as related to a particular group of churches, or an entire city or metropolitan area as related to all of its churches. The particular community must first be identified in either case, by the use of criteria indicated in the next chapter.[1]

This chapter does not attempt to give complete directions for social surveys. It is assumed that the study will be made as part of the community religious survey described in the following chapter. It is only under such circumstances that there is likely to be a demand for the collection of extensive social data under religious auspices. The social interest, however, is subordinate, and the data are limited. If a single church wants to sketch in its social background beyond the limits provided for in chapter ii, it may select additional phases of investigation from the present chapter.

PLANNING THE STUDY OF THE COMMUNITY BACKGROUND

SCOPE AND EXTENT OF EXISTING SOCIAL DATA

Any plan for the study of the community background of the church must depend upon the scope and extent of existing social data. The creation of social data of any importance is expensive and time-consuming. The first step should then obviously be to discover, inventory, and critically appraise, all old sources. Their scope and variety, as gathered by public and private agencies in any great American city, will surprise one not familiar with the facts.[2]

CHARACTER OF EXISTING DATA

Equally surprising will be the gaps in the data, the lack (in spite of their bulk) of direct applicability of most of the data to the questions the church wants answered. This is matched only by the failure of the churches themselves to depend upon precise knowledge,

[1] See p. 197.
[2] For a discussion of the character and types of such data, see Carpenter, "The Research Resources of a Typical American City as Exemplified by the City of Buffalo," *Proceedings of the Twentieth Annual Meeting (1925) of the American Sociological Society* (University of Chicago, 1926).

or to create, as they go along, records comparable in extent and accuracy with those of the other constructive agencies. So soon, therefore, as the student of religious community has initially defined his problem, he should find out what has already been done that throws light upon it.

In a few cities, previous religious surveys, or field investigations, and statistics gathered by church federations, have assembled more or less adequate data for study of social backgrounds; and important studies of limited areas will sometimes be found. In the main, however, the problem will be that of the examination, reorganization, utilization and interpretation from the religious standpoint, of large bodies of exceedingly varied data. These have to be fitted together in harmony with the present purpose, along with products of the more definitely social studies described in preceding chapters; such as those of church constituencies and of parish distribution.

SCOPE OF SOCIAL BACKGROUND STUDIES

Logically following upon the determination of the community to be studied and the appraisal of existing data, comes the decision as to what new data are to be sought, how much of the existing data are to be used, and from what points of view they are to be regarded. The use of existing data means, of course, that the fundamental ways of regarding any given phenomena have been predetermined by those who first gathered and analyzed the data. Accordingly the present problem is one of selecting what is profitable, and perhaps of recombining data from new points of view within such limitations as their form and nature impose.

As elsewhere noted,[3] the degree to which the study of an individual church's social background should be carried depends upon the importance of the environmental factors relative to others in determining the church's fortunes, or as indicating its opportunities for service. This principle applies equally to a group of churches. If the churches are located in a rapidly changing part of the city, or one in which problems of poverty and delinquency converge, studies throwing light on social phenomena will probably seem more pertinent than they will if the churches are in static residential sections or prosperous suburbs.

CONTENT OF BACKGROUND STUDIES

The study of the church's background should obviously include the more significant structural aspects of the environment, such as the number and distribution of people of different sorts; the physical structure of the city or district; the distinct economic and social com-

[3] See p. 21.

munities or levels of population occupying the area; the distribution of religious population and of institutions sharing constructive social responsibility with the church. It should also be concerned with the course of social evolution as revealed in environmental changes in the area concerned, especially as they may have affected the fortunes of the churches and their allies. Still again, the study of social background must include some account of the regular movements of population from place to place within the city, such as the daily ebb and flow between the peripheral areas and suburbs and the centers of industry, business and recreation. This phase of the study must particularly deal with the fixed paths of travel and the habits of going back and forth over given routes which may be translated into the practice of churchgoing. Finally, the study should generalize its discoveries and draw reasonable conclusions from the standpoint of the church's problems.

A "moderately full" treatment of the social background relative to community religious study is illustrated in the following sections.

METHODOLOGY

STUDY OF POPULATION

The church needs, of course, to know how many people live in its parish, who and where they are, and particularly whether they are of the sort that it can probably reach directly or for which it ought to feel responsible. It also needs to know how, if at all, its tributary population varies from normal population as to age and sex and marital status.

SOURCES OF INFORMATION

The standard source of such information is the United States Census, which publishes data covering these points by wards for (nearly) all cities of 100,000 population and over.[4] Certain states take censuses at intermediate periods and publish the results in a form similar to the decennial Federal census.

Short methods (yielding approximately accurate results) of using the census material were set forth in connection with the environmental study of the single church.[5] But groups of wards do not always correspond closely with communities; and wards are not individually homogeneous. An adequate survey must therefore have data for smaller units of population than records afford.

The local unit of census enumeration is a small precinct or district consisting of a few blocks. This furnishes the unit for all tabulations

---

[4] *Fourteenth United States Census, 1920*, Vol. III, Table 13, under each state containing cities of 100,000 population and over.
[5] See pp. 22 f.

of data in the Census Bureau at Washington. Transcriptions of the data for certain cities have been made in terms of these original units. Local chambers of commerce, public libraries, and universities should be consulted to see whether the data in this form exist for any city in which a survey is to be undertaken. The importance of the precinct data is that they can be recombined with great accuracy for any particular area desired. Such a process yields very precise social

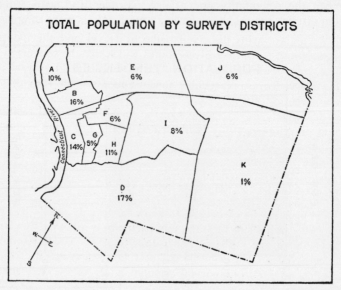

CHART XIII—GEOGRAPHICAL DISTRIBUTION OF THE INHABITANTS OF SPRINGFIELD.

information as to the number, composition and characteristics of population. In a large community survey it would not be unreasonable to go to the expense of having such a transcription made in the Census Bureau.[6]

While local estimates of the growth of population between censuses are highly unreliable, and are generally not attempted for small areas within the city, the rates of growth indicated by school enumerations, city directory canvasses, etc., may be conservatively used as the basis of guesses in this matter.

Occasionally, also, dependable censuses are taken under local authorities (sometimes with federal coöperation) or under private auspices. The house-to-house canvass for economic data conducted by the *St. Louis Post Dispatch* in 1925 was of this sort.[7] The unit

[6] For an example of the practical use of precinct data, see *The Springfield Church Survey*, p. 263.
[7] See p. 22.

of its enumeration was the small precinct largely corresponding to those of the Federal census.

By means of any such reliable data for small areas, the population of any church's parish or community, or of any district within a city, can be very closely approximated and its composition and characteristics determined in whatever categories the particular census provides.

When the community under survey is identified with a metropolitan district, the problem of using census data is more complicated.

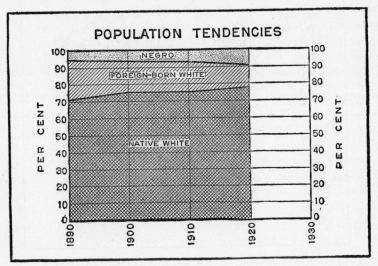

CHART XIV—FOREIGN-BORN POPULATION IS DECREASING, NATIVE WHITE POPULATION INCREASING, IN ST. LOUIS.

Precinct data are likely to be obtainable only for the major city; while larger suburbs are reported by wards and smaller ones only in totals for incorporated places or minor civil divisions. Totaling the figures for all these divisions will, however, give the population of the total community involved, and the composition of population of its several parts may be approximately arrived at and compared.

The importance of the ability to recombine data for small areas is especially marked in the study of colonies of foreign-born or Negro population. Thus, in a certain urban district, the 1920 census found 12,109 foreign-born people living within four different wards, along with nearly 26,000 Negroes. The precinct data combined with field observation showed that nearly all of these were located within three distinct, but contiguous, colonies occupying less than one-fourth of the area of the district. Each of these contained about 5,000 Negroes, and considerable minorities of Irish and German birth. An

165

adjoining area included a compact Jewish community of over 3,000 people. The boundaries of these colonies were accurately traceable by the method described. Between and among these alien populations remained a large element of stranded American population. This had recently been reënforced by strong rural immigration. The evidence of these last facts was found in a school district census in which was reported the race of each school child and the state in which he was born. It was clear that the parents of children young enough to be in low elementary grades and born in other states, could not have lived many years in the city; and that where this school population was almost entirely from one or two states a recent colonizing movement had taken place. These items marked off the American-born rural immigrant from the older, stranded American population.

Similarly, census precinct data enable one to analyze the population from the standpoint of its age and sex variation. Thus a group of precincts in Ward Seventeen in St. Louis showed a marked excess of adult male population. The racial analysis of the census located one-half of this excess with native-born whites, one-fifth with foreign-born, and three-tenths with Negroes. In another direction in the same ward were precincts showing a smaller excess of adult females. But virtually all of these fell within the native white population. The number of children fell below the normal level in exact proportion as there was an excess of unmarried adults of either sex.

STUDY OF PHYSICAL STRUCTURE

A city's population is related to a particular physical structure, natural or artificial, consisting of land and water, streets and buildings, and the major facilities which make large demands upon space. The original physical basis of a city is topography. This governs the essential city plan. Such structural aspects of the community, particularly the location of its homes, its business and its industry, concern the church because they determine the distribution of population with which the church deals, the channels and directions of the population's going and coming which concern church attendance, as well as the directions of probable growth in which the church may share. Besides this, the use to which any area of the city may be put, as expressed by these structures, is now being increasingly determined by zoning requirements and regulations. These fix the physical structures legally; and largely settle what kind of people will live in any area, and the consequent fortunes of any institution that may be identified with them. Zoning regulations have sometimes even prohibited the building of churches.

STUDYING THE COMMUNITY BACKGROUND

Sources of Information

Municipal or regional city-planning authorities, when such exist, or the engineering departments of cities, together with large fire insurance and public utility companies, possess the most elaborate and reliable information concerning the city's physical and structural aspects. Many of their studies are published; others remain in maps and raw data. It is important to interest such agencies in assisting community religious surveys. In any large-scale survey, the officials of the city-planning commissions should be invited to become members of its advisory board, to which they can contribute invaluable information.

INDUSTRIAL, COMMERCIAL & RESIDENTIAL DISTRICTS

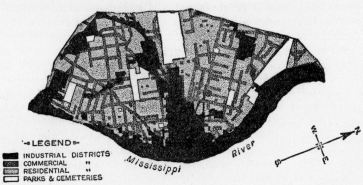

LEGEND
- INDUSTRIAL DISTRICTS
- COMMERCIAL "
- RESIDENTIAL "
- PARKS & CEMETERIES

CHART XV—THE ZONING OF ST. LOUIS (ADAPTED FROM MAP OF THE CITY PLAN COMMISSION).

Tracings of various mappings of religious phenomena, such as the distribution of religious adherents according to parishes, denominations, and faiths, should be superimposed upon map after map prepared by a city-plan commission in illustration of various points covered by its investigations. The limiting effect of topography on the typical parish will then be clearly seen. Natural barriers have ordinarily been reënforced by artificial ones. These latter have then been fixed by zoning law. The parishes have ordinarily grown along the major axes of the city's growth, and reach out farthest in the direction of the best transit facilities.

Thus, in a certain St. Louis church, the points specifically observed were: (1) the parish was sharply divided toward the south by the shallow valley of Mill Creek, now occupied and paralleled by railways and the industrial zone. The early occupancy of this valley by the railways permanently bisected St. Louis into a north side and south side; and since the major movement of the city was from east to west, the two sides have never been united by numerous major

167

thoroughfares. The city's greatest growth has been westward, but on the north side rather than the south. This is true also of this particular church. It stands at the gateway in the narrow sector where numerous east and west lines of traffic converge and almost at the focus of the main line of automobile traffic. In its location just off Grand Avenue, however, the church also enjoys the benefit of the city's chief north and south streets. This partially overcomes the effect of the dominent east-west movement, and gives the parish a balance that few of its neighboring parishes possess. All told, the study of the physical structure of St. Louis showed this church standing almost at the crossroads, at the city's most focal point outside the down-town business district itself.

Every other church or group of churches is similarly either helped or hindered by the city's physical structure. The distribution of constituencies should be measured and expressed in terms of the directional categories applied to the single church in chapter i.[8]

ECONOMIC STRUCTURE

It goes without saying that the institutional fortunes of a church are largely bound up with the wealth or poverty of the people to whom it looks for support. The ordinary observations of persons familiar with a city discriminate the more glaring economic contrasts from district to district—the slums, the "Gold Coast," the blighted area, the desirable suburbs. In many cities, business research has made careful studies of economic levels of population by areas to determine the market for goods. The *St. Louis Post Dispatch's* study of its city's metropolitan district has already been referred to.[9]

Method

The use of the *Post Dispatch* data in determining the economic levels of population with which the St. Louis "West End" churches have to do, and comparison of these levels with those of population tributary to other groups of churches, illustrate the general method of using such data. Calculations were made for areas within a mile of eight important Protestant churches; the churches being so located as to describe a cross section of St. Louis on an east and west axis from the center to a point beyond the western boundary.[10]

The points covered in the comparison were: (1) average rents paid (primarily reflecting differences in land values), and (2) the character of housing. The results appear in the following table (with the number of charity cases reported by the St. Louis Provident Association added as an additional index).

[8] See p. 19.
[9] See Chart XVI, p. 170.
[10] The St. Louis churches are so located in clusters that these eight locations accounted for thirteen churches. The approximate status of the population surrounding fifteen or twenty other "West End" churches could be obtained by splitting the difference between the figures for churches between which any other given church was located.

TABLE XXX

TABLE —FAMILIES, RENTS, TYPES OF DWELLING AND CHARITY CASES WITHIN A MILE RADIUS OF SPECIFIED WEST END CHURCHES

	Churches Designated by Number in Order of Location from East to West							
	1&2	3	4	5&6	7&8	9,10,11	12	13
Number of families:	21,749	19,023	12,767	13,844	17,683	15,984	12,431	3,320
Per cent. paying								
Very high rents	7	19	61	57	42	55	79	78
High rents	12	15	19	23	38	32	12	22
Slightly above average rents	36	41	20	18	18	10	5	0
Average rents	19	25	0	2	2	3	4	0
Slightly below average rents	0	0	0	0	0	0	0	0
Low rents	26	0	0	0	0	0	0	0
Very low rents	0	0	0	0	0	0	0	0
Per cent. living in								
Residences	16	23	29	28	31	30	29	48
Flats	58	51	44	42	45	43	21	22
Apartments	4	9	17	27	22	25	50	30
Lodging houses	7	5	3	1	1	1	0	0
Light housekeeping rooms	15	12	7	2	1	1	0	0
Number of charity cases:	343	160	110	71	73	43	19	6

In the cases of churches 1 and 2, for example, the table shows that no portion of the population living within a mile pays the very lowest rentals such as are found in St. Louis only in the river wards of the older city. But over a fourth are paying very low rentals; while no part of the population surrounding any of the other West End churches compared was living on this level. Furthermore, the economic levels within the parishes of the two churches revealed a distinct gap. About a fifth of the population was paying average rents, and about a fourth low rents; but no part was paying slightly below average rents. In brief, one economic stratum was left out. The break came at Grand Avenue. The population living east of Grand Avenue was very much poorer than that living west. Such immediate contrasts, as distinguished from the more usual shading-off of one economic level into another, are of obvious significance for church fortunes.

As to housing, quarters for rooming and light housekeeping were decidedly characteristic in the parishes of churches 1 and 2; while single-family houses and apartments were much less characteristic than in the parishes of the other churches measured.

These two measurements of economic status afforded a very lively

impression of the complexity of the "West End," as well as of the
rapid increase of wealth as one passes westward toward the suburbs

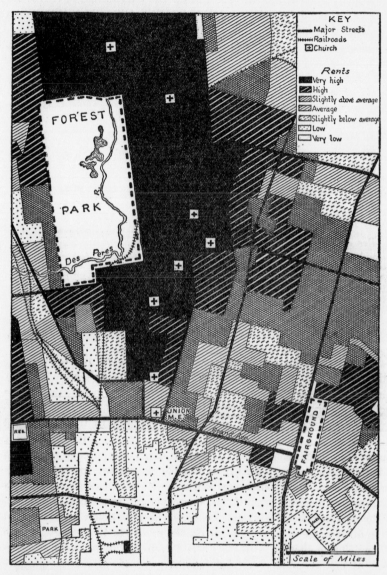

CHART XVI—ENUMERATION PRECINCTS USED AS THE BASIS OF AN ECONOMIC
SURVEY SHOWING AVERAGE RENTS.

along the line of the city's major growth. Something similar should
be worked out from economic data that may be available in any city
in which a community-wide survey is undertaken.

A measure of the economic levels of population is at the same time a measure of its general social fortunes, good or bad. But a more careful determination of the social structure of the city or community must be made, on the basis of a variety of criteria, in terms of homogeneous districts or relatively small areas, such as are shown on Chart XVI. In the St. Louis Church Survey, for example, the basis of comparison consisted of eleven independent social criteria finally combined into a general ranking scale.

Method

The method for deriving and using similar data is as follows:

Criteria for determining social levels, data concerning which are likely to be available, include the following: (1) proportion of foreign-born population; (2) proportion of Negro population; (3) congestion of population; (4) gain and loss of population; (5) degree of industrialization; (6) degree of home ownership; (7) infant mortality; (8) juvenile delinquency; (9) illiteracy; (10) poverty; (11) tuberculosis mortality. It may be assumed that a district with a large population of foreign birth, many Negroes, high degree of industrialization, and congestion of living conditions; with much illiteracy, juvenile delinquency and poverty, represents a less desirable combination of human fortunes than one in which opposite conditions exist—so that ranking of areas on this basis approximately places their residents in the scale of human welfare.

The methods for determining the rank of any given district in terms of the individual criteria have to be varied according to the nature of the existing data. For juvenile delinquency, poverty and tuberculosis mortality, the case records of public or private agencies dealing with these phenomena have to be drawn upon. The cases are located by residence, mapped for the entire city, and the number of cases falling in each district directly counted. Infant mortality and tuberculosis mortality data can probably be secured from records in the city health departments. Very likely they have already been transcribed and the results mapped by some health agency. If not, they will have to be tabulated for a sufficient number of years to rule out fluctuations. This will involve the handling of some thousands of birth and death certificates. Infant mortality is expressed as a ratio of infants dying under the age of one year per thousand live births. Juvenile delinquency data may be similarly transcribed for adequate periods from the city court records. They may be expressed as a rate per thousand total or per thousand juvenile population. The data on poverty and social maladjustment should be drawn from the records of the most representative charity organization. When, as is frequently the case, Jewish and Catholic poverty is largely cared for by separate agencies, it must be recognized that these data will not be as nearly adequate as though cases from these agencies had been included. The records of a single large society serving all faiths, however, probably furnishes a fair index of the distribution of poverty and social maladjustment throughout the city. Poverty cases may be expressed as a rate per thousand total population.

The period covered by each of the above lines of information should terminate with the year corresponding most nearly to the date of the survey.

Total population, foreign-born population, Negro population, illiteracy, congestion, gain and loss in population, and home ownership are derived from census precinct data in the manner described in a preceding paragraph. (Note that illiteracy is calculated with reference to population of ten years of age and over.) The data for any survey district are easily secured simply by combining those reported for the precincts that fall within it.

The degree of industrialization of any district has to be determined by a series of judgments, rather than by calculation. Zoning Ordinances commonly divide the city into use districts as follows:

1. Those open to all industries.
2. Those open to industry that does not constitute a nuisance.
3. Those open to retail business.
4. Those open to residential use only.

The area of each district open to, and actually occupied by, structures devoted to these various types of use has ordinarily been mapped by the City Plan Commission.

While, therefore, the per cent. of the area any district actually occupies by industries is easily discovered, another factor remains; namely, that of the distribution of industries. A certain district, for example, is in the main protected from future incursion of industry and is not actually occupied by concentrated industries at any point; neither is a large part of its area occupied by industries. It has, however, very many small industries so scattered throughout its area that the district as a whole is seriously impaired from the standpoint of desirable residence. It must, therefore, be judged more highly industrialized from the social standpoint than another district with more industries might be; because in the former case they are not so concentrated and their social effects are greater. The estimates of the survey as to degree of industrialization will thus be the result of a balancing of these various factors, carefully checked by field observations.[11]

The ranking of each district with respect to each criterion, expressed as a per cent., or rate, as the case may be (except in the case

11 *The St. Louis Church Survey,* pp. 280 and 284.

of industrialization as just explained, may now be easily calculated. The results should then be summarized in the form shown in the following table. It should be noted that on all criteria but two the ranking is from least to greatest. For example, the district with the fewest foreigners or the least illiteracy stands first. With respect to gain of population and rate of home ownership, on the other hand, the district with the largest amount stands first.

TABLE XXXI

TABLE —SUMMARY OF SOCIAL DATA USED IN RANKING DISTRICTS

CRITERIA	DISTRICTS BY RANK						
	1st	*2nd*	*3rd*	*4th*	*5th*	*6th*	*etc.*
I. Foreign-born Population							
Number							
Per cent. of total							
II. Negro Population							
Number							
Per cent. of total							
III. Illiteracy							
Number							
Per cent. illiterate							
IV. Juvenile Delinquency							
Number							
Rate per 1,000 population							
V. Industrialization							
Rank							
VI. Gain or Loss of Population							
Amount							
Per cent.							
VII. Congestion							
Number of Families per Dwelling							
VIII. Home Ownership							
Number homes owned							
Rate per 100 population							
IX. Infant Mortality							
Number dying under one year							
Per cent.							
X. Poverty							
Number charity cases							
Rate per 100 population							
XI. Tuberculosis Mortality							
Number cases							
Rate per 1,000 population							

Rank on Combined Criteria

To obtain the ranking of the districts according to the combined weight of all the criteria, make a table showing how many times each district occupies first place, second place, etc., with respect to the eleven separate criteria.

Devise a series of numerical values (greater than the number of the districts) and assign a fixed value to each position—say, twenty-five to first place, twenty-four to second place, etc. A similar method is in common use in the scoring of games. Count up the score of each district by adding together the products secured by multiplying the values assigned to the several ranks by the number of times each rank is reached, thus:

Position	Values	Districts					
		I		II		III, etc.	
		Times Ranked	Score	Times Ranked	Score	Times Ranked	Score
1st place	25	6	150	3	75	0	0
2nd place	24	3	72	2	48	2	48
3rd place, etc.	23	2	46	2	46	4	92
Total score	X	X	268	X	169	X	140

The total scores of the districts rank them with respect to the combined criteria of social quality. The ranking has no absolute validity, because the criteria do not have equal values. Probably a low illiteracy rate is socially less significant than a low death-rate for infants. Note, however, whether the scores of most of the districts according to the separate criteria tend to "bunch" in the same

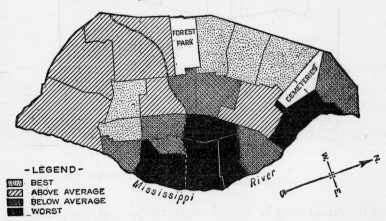

RANK OF SURVEY DISTRICTS
BY ELEVEN SOCIAL CRITERIA

-LEGEND-
BEST
ABOVE AVERAGE
BELOW AVERAGE
WORST

CHART XVII—THE "GOOD" DISTRICTS IN ST. LOUIS TEND STRONGLY TO BE GOOD ALL AROUND AND THE "BAD" ONES TO BE BAD ALL AROUND.

range of the scale—at the bottom, top, or in the middle. If the results are thus consistent in their details, the final ranking of a district may be accepted as a rough measurement of its actual social level. When they are not consistent in detail, the district should be isolated for special study directed to finding an explanation.

After ranking, the districts may then be divided into four equal classes, as follows, and the community mapped on this basis.

A—The upper fourth in rank.
B—The fourth just above the average.
C—The fourth just below the average.
D—The lowest fourth.

An example of the results of this method is shown in Chart XVII.

The differentiation of neighborhoods within districts is not fully discovered even by the above elaborate analysis, for the reason that people on the same economic and social level may belong to different races, cultures and periods of migration. A homogeneous area according to the criteria has still to be analyzed according to such components.[12] This must finally be done through field observation;

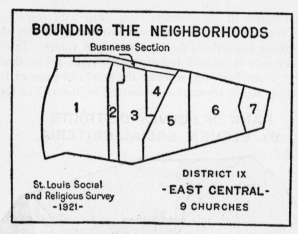

CHART XVIII—NATURAL NEIGHBORHOODS WITH COMMON INTERESTS—NOS. I AND 3, NEGRO DISTRICTS, DIVIDED BY "AUTOMOBILE ROW," CHIEF THOROUGHFARE OF THE CITY FROM DOWN-TOWN TO THE WEST END; NO. 4, RECENT RURAL IMMIGRANTS; NO. 5, RUSSIAN JEWS; NO. 6, IRISH CATHOLIC AND INDUSTRIAL; NO. 7, CHIEFLY RESIDENTIAL—GERMAN-AMERICAN WITH EVANGELICAL AND LUTHERAN TENDENCIES.

and the details must be worked out on the basis of conference and testimony as to the actual feeling of residents as to social identity and social distance. District IX, for example, as shown on Chart XVIII, was thus found to include seven natural neighborhoods, differentiated chiefly by race and nationality, and divided and bounded in the main by major arteries of traffic. It is important to check back from the social to the economic and physical data previously studied, to see whether the areas of low social fortunes approximately coincide with those characterized by low rents, or by physical handicaps, such as low elevation, isolation by barriers, poor transit

[12] See chap. vii, pp. 199 f.

facilities; and with those occupied by industries. Churches may then be studied individually to discover the relation of their locations and parishes to the social and economic structure of the city.

Parish maps should be compared with the city map showing the social levels by districts. These will show how many churches are wholly or chiefly identified with one particular level of social fortunes. These are the class churches. For those that draw widely from various parts of the city, calculations will have to be made showing what per cent. of their constituents come from Class A areas, Class B areas, etc.

Acute Phases of Mobility and Change

The social criteria thus far considered give the status of different parts of the city as it exists at a given time. But cities change rapidly. When the social phenomena of a district appear to be inconsistent, it may be because one of the generally associated factors has been modified somewhat by advance of, and independently of, the others. These portents of further change, the advance signs of adversity or prosperity, are peculiarly worth study from the church's viewpoint.

Rates of change may be calculated for any of the social factors covered by census data by a comparison of the returns for two or more census periods, according to the methods discussed in a subsequent paragraph.[13]

Mobility of population, in the sense of the rate of its removal from one place of residence to another, is in general an index of the degree of social transience or permanence. This rate may be directly calculated for one or more dates, by districts, by means of a count of the number of changes of address in a sufficiently large sample of the population as listed in the city directory. A still more refined process of calculating mobility is afforded in cities that print annual poll-lists of voters, giving both the old and the new addresses of those who have moved within a year. This makes it possible to calculate separately those removals that are a mere milling around within the same neighborhood and those that are real changes of residence to other neighborhoods and districts of the city. In typical cities, from one-fourth to over half of all addresses will be found to change annually. The prevalent rate of mobility in the vicinity of each church should be calculated, and its relation to the rate of membership-turnover noted.

The geography of families occupying lodging houses and light housekeeping rooms is perhaps the best single index of the approach of deterioration and of the invasion of a district by transient and

13 See pp. 185 ff.

socially undependable population. Housing surveys often afford means of charting the advance of these conditions. Chart XIX is

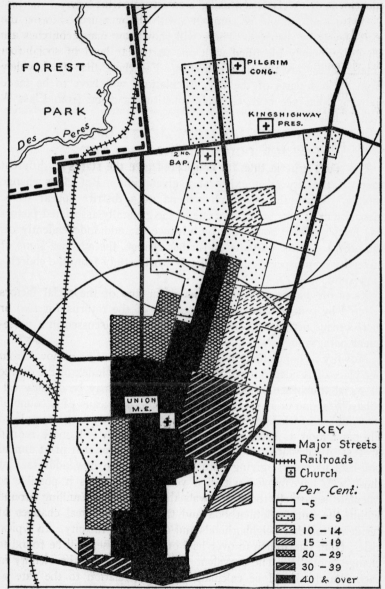

CHART XIX—ROOMING-HOUSE AREA, ST. LOUIS (SHADING SHOWS PER CENT. OF FAMILIES LIVING IN ROOMING-HOUSES OR LIGHT-HOUSE-KEEPING QUARTERS).

based on the underlying data that are summarized in the table on page 169.[14] It shows a relatively compact area in St. Louis in which

[14] See p. 170 for chart showing average rents in the same area.

from 15 to over 40 per cent. of all families are in lodging houses or light housekeeping rooms; and also locates the further westward movement of deterioration along axial streets where as yet the proportion of families in lodging houses and light housekeeping rooms is only from 5 to 10 per cent. Here a second zone of transient residence is clearly forming. The menace of this secondary zone of deterioration for still favored churches of the residential regions is quite obvious in this case, from the map.

By means of similar maps, any city can show the direction in which a given social condition is moving and trace its line of advance.

ENCIRCLING MOVEMENTS OF POORER POPULATIONS AND THE PATHS OF WHITE PROTESTANT RETREAT

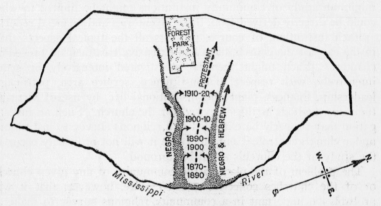

CHART XX—PARALLEL WESTWARD MOVEMENTS OF NEGROES AND HE-BREWS IN ST. LOUIS HAVE BEEN EVICTING WHITE PROTESTANT POPULATIONS FROM THE CENTER OF THE CITY FOR FIFTY YEARS.

This is a very essential phase of the study of the background of religious institutions.

Institutional Structure

The study of the church's social background must, of course, include institutions other than churches. In cities, these are exceedingly numerous and take on perplexing variety.

The territory adjacent to a business center of any size is likely to be a focal area for the location of numerous civic and social institutions such as clubs, lodge headquarters, hospitals and working women's homes. Here will be found the chief recreational institutions of the city, massing large numbers of theaters, moving-picture houses, dance halls, billiard- and pool-halls, etc. It is also likely to be a school center, including perhaps some denominational university, a city high school, and numerous schools of business and music.

These all serve widespread constituencies. The more strictly residential areas, on the other hand, will show only purely local institutions, like ward schools and local moving-picture houses. Some of these institutions are organized and supported by churches, others are acknowledged allies of the church, others rivals; while some are allies in one sense and rivals in another. The interest of the church in conducting a survey of these institutions is naturally colored by the degree of affiliation or antagonism involved.

The chief sources of information about social agencies are classified directories, which are found in all large cities and which often give compressed information concerning the work of each; and their own formal reports and promotional literature. Community Chests and Councils of Social Agencies now commonly compile certain statistical information annually, chiefly of a financial nature. A minimum study of community institutions might be limited to what could be directly derived from these inventories and financial reports.

Each institution, of course, presents all the typical aspects that, in the case of the church, have had extensive treatment in preceding chapters. Each might then be investigated intensively or semi-intensively, with respect to constituency, service area, patronage, leadership, finances, plant and institutional life, by use of virtually the same methods as those devised for the church. Such an investigation may properly be extended in a religious survey to institutions under church control;[15] but otherwise it will not ordinarily occur in the study of the church's social background.

The problem of the place in the community of any given church, or of the churches collectively, is so acute, however, that it will probably be important in a community religious survey to make at least certain minimum investigations that require the securing of new data through first-hand study of institutional records. The following paragraphs indicate limited researches of this type.

Study of Social Institutions from Data Already Collected

The data relating to social institutions must first be assembled, edited for comparability (often a difficult task), tabulated and summarized. Social agencies are classified more or less closely in directories and the lists of Community Chests, etc. Maps should be made locating each agency in the city or district, by geographical subdivisions; a separate symbol being used for each kind of agency, with a separate color to show the general auspices under which it is conducted.[16]

Social institutions may be maintained by the public for all of the people who may need their services; or by private groups for their

15 See pp. 58 f.
16 For a standard form of symbols to be used in mapping social institutions, see leaflet of the Russell Sage Foundation (New York City, 1926), entitled "Social Map Symbols," with price-list of symbols that may be purchased for pasting on maps.

own use; or under mixed auspices and for various constituencies. A first result of the study may therefore naturally be a classification

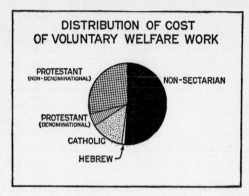

CHART XXI—FINANCIAL CONTRIBUTIONS TO COM-
MUNITY WELFARE IN SPRINGFIELD,
ACCORDING TO SOURCE.

and distribution of cost and investment according to the auspices under which they are supported and controlled. The following form may be used as a summary:

TABLE XXXII

TABLE —INVESTMENT IN PROPERTY AND ANNUAL COST OF OPERATION OF SOCIAL AGENCIES CLASSIFIED ACCORDING TO AUSPICES OF SUPPORT AND CONTROL

Auspices	Number of Institutions	Property Invest-ment in (Dollars)	Annual Cost of Operation (Dollars)
Public (tax supported)			
Private			
Non-sectarian			
Sectarian			
Protestant			
Denominational			
Non-denominational			
Catholic			
Jewish			
Other			

This summary shows the division of the social burden of the community among the several supporting constituencies. Further subdivision by Protestant denominations or special agencies may also be shown. Such data may be graphed effectively as is illustrated in Chart XXI.

The classification of agencies according to kind should next be tabulated, in total and also for the separate constituencies, in the following form:

180

TABLE XXXIII

TABLE —NUMBER OF SOCIAL AGENCIES CLASSIFIED AS TO TYPE AND AUSPICES

TYPE	TOTAL PUBLIC	PRIVATE					
		NON-SECTARIAN		SECTARIAN			
		Protestant		*Catholic*	*Jewish*	*Others*	
			Non-				
		Denomi-	*denomi-*				
		national	*national*				

Health
  Hospitals
  Other
Charity
  General Relief Agencies
  Children's Agencies
  Institutions, etc.

The classification of agencies in the left-hand column should adopt the best usage of the local community. Tables in the same form should be made out for each district of the city, listing in separate columns the local agencies serving the vicinity only, and the remoter ones serving the whole community and available for residents of the district.

A financial table in similar form should also be made by substituting amount of annual operating costs for number of institutions.

The support of social agencies is generally divided between the beneficiary and the supporting constituency; and, with respect to the constituency's share, between past givers (whose gifts have been funded) and present ones; also between the taxpaying public and private supporters. These divisions should be calculated, if local forms of institutional accounting permit, in a form similar to the following:

TABLE XXXIV

TABLE —SOURCES OF CONTRIBUTIONS TO SOCIAL AGENCIES CLASSIFIED BY TYPE

SOURCE	AMOUNT BY TYPE OF AGENCY			
	Health	*Charity*	*Recreation*	*Etc.*

Taxation
Private Supporters
Current Gifts
Income from investments
Fees, dues, etc., from beneficiaries

This calculation should be carried out for each group of institutions classified according to auspices. In this respect the results may show great differences as to sources of support, and also in the types of agencies. Other data of this sort may be found in published reports and arranged from the viewpoint of the church as a large supporter and ally of social work.

Investigation Involving Securing of New Data

Methods of investigating certain formal relations of churches and other community institutions have already been shown in chapter ii.[17] These methods should be followed at this point. The livest problems of the relationships of churches and social agencies, however, are areal. They ask about the division of responsibility and services in this or that district or part of the city. These problems can be investigated only by the gathering of data not ordinarily reported. The grouping of the cluster of neighboring churches and the pattern of their several parishes is itself a prime factor in the institutional structure of the community.

A method of studying problems of division of responsibility among churches, by means of parish maps, has already been developed.[18]

Spot-maps should be made of the parishes and Sunday schools of all the more important of the neighboring churches. From these the degree of identification of each church with any given area may be directly calculated. The density of membership of the several churches in various subdivisions of the area may also be calculated, relative to the total population of the subdivision.

The facts may also be expressed graphically by transferring the spot-maps of the four or five larger churches to a single map on which spots of a different color are used for each church. These will be likely to include the great bulk of the church constituency. Adherents to all other churches may then be indicated by still a different color. This avoids covering the map by an unintelligible number of colors as is the case when every church is separately indicated.

But not all churches are institutional equivalents. The mere fact that a church has adherents in an area by no means assures that it is doing anything like the same thing for these adherents. And, of course, churches doing very different things cannot strictly be rivals.[19] It is desirable also, therefore, to chart the service areas of their several subsidiary functions by locating, for example, all members of men's brotherhoods, women's missionary societies, boys' or girls' clubs, etc., within given areas. These show how much each church contributes to the territorial community in each of these lines, in some of which certain churches with many members but narrow programs may not figure at all.

Some churches are also doing a good many things that specialized social agencies are particularly established to do. They have health

17 See pp. 58 ff.
18 See pp. 146 f.
19 See p. 144 for means of classification of churches by similarity of functions.

activities, as do health agencies; they carry on recreation, instruction, employment service, etc., all of which are also provided by separate institutions. It is important to find out just how much these other agencies are doing in a given area.

At this point, the investigation will best be topical. It will be easy to map all the centers of health activity of each given kind, giving separate symbols to church and to social health agencies, and different colors to the different denominational or other auspices. It may also sometimes be possible to indicate by spots the exact residences of persons served in the same capacity by the different agencies. But since beneficiaries often do not "join" an agency as they join church activities, and since they are often very numerous, the spot-map method may be too cumbersome. In this event, direct calculation of geographical distribution from lists of addresses may be necessary. In the end, however, the research worker ought to be able to arrive at an approximately accurate statement of how much social work of a given sort each agency is doing in a given line and a given area.

Before attempting to arrive at a division of responsibility on this basis, it will be necessary to discount the presence of institutions— both churches and social agencies—that are in local communities but not of them. Here, for example, is a church that draws only 16 per cent. of its adherents from within a mile. All the neighboring churches draw most of their adherents from less than this distance. The buildings of two churches may be immediately adjacent; yet they may belong to different communities, or to the same community only in very different senses. The same thing is true of numerous important social agencies of the city. Those that are located in or near the major center are often there because of the focal character of centers in the structure of the city. Most of them are not there primarily, or in any special sense, to serve the local population. The study of the distribution of service-functions will distinguish accurately between the localized and the city-wide agencies. The two cannot be held to areal responsibility in the same sense.

Another set of distinctions that must be investigated are those between agencies that work for broad classes of population and those that are limited to a clientele of one sex, of some specified age, or of a given type of need or disability. It takes a study of charter limitations and administrative red-tape to tell whether an agency is really at liberty to meet the demand of human need as it actually occurs in a given area; that is to say, whether it is really where it purports to be when it is wanted.

Until fundamental analysis has made plain wherein the whereness of urban institutions consists, it will not be possible to fit them with any exactness into localized programs of social betterment.

Mere inventories, then, of agencies that happen to have their buildings or offices located in given areas are of little real social significance.

A special type of relationship between churches and social agencies is presented by a group of agencies part of whose theory is to make the churches the sects of their local units. This policy is illustrated by the Boy Scouts and similar organizations. Churches become organizers and sponsors of Scout troops that are at the same time regarded by the Scout Councils as primarily their own organizations. The frequency of this two-faced type of institutional structure, and the agencies involved in it, should be studied.[20]

Very many of the problems that emerge from institutional studies cannot be settled by survey methods or results, because of the lack of authoritative criteria. It is not at all settled how social responsibility is best divided among agencies. What surveys can show by the methods suggested is how it is divided at present, and what the total service of all agencies amounts to with respect to any given function.

Partial solutions of this problem may best be got at directly by conferences of representatives of religious, educational and social agencies in the several districts surveyed. In the course of the St. Louis Survey, for example, such conferences were held in ten of the twenty-three survey districts. The object is to check up on the tabulated data and field observations as to the field and functioning of institutions; and, through discussion, to bring out such factors as the sense of obligation to coöperate, habits of coöperation, and the degree of felt identification with the neighborhood, as well as local opinion as to the location of boundary lines between spheres of service, both logical and geographical. In cases of doubt, representatives of apparently competing agencies should be brought together to consider such concrete questions as who is responsible for a given function, in what area, and for what part of the population.

The working postulates that the group is willing to accept should be discovered by discussion and adopted as a basis of judgment upon the facts till such time as more permanent criteria may emerge.

A study of institutions regarded by churches and social agencies as anti-social, or under suspicion, is the necessary part of the background of a community survey. These include (a) such frequently exploiting agencies as lodging houses for the homeless, and employment agencies; (b) such agencies of commercialized recreation as dance halls, pool-rooms, movie houses, theaters, and amusement resorts; and (c) such definitely vicious and illegal places as gambling houses, houses of prostitution, and places for the sale of intoxicants. Much the same aspects should be studied as were chosen in case studies of the church; for example, who are their constituents?

[20] An extensive methodology applicable to the urban forms of this relationship is to be found in Douglass, *How Shall Country Youth Be Served* (Doran: New York, 1925).

What areas do they serve? Who operate them? How are they financed? etc. But the peculiarities of many of these institutions involve highly specialized techniques of investigation into which a community survey can hardly go unless it is decided to intensify this phase disproportionately. In such a case, methods of study may be derived from the reports listed in the bibliography.[21]

Evolutionary Processes

The foregoing studies of the church's background in social structure should obviously be supplemented by studies of social history showing how existing conditions have come to be and the direction in which change is now moving.

A considerable part of the data studied contemporaneously under previous topics is directly available for study over periods of time. With respect to urban conditions generally, the populational data of the successive United States censuses are thus available, provided the boundaries of the wards and enumeration precincts (in terms of which they are reported) have not changed during the intervening periods. (The contents of these data are indicated in a preceding paragraph).[22] Unfortunately for the study of social trends, ward and precinct lines are frequently modified for political or administrative reasons. Very ludicrous blunders have appeared in statistics issued by supposedly reputable organizations as a result of forgetting this fact. City plan offices, however, generally have carefully calculated the trends of population in terms of small areas. The monumental studies of the New York Census Committee[23] have even recalculated population data for 1910 and 1920 on the same units, even when the census used different ones; and competent statisticians can reach approximate results for other areas even when the enumeration areas are not fully identical. The fundamental methods of dealing with data of this type have been discussed earlier in this chapter, and may be easily applied to this material.

Of data relating to the church itself, the most important as throwing light on social conditions are those relating to removals of location. A study of such removals by dates, and causes, and of locations, results in an epitome of community changes.

Such a study may be conducted by means of the historical records assembled in case studies of churches, or by a special questionnaire supplemented by the study of statistical records of the churches concerned.[24] The questionnaire should cover (1) dates of church's first location and subsequent relocations (from which the duration of occupancy of each site may be calculated); distance covered by each removal; and disposition of old property. It may be supple-

---

21 See pp. 214 f.
22 See p. 163.
23 See *Statistical Sources for Demographic Studies of Greater New York,* 1920.
24 See Douglass, *The St. Louis Church Survey,* p. 305.

mented by questions calling for opinion relative to the facts by persons who have some knowledge of the facts on the following points: Why did the church move? What was the effect of its removal on the neighborhood that it left? Why did it relocate where it did? What was the effect on the new neighborhood? What did the church lose in the removal? What did it gain?

The facts as to removals are most usefully summarized by decades (for any length of time during which the process of relocation has been active) in terms of survey districts, as in the following form:

TABLE XXXV

TABLE —GEOGRAPHICAL REMOVALS OF CHURCHES BY
DECADES AND DISTRICTS

Decade	Removals					
	FROM DISTRICT		TO DISTRICT		WITHIN DISTRICT	
	District	Number	District	Number	District	Number
1870–1879						
1880–1889						
1890–1899						
Etc.						

The disposition of old church property in cases of removal should be tabulated, in cases of sale to other churches, according to the faith, race, and denomination of the purchasing church; in other cases, according to purpose for which it was purchased.

THE WELL-WORN WESTERN TRAIL

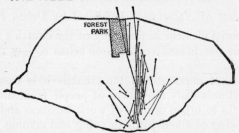

CHART XXII—MIGRATING ST. LOUIS CHURCHES
HAVE LARGELY FOLLOWED A COM-
MON PATHWAY TOWARD THE
PROSPEROUS WEST END.

Parallel studies should then be made of the following data: (1) populational census data by ward or precinct, to see what changes in the number and character of population were actually coincident with the removals of the churches; (2) geographical data relative to the founding of churches, to see what races, faiths and denominations were coming into the area when others were moving out; and (3) any other available data showing changes in economic and social structure. Such studies make it possible to map the lines of advance of, and the exact pathways followed by, the lower-grade and alien populations before whose advance the churches probably fled. The progress of such populations will obviously be measured by the dates of organization of their peculiar institutions and of their second-hand occupancy of religious buildings taken over from their previous owners. It is likely to be found that districts losing churches were, at the same time, receiving in their place churches on lower economic levels than the former ones, some moving into the district, others being newly organized there. Map these phenomena for a period of years.

The investigation of these movements of churches finally yields a very complete story of social evolution with its succession of peoples and changes of economic and social levels within the same areas.

On the basis of these studies, judgment can be rendered as to the probable truth of opinions held as to the reasons for church removal. Finally a summary of social history of the community may be written showing what areas were desirable in each decade, the progress of deterioration in certain (generally old) areas with the growth of the city; the formation of centers of vice and disintegration; and the succession of religious forces. It should be shown whether the rate of social change was gradual, or whether there was a sudden break; whether the faiths and denominations gave way at the same time, or whether some remained longer than others before moving their churches (or did not move at all); and in general what happened after the churches had gone?

Distinctive Habits of Association Exhibited by Urban People

Another essential element in the study of the church's social background concerns the distinctive habits of urban society that directly affect the church.

One of the most important of these habits it is easy to study; namely, the rhythmic daily movement of people from the peripheral areas and suburbs to urban centers of work, business and recreation, and their following of fixed paths in going and coming. That city people acquire the habit of going to centers and feel at home in so doing, is important to the church; because churchgoing, in considerable measure, already spontaneously follows the paths thus fixed, and may be further induced to do so as the city man's city is primarily that part of it with which he has to do in his regular routine of movement. For this part only he acquires the sense of familiarity and "belonging." In the largest sense, where he lives is where he goes and feels adjusted. Centers of churchgoing become such because habits already established have made them centers of congregation for other leisure-time purposes, such as recreation, as well as for business and industry.

The chief sources of information concerning the volume, particular paths, and general pattern of urban movement, are the transit studies of city plan commissions and transportation companies. These studies have asked: How many people come to the main city center and to each subordinate center daily and weekly? Whence and over what distances do they come? What do they come for? How long do they stay? Most of these questions are involved in studies to determine the need of transportation facilities in various directions and at the different hours of the day. The magnitude of the daily movement of population in and out of each district of the city may thus be discovered with sufficient accuracy. The relation of these transit habits to churchgoing may then be observed by comparison of the parish distribution of churches that are located at centers with those that are not. The replies to a questionnaire sent out by a church would further answer these questions in terms of the experience and attitudes of its own constituents.

The parish data already gathered by the community survey furnish the means of studying the varying degrees in which any district is able to attract adherents from a distance to its churches. Spot-maps have been prepared accounting for the movement to and from church of every church-member of the city. These show certain districts receiving from a distance great numbers of churchgoers for whom the churches of their districts of residence were for some reason not adequate; and other districts losing many, if not most, of their churchgoing people, and receiving few in return. The survey should calculate whether a given district is a center to which people come to church from a distance in about the same ratio to total churchgoing as it is a center of week-day commuting relative to the total of such commuting; and similarly whether other districts send out Sunday churchgoers and week-day workers in comparable ratios.

The study, through the parish data, of the total churchgoing movement, will doubtless also show minor cross-currents. Certain churchgoers will turn their backs on centers and seek religious fellowship elsewhere. There will be a wish to discover whether this also is significant evidence of some distinctive habit. Are those who thus cut across the main stream of churchgoing traffic foreigners, or members of particular races, who do not share the sense of proprietorship in the big center of the city but seek little centers of their own—this marking their segregation from the main social process? Much incidental light will be thrown on this inquiry by other phases of the studies of social background; but to gather them together is the work of interpretation rather than strictly of survey.

As a final step in the study of social movement, however, an attempt should by all means be made in the survey to formulate answers to the following questions:

(1) In each given area or district, how many people are there, and what people are they, whose habits of coming and going within

the city have established in them such feelings of attachment to some other area of the city that they feel more at home there than they do "at home"; who are hence not easily available for cultivation by local institutions, but who may be expected to go elsewhere for their social relationships; as for example, for church fellowship?

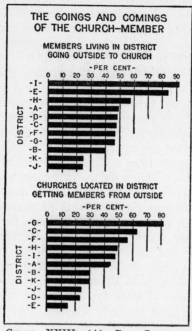

CHART XXIII—(A) PER CENT. OF CHURCH-MEMBERS IN SPRINGFIELD LIVING IN SPECIFIED DISTRICTS WHO BELONG TO CHURCHES LOCATED OUTSIDE OF THESE DISTRICTS; AND (B) PER CENT. OF MEMBERS OF CHURCHES LOCATED IN SPECIFIED DISTRICTS WHO COME FROM OTHER DISTRICTS.

(2) What organizations located outside of a given area reach into it with an effective appeal, and consequently belong to it in a vital sense other than that of being physically located there? What organizations located in a given area are not closely related to it as a field from which to draw constituents?

(3) What consequently is the proper division of responsibility, and what are the right terms of coöperation, between churches with city-

wide "pull," whose people live all over the city, and churches closely identified with local areas?

Up to date, the best of surveys have not been able to answer these questions satisfactorily; but it is important that the formula be worked with and improved so that it may ultimately become a real guide to the founding and support of churches in just the right numbers and places.

Projection of Trends

Since churches are strongly affected by radical changes in their environment, obviously one would like to know what are to be the future environmental fortunes of the church. The best ground of prediction is reached by projecting established tendencies into the future. The ability to follow out the lines of such trends throws light upon the prospects of the churches.

The most precise evidence that the past can bring to bear upon the future is the determination of the rates of change in the past. By this means one sees whether the tendency in a given direction is diminishing or accelerating; and can prophesy about how long it will take to reach a given degree of change, provided the trends of the past continue. These phenomena may be calculated for any of the aspects of social background for which data exist over a period of time. The method of studying past time-trends has already been presented in chapter v. They should now be projected into the future, say, for five, ten, and twenty-five years.

As to the future, the probable rate of increase or decrease of population has undoubtedly been studied by city-plan officials and by agencies that have to provide the layout of public facilities for years in advance. The estimates of the local branches of the American Telephone and Telegraph Company are particularly reliable.

The interpretation of trends of population is especially important as related to the growth of Negro population or of foreign population in areas on which the older churches depend. The rate of increase of these populations should be calculated by decades; but its course within the last decade was so generally affected by the World War and restriction on immigration, that shorter time-trends will have to be regarded. Conferences with real-estate boards and operators, and a study of the trend of land values, should supplement these efforts to foresee the probable areas of expansion of populations of any given character.

The study, already presented, of the advancing area occupied by transient rooming-house and lodging-house population, illustrates another way of predicting probable social change in the future. Finally, of course, the general trend of fortunes of churches of a given type, especially when coupled with a contrary trend in the fortunes of those of another type, afford reliable institutional omens for the future. Are more churches occupying rented "store fronts"? Are cruder types of religion being substituted for the older and more regular denominations with white constituencies? Are churches of Spiritualists, Latter Day Saints, and the Pentecostal sects concen-

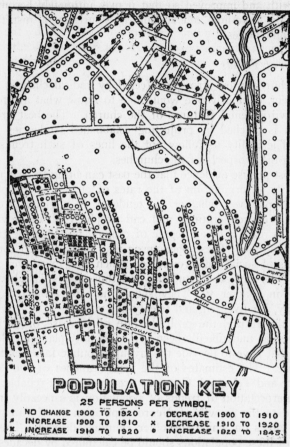

POPULATION KEY

25 PERSONS PER SYMBOL

• NO CHANGE 1900 TO 1920	✓ DECREASE 1900 TO 1910
⌀ INCREASE 1900 TO 1910	✕ DECREASE 1910 TO 1920
✱ INCREASE 1910 TO 1920	○ INCREASE 1920 TO 1945

CHART XXIV—DISTRIBUTION OF POPULATION, TYPICAL DISTRICT (CITY PLANNING BOARD). THE ESTIMATED DOUBLED POPULATION IN 1945 HAS BEEN DISTRIBUTED THROUGHOUT SPRINGFIELD ACCORDING TO THE CONTROLLING EFFECT OF THE ZONING ORDINANCE. THE CHURCH MUST PLAN FOR THIS INCREASED POPULATION IN ITS PROBABLE FUTURE LOCATIONS.

trating in a given area? Then, clearly, the future of the area for the more standardized denominations is not hopeful.

Institutional prospects may be still more completely determined by the statistical study for two or more decades of the group of churches occupying a common area. When their trends as to total and net gains and losses are carefully computed and summarized, conclusions may be reached for different types of churches whose prospects of survival and future usefulness greatly differ in spite of their common experience of social change. (1) Some stocks of people are more resistant to such change than others. Thus two or three churches of German or Scandinavian origin, supported by a considerable residual population of German antecedents in a district and by the accessibility of a much larger population within a short distance, may maintain themselves after most of the other Protestant churches have "gone West." (2) Socially adapted churches with broad programs of community work, large staffs, and special facilities, may succeed if adequately supported from the outside. (3) Churches of the "wild religions," indigenous to and having special affinities for rural immigrants, or Negro churches, may be just entering into their own when the others fail. (4) Churches located immediately at the focus of some secondary central district, and capable of making a city-wide appeal and of drawing on constituencies not affected by changes in the local community, may even be strengthened by adverse change all around them because their strategic value grows as the old character of the area departs.

In all these lines, a survey should cautiously and discriminately, but faithfully, show what the continuation of present trends into the future will mean if it occurs. It is clear, however, that the degree of certainty with which future changes can be predicted depends upon whether the movement exhibited in the past is deep-seated and consistent, whether it is reënforced by general and parallel tendencies; and upon the absence of other forces that might thwart or deflect it. With these limitations, the study of environmental background throws dependable light upon institutional prospects.

THE UTILITY OF STUDIES OF THE CHURCH'S COMMUNITY BACKGROUND

At the outset, the obvious fact was stressed that it must be decided on specific evidence in the individual case how far to carry such studies of the church's social background. If one is undertaking to study the church, one must not spend too much time upon other matters even though these be closely related; but neither should one ignore them. The more general values of reasonable background studies are fairly clear from the preceding paragraphs. On the one hand, a study of the phenomena of the urban church helps the city to understand itself in one of its important manifestations. On the other, social analysis furnishes an important guide to the church's policy and methods. Often, however, its chief value is negative as showing what cannot be done or expected here or there, or as explaining the limitations and failures. Often it reveals social bias in the church which the church itself may not have suspected. It ought to throw light on problems of religious coöperation. It clearly reveals tendencies, and probably warrants the criticism of certain present policies. All these aids to the understanding of the church have been illustrated in the immediately preceding paragraphs.

Finally, as related to groups of churches, the study of social background furnishes a basis for the analysis and classification of the characteristic reactions that churches make to changed environment. Some avoid the consequences of change by various devices, the most radical of which is removal to a new locality. Others compromise with change in more or less successful ways. Still others accept the consequences of change with varying degrees of sincerity and adaptability. The passage from one of these phases to another is accompanied by numerous transitional stages.[25] A generalized statement of the reactions of churches to their social background such as can be made at the end of a comprehensive survey, distinctly contributes to the understanding of the city church.

SCHEME OF STUDY

(Chapter VI)

(It is assumed that the community background will be studied as a phase of a comprehensive community survey, with adequate organization, and that identification and scientific districting of the community has already been made.)

PLANNING THE STUDY

1. Determine scope and extent of existing data.
2. Study character and appraise value of existing data.
3. Decide scope and contents of background study.

MAKING THE STUDY

I. Population
1. Calculate population of the community and the districts or subdivisions.
2. Calculate composition and characteristics of same population.

II. Physical Structure of Community
1. Map topography.
2. Map transit facilities.
3. Map physical structure as limited by zoning laws.
4. Map physical structure as related to urban centers.
5. Study relation of physical structure to the churches.

III. Economic Structure
1. Measure economic levels of population.
2. Tabulate relative to church parishes.

[25] See Douglass, *The Church in the Changing City* (New York: Doran, 1927), for a classification applicable to the churches of any single city.

3. Note gradients in economic fortunes along major axes of community growth.

IV. Social Structure

1. Determine measures of social quality for which data are available.
2. Calculate standing of subdivisions of community by these measures.
3. Rank subdivisions on combined weight of all social criteria.
4. Map results.
5. Differentiate smaller neighborhoods by field study and local conferences.
6. Note correlation between physical and economic structure and social structure.
7. Calculate distribution of population according to social levels.

V. Acute Mobility and Change

1. Calculate rate of internal mobility of community from change of residence.
2. Trace and map movements of deterioration from housing or economic surveys.

VI. Institutional Structure

1. List and classify constructive community agencies.
2. Assemble data already existing concerning them.
3. Locate community agencies on maps.
4. Summarize existing financial data for community agencies.
5. Map the overlapping parishes of groups of neighboring churches.
6. Calculate density of church adherence by community subdivisions.
7. Map service areas of churches in various functions.
8. Map service areas of community agencies performing similar functions.
9. Make approximate statement of total amount of social work by districts.
10. Distinguish between city-wide and localized community agencies.
11. Classify community agencies relative to specialization and restrictions upon services.
12. Make special study of social agencies that use churches as units of operation.
13. Hold conferences of representatives of community agencies and churches to develop basis of judgment on the facts discovered.
14. Study anti-social agencies of community.

VII. Evolutionary Processes

1. Calculate by districts gross changes and relative changes in number and composition of population and summarize by districts.
2. Secure data relative to the removal and relocation of churches.
3. Note and map lines of expansion and rate of progress of different types of population.
4. Write summary of evolutionary processes and tendencies underlying the city's growth.

VIII. Distinctive Habits of Association Exhibited by Urban People

1. Map paths and centers of daily movement of commuting population and calculate amounts.
2. Map paths and center of movement involved in churchgoing and note correspondence.

3. Calculate number of churchgoers who go beyond their neighborhoods for religious association.
4. Reach conclusion as to proper division of responsibility between churches of local and of city-wide influence.

IX. *Projection of Trends*

1. Secure most reliable estimates of probable size and distribution of population in five, ten and twenty-five years.
2. Estimate trends as to composition of population, e.g., future per cent. of foreign and Negro.
3. Project into future, trends in church fortunes revealed by statistical study of the history of the churches.
4. Distinguish probable difference in fortunes of the varying types of churches.
5. Summarize and interpret total trends as bearing upon church and community fortunes.

X. *Conclusion*

1. Consider what light social data throw on church policy.
2. Analyze characteristic types of behavior of churches confronted by social change.

SUGGESTIONS FOR SUPPLEMENTAL RESEARCH

1. Make a socio-religious survey of a community from some limited viewpoint; for example, Religious Education and the Social Welfare of Boys and Girls; or The Church and the Negro (or some other racial group).
2. Work out the census data relative to the characteristics and composition of population, by districts, as the basis for a possible definite division of responsibility or a coöperative program for groups of neighboring Protestant churches.
3. Make and provide for the exhibition of a series of permanent maps covering the major social phenomena investigated in the survey, and prepare materials for making tracings of parish maps. Whenever a new pastor moves to the city, call his attention to these facilities for rapidly reaching an understanding of his field.
4. Make more intensive studies of any of the social phenomena felt to be intimately related to the church's duty and welfare.
5. Calculate the increase or decrease of social advantage or disadvantage from one district of the city to another along typical axial lines; for example, a line drawn from the center of the city to the best residential suburbs, provided physical barriers do not intervene to disturb the natural distribution of population.
6. Make intensive studies of one or more urban areas of rapid and acute change.
7. Make individual studies of typical Protestant social and philanthropic agencies as related to the church's social background.
8. Make studies of anti-social agencies that affect the church's problem, by districts.
9. Study the effect of distance of residence from the church upon the closeness and regularity of the adherents' relation to it.

BIBLIOGRAPHY AND REFERENCES

Byington, *What Social Workers Should Know About Their Own Communities* (New York: Russell Sage Foundation, 1924).

Carroll, *The Community Survey in Relation to Church Efficiency* (New York: Abingdon Press, 1915).

Douglass, *The Springfield Church Survey* (New York: Doran, 1926).

Douglass, *The St. Louis Church Survey* (New York: Doran, 1924).

Douglass, *1,000 City Churches* (New York: Doran, 1926).

A Health Survey of 86 Cities (New York: Research Division, American Child Health Assn., 1925).

Mangold, *Challenge of St. Louis* (New York: Missionary Education Movement, 1917).

Marsh, *Challenge of Pittsburgh* (New York: Missionary Education Movement, 1917).

Shriver, *Ten Steps Toward Your Neighborhood Community* (New York: Federal Council of the Churches of Christ in America, 1926), pamphlet, 16 pp.

CHAPTER VII

Community Religious Surveys

The situation assumed in this chapter is one in which an urban community wants to make a comprehensive study of the institutional aspects of religion. This means that the churches and their allies are to be investigated severally, and in their interrelations, and with reference to their setting in community life.

In such a comprehensive study, all the types of researches already discussed would find place: time studies by churches and denominations; contemporaneous studies of groups of churches or their allies by denominations, geographical areas, or type of institutions; case studies of representative churches; studies of religious population; and various intensive topical studies; each with so much of the historical element as is necessary to orient it, and all set against the social background necessary to explain the whole.

It is precisely this combination of all these limited studies in a given field into a unified scheme of research, and one relating to the same general object of investigation, that constitutes a survey in the completely technical sense.

Planning the Community Survey

IDENTIFICATION OF THE COMMUNITY

Decision as to what area and population are to be regarded as constituting the community to be surveyed may be conventional and arbitrary; or it may constitute the first step of scientific research. In the first case, it is taken for granted that everybody ought to know what constitutes the community to which he belongs, and that any uncertainty may be met by a practical ruling on the part of those making the survey. In the second case, the conception of the urban community, and the discovery of criteria for determining what objective phenomena correspond to the concept, are involved.

If the second position is adopted by the surveyor, how shall he go about it to identify the urban community?

Assuming that a community-wide survey is in mind, the first problem is how much, if any, of the suburbs should be included with the central city? In its gross population figures, for cities of 100,000 and over, the U. S. Census recognizes the "city and adjacent territory," and for cities of 200,000 population and over, the "metropolitan district," as defining a type of community larger than the political city. All sociologists would agree to this point of view. The criteria on which the census defines the extent of the metropolitan area beyond the central city are those of distance and density of population.

> The city with its adjacent territory includes, in addition to the central city, all cities, towns, villages or other civil divisions located within ten miles beyond the boundaries of the central city; while the metropolitan district includes, besides the central city, only those divisions within the ten-mile limit, in which the population of the last census was at least one hundred fifty per square mile. (*14th Census,* Vol. I, "Population," 62 ff.)

City and regional planning uses a large number of additional criteria in determining the urban community; all of which, in the case of a given city, should be investigated. Daily commutation to work and trade is one of the most important. This involves closeness of connection with the central city by means of transit facilities. Fluctuating contour lines are drawn showing zones of equal time and cost of transportation. These define the community limits more accurately than do simple distance or density of population.

Another excellent mark of the urban community is the limit of daily free delivery of purchases by great central department stores.

There is a still more vital factor, however, namely psychology. Subdivisions within a metropolitan district feel nearer or more remote from the center according to whether their interests and those of the center are identical or distinct. Holyoke, Mass., for example, by census definition is part of the Springfield metropolitan territory; but in every emotional sense it is a distinct and rival city, largely because it is occupationally so different. State lines, especially when they mark physical barriers like rivers, reduce the feeling of unity in the metropolitan district even when conquered by transit facilities. Camden, N. J., is another case in point. In distance and time, it is now very near the center of Philadelphia; but it maintains the attitude of a separate city.

The practice of church bodies (such as denominations and interdenominational councils and federations) with respect to the administration of community-wide enterprises is illogical as a whole; but is based on a variety of sound practical considerations. The spheres of operation of these bodies are likely to reach somewhat outside of city boundaries, but not to cover the whole community as the sociologist defines it. The Philadelphia Federation of Churches, for example, covers the nearest Pennsylvania suburbs, but not those in New Jersey. The St. Louis Federation, on the other hand, attempts to include the Illinois suburbs as well as those in Missouri; but it experiences difficulties, because the people in Illinois feel more remote from the city than do people living the same distance out in the other state.

The same mixture of considerations that govern church practice is likely to govern surveys undertaken in religious interests, unless still other practical considerations intervene. Thus, on many points on which data are available for the city proper, it is difficult to get comparable data for areas outside the city; and the cost of survey work is correspondingly greater. It is legitimate to let the decision in any given case rest on such factors as these.

But whatever the decision as to the extent of the community for the purpose of the survey, the theoretical issues determining community should be understood; and, if the whole urban community in the social sense is not included, the fact should be recognized and admitted as a limitation upon the results.

FIXING AREAL UNITS OF INVESTIGATION

Following the identification of the community comes its subdivision into units of investigation; that is to say, the minimum areas concerning which data are to be sought.

All surveys of groups of churches occupying common territory are bound to require such subdivision. Popular usage already distinguishes the "North Side," "West End," "Southern industrial district," etc. What is now needed is a scientific basis for these discriminations.

The underlying logical requirement involved in breaking up any whole into parts is that each part shall be relatively homogeneous. Accordingly what one must look for in subdividing a city are its relatively homogeneous areas.

Means for discovering to what degree an area actually is socially homogeneous are shown in the sections of chapter vii entitled "Economic Structure" and "Social Structure." In the actual conduct of a survey, the processes traced in these sections should be carried out at the outset, so far as they relate to already existing data in the census, city-plan studies, and histories of institutions. In other words, what can be ascertained from books about the community should be ascertained in advance, as a basis for determining the units of investigation that are to be used, in turn, in securing new data. When a survey goes forward without this precaution being taken, it may spend much time and money and then discover, when it is too late, that its data have been wrongly classified; and that, consequently, valid conclusions cannot be drawn from them. Another reason for spending plenty of time on the determination of homogeneous areas is that the process reveals what recasting and rearrangement of existing data may be necessary before they are valid for the study. All told, the issue presented by the choice of units of investigation is one of the most crucial of the entire survey; and only the results of the entire study can tell success or failure.

The most important marks of the homogeneous district, as the processes described in chapter vi have discovered it, are:

(1) It is a natural area more or less clearly set apart by physical barriers, natural or artificial, with a system of streets relating it to some center of its own and ordinarily a common transit system relating it to the city as a whole.

(2) It has experienced a common or closely similar social history, going at the same time through some part of the characteristic cycle of changes incident to city growth.

(3) Its people are living upon a common level of economic and social fortunes.

(4) It is served, in large measure, by common institutions. This, of course, includes the churches.

The area with which the churches of each district as a group are most closely identified will have been calculated in the survey from the parish distribution maps. Limits will be found within which most of the churches get most of their adherents. A few adherents will come from outside; and a few churches may be drawing most of their adherents from outside. These exceptions may be ignored in favor of the central tendency. They prove, of course, that the smaller urban communities are not wholly separate; and, after the central tendency has been studied, they should be accounted for independently.

(5) The homogeneous district may also be devoted to the same types of economic activity and be inhabited by people engaged in the same occupation.

(6) It may also be occupied by a single racial or language group. Base maps should be drawn subdividing the community on the basis of these criteria, each criterion first being separately mapped by means of processes shown in chapter vi. Tracings of these maps should then be superimposed one upon another. Most of the area covered by any one of them will be covered by all. But the limits will fluctuate more or less; one criterion relating to a little larger, another to a little smaller, territory. The exact boundaries of the district will finally thus have to be more or less arbitrarily chosen by the process of striking a rough average, and by smoothing boundary lines to correspond to the major tendencies revealed by the various criteria.

In making the final decision as to the limits of homogeneous districts, two other factors will have weight. First, previous usage. The city has been districted for various purposes a good many times; and those doing the subdividing have more or less definitely felt after logical principles. Important data may have been gathered in terms of these subdivisions, say, by school districts or city wards.

It is important to make survey districts coincide with previously recognized districts so far as the latter are actually homogeneous.

But the feelings of people as to an area should also be consulted. How far do they recognize their part of the city as extending, and where do they draw the line? Series of consultations with local community leaders in various lines are a necessary supplement to the study of objective data, and the existing districting, before reaching a final decision.

It has already been noted that neighboring people living on the same economic and social levels, and recognizing the same larger district boundaries, may be of different races and feel as distinct from one another as possible. The means of breaking up the so-called homogeneous districts into still smaller units based on social and cultural likeness is furnished by the small enumeration precincts in which census data are originally gathered. Means of securing and using these data are shown in chapter vii,[1] which should be consulted at this point.

The entire process just outlined is necessary to a really scientific districting of an urban community.

In case a survey under church auspices is related to only a portion of the community, say, the "North Side" or "West End," it may be enough to start with the fact that the churches of some territorial group believe they have common problems to be surveyed and are about to take common action in making a survey. This is in itself prima facie evidence of the existence of some sort of common field of service for these churches. How far it is actually homogeneous, and how far it must itself be subdivided are matters determinable only by the methods just expounded as applying to the entire community.

SCOPE AND CONTENT OF A COMMUNITY SURVEY

What would naturally be included in a community survey may be crudely arrived at by combining the topical outlines of chapters ii to v, eliminating duplicate topics; and, in case it is desired to put the religious data upon a social background, by adding those of chapter vi. The resulting outline should then be supplemented and the whole reorganized.

The points at which it needs supplementing are chiefly three:

Historical

(a) A historical background must be provided for the community study as a whole, similar to that provided for the single church. A sketch of community history should therefore be prepared by using the methods illustrated in chapter i.[2]

[1] See p. 185.
[2] See pp. 9 ff.

(b) A parallel sketch dealing with the history of religious institutions should be produced by a continuation and generalization of historical material gathered for each church and religious agency. Existing local histories will probably furnish condensed material from both these viewpoints.

(c) The historical study of the community in more recent times (say, for the same period that is covered by the study of church records in chapter v), should be intensified by the use of statistical data from the census and elsewhere. These should be treated by the method illustrated already for church data.[3] The object, in brief, is to show how the community was changing during the period for which church growth or decline has been carefully studied.[4]

(d) The geographical expansion of the city, and the corresponding evolution of the city's structure as analyzed in chapter vi,[5] should also be informally studied, and maps showing its growth by epochs consulted.

This will complete the necessary historical orientation. These data should be kept subordinate in quantity, and need not follow rigidly predetermined form (except as to paragraph [c] above), but should be carefully verified as far as they go.

Enlargement of Study of Religious Population

In chapter iv directions were given for the study of religious population of the parish of a single church in part or in whole. When this study is extended to include the population of an entire community (studied either in total or by sampling), it should use as subdivisions those homogeneous districts that an earlier paragraph of this chapter insisted upon. They may be still further subdivided for administrative purposes; and the further subdivisions should also be as homogeneous as possible. All the items on the schedule-card should be tabulated. (For card, see p. 108.) Tables based on the first column will be very similar to those illustrated in chapter i;[6] and the remaining tabulations will simply follow the analogies of many tables previously shown.

Study of the Church's Extensions and Allies

Ministerial alliances, city mission and extension societies, women's missionary unions, young people's unions or men's club organizations, denominational philanthropies, church federations, councils of religious education and other interdenominational agencies, the Y.M.C.A. and Y.W.C.A., and numerous other agencies, express the larger aspects of organized religion; and must be included in a really inclusive community religious survey. In any given city, these

3 See pp. 125 ff.
4 See p. 176.
5 See pp. 185 ff.
6 See pp. 16 f.

agencies have first to be inventoried and classified. Schedules and methods of study of a few aspects of some of these, as related to the social background of the church,[7] are included in the section entitled "Institutional Structure" in chapter vi. But these agencies also require direct institutional study, as forms of organized religion, by methods essentially the same as those used in the contemporary study of groups of churches.

The agencies in question are, however, so varied in purpose, and belong to so many different types, that the limits of this book do not permit it to present schedules in detail, nor to discuss the special adaptations of methodology. Typical research studies of some of the more important of these extensions and allies of the church are listed in the bibliography.[8] These afford models for the application to related fields of the methods of institutional research set forth in these chapters.

Summary of a Community Religious Survey

When the studies separately presented in other chapters have been combined and supplemented, they must be boiled down to consistency in some form analogous to the following. After each topic is given the chapter of the present book in which details of scope and content and methodological directions are to be found.

    I. Historical Background of the Community and Its Religious Institutions. (Chapter VI.)

    II. Recent Tendencies of Religious Institutions as Revealed by Published Records. (Chapter V A.)

    III. Religious Antecedents and Status of Population. (Chapter IV.)

    IV. The Present Churches. (Chapter V B.)
       1. General aspects; by denominations.
       2. General aspects; by geographical groups and types.
       3. Religious education.
       4. Parishes and the geography of churchgoing.
       5. Case studies of representative churches. (Chapter II.)

    V. The Church's Extensions and Allies. (Chapter VI.)

    VI. Social Background of Religious Institutions and Activities. (Chapter VII.)

    VII. Community Relationships of Religious Institutions. (Chapters V B and VII.)

    VIII. More Intensive Supplemental Study of Selected Topics. (Chapter III.)

The generalized outline of a community religious survey serves the same purpose as would be served by a picture of an average man. Any actual survey will have individuality. It will be thinner or fuller, and will emphasize or minimize this or that feature, as its particular antecedents and interests dictate.

7 See pp. 178 ff.
8 See pp. 214 f.

If the survey is conducted under the auspices of some particular agency, its basic plan is likely to reflect some particular viewpoint. This is all right so long as the bias is exposed and confessed, and not allowed to distort the interpretation of particular facts. In so large-scale an enterprise, however, it is particularly important that no unconfessed philosophy whose implications are unsuspected be allowed subtly to determine the foundation of the investigation.

THE COMMUNITY SURVEY AS A PRACTICAL PROJECT

In considering large-scale surveys, it will be worth while here to follow the essential phases in their natural history, step by step, from the nebulous beginnings to full definition and organization, through the various practical and technical procedures involved in getting data, handling and interpreting them, through the phase of formulation into a literary report to the final presentation to the public toward which it was directed, and to any measures that are taken to get this public to act upon what the survey discovers.

INITIATION

The first step is to consider what, in general, are the practical requirements of such surveys. The necessary detail of a community survey is very great; and its technical requirements are exacting. It is useless to conceive of such research unless its organization and resources can be put upon a commensurate scale. Its conduct is not a matter of weeks, but of months. Even in a city of 100,000 population, cost must be counted by tens of thousands of dollars. Resources necessary to finance and carry out research on this scale cannot easily be secured. When happily they are available, they must be used with the completest competency. In brief, such a survey almost certainly will have to be put into professional hands for technical execution. But ordinarily it will be projected, and its administrative details will be handled, by officials of ecclesiastical bodies or church federations. Throughout the survey, much dependence will have to be put on lay coöperation. All parties should understand the principles governing such large-scale processes and be able to see their applicability to the special case.

If the degree of intensiveness necessary to get results cannot be paid for on the scale first projected, the scope must be narrowed. It is even conceivable that by such a scaling down, a community religious survey may, in the main, be conducted by coöperating local agencies. Procedure under such limitations is suggested in chapter v.[9] On the other hand, it might very well be extended beyond the proportions assumed in this study and merge with continuous survey

9 See p. 138.

processes which, some day, will be required by public opinion of the supervisory agencies in charge of religious work.

Certain other general considerations of a fundamental nature operate to limit and control the planning of comprehensive research projects undertaken in relation to particular communities.

Coöperation

First, such a project is in itself a large-scale experiment in community coöperation. No matter how influential and well established the organizations initiating the project, and however catholic the scope of the proposed investigation, there are hundreds of lesser organizations and individuals on whose voluntary coöperation its success depends. All these must be made to "open up" both as regards information and attitudes. They will have to have the project "sold" to them one at a time. No force can command their labor in furnishing and assembling the data required of them, nor compel their interest in the long, long line of particular acts that lead on so slowly to the final conclusion. But selling implies bargaining. Frequently it requires that the coöperators be made to feel that they will get some immediate benefit as well as indefinite ultimate returns for the processes they undertake in the survey. This in turn compels the projectors of the survey to leave a measure of elasticity in their plans, a requirement that conflicts to a degree with the ideals of clear definition and predetermination of detail that characterize scientific precision and make for economy of procedure.

In the Springfield Church Survey, for example, certain supplementary schedules for use by single churches were devised, and the churches were told that the survey would help them to go as far as they individually desired beyond the minimum requirements of the investigation.[10] The final report on a case study, such as was considered in chapter ii, virtually has to be shaped so as to meet the particular interests of the particular church.[11]

Participation as Education

Second, the presuppositions in a survey as to the means by which truth is arrived at and communicated to others also condition the survey methodology in important ways. Particularly is this true in the study of a complicated community situation. Relative to organized religion in a city, is truth something that is arrived at through technical processes and then embodied in a report and read by, or talked to, the community? Or is it something chiefly acquired or disseminated through the process of participation in its discovery? Are the survey's chief values reserved to be distributed at the end, or are they dispensed all along during the progress of the study?

10 Douglass, *The Springfield Church Survey* (New York: Doran, 1926), pp. 395 f.
11 See p. 63.

Are the final generalizations more important, or less, than the fragments of facts that are uncovered bit by bit for individual organizations or groups, that are immediately thought about by the members of these organizations and groups and quickly entangled in the ongoing stream of conceptions, plans and decisions relative to action? Even with respect to formal procedures, which is the more important: the chance that several churches, say, will permanently improve their bookkeeping because they have learned to use the more exact forms required by the survey, or the chance that when the study is over, better bookkeeping for the churches in general will be resolved upon, and the policy be put into practice piecemeal, as it will have to be if put into practice at all? In brief, which is the major product, and which are the by-products of the survey process?

Obviously both of the above interpretations of the values of surveys may be partially accepted; but a community survey will be much less rigid and less fully predetermined if its incidental values are regarded as more than incidental; and if it is decided in advance to stop and help people get the good out of the parts of the process instead of to stake all upon some remote scheme of utilization after the process is finished.

Ordinarily the coöperation required for the success of a community survey cannot be secured unless those responsible for the work are willing to coöperate in gaining the separate ends of the allied forces, as well as their own ends.

These are considerations of which the theoretical projectors of surveys sitting in offices have little sense; but which, when they are ignored, exact their penalties in the shape of disrupted plans and financial deficits on the one hand; and, on the other, in the failure of the survey to cause anything significant to happen in the community when the work is done.

Conditional Adoption

When a provisional policy with respect to these matters has been determined upon, a tentative decision will be reached to go ahead if general support for the proposal can be won. The persons and agencies whom it is proposed to include will then be approached in behalf of the partially digested project; and their reactions will determine the final decision. The technical plan, involving the identification of the community to be studied, and the scope, content and method of research, will then be worked out. This brings the matter down to the planning of the survey's practical procedures.

ORGANIZATION AND EXECUTIVE AGENTS

First to be considered are the executive agents of the project. If the community survey were small enough to be conducted in connection with the routine processes of an organization, as the survey of a single church or agency sometimes is, its executive direction would naturally fall to the minister and official board or comparable officers. A survey creating separate machinery will ordinarily need an executive committee and one or more executive secretaries or directors who must be competent to carry out both the technical and the practical phases of the enterprise. The first requires the expert; the second, a business manager. The two functions may perhaps be combined in one person. If there are two executives, the prime question is which is to be chief?

In case an agency or group is conducting a community survey for its own acknowledged practical ends, it may seem only natural to keep at the helm the man who best represents it to the community and can handle the community best. If, on the contrary, the dominant objective is to conduct an unbiased survey that shall result in the discovery of truth, it will be natural to make the technical expert, who plans the gathering of data and interprets the results, the chief administrator; and to give him, as a right-hand man, a practical executive in close touch with the community. In either case, as a later paragraph will show, certain matters naturally fall to each man for final determination.

Repeatedly, in earlier chapters, it has been stated or implied that some one will take the general directions given for the making of a particular kind of survey and adapt them to the particular case. Who shall do this? First, of course, the expert technical director; but he should be aided by competent local advisers.

A community survey should consequently be administratively departmentalized in general correspondence with the logical framework of its outline; and more or less independent subcommittees should be created to assist in planning the detail of the various researches that make up the whole, to assemble existing data, to secure new data, and to study the results. The members of these subcommittees should be persons especially interested in, and well informed concerning, the survey's several fields of research, as for example:

Subcommittees	Chief Sources of Committee Members
Historical Background	Local historians
Statistical Records of Religious Bodies	Denominational statisticians
Religious Status of Population } The Present Churches }	Ministers and leading laymen
Religious Education	Sunday-school experts
The Church's Extensions and Allies	Denominational, Y.M.C.A. & Y.W.C.A. officials
Social Backgrounds	Social-work experts

Such committees actively engaged in the work will save money and diffuse interest and knowledge. They will also add influence and yield valuable suggestions, even in a survey largely conducted by paid professionals.

In any case, the planning of the professional force is dependent upon the kinds of highly specialized services involved in the conduct of the survey.

FUNCTIONS REQUIRING PROFESSIONAL SKILLS

References to the general outline,[12] and then back to the several methodologies, show what distinctive methods characterize each major investigation, and what sort of specialized (and often professionalized) ability and experience are required to carry it out. These are summarized in the following table:

Department of the Survey	Chief Methods	Specialists Required
1. Historical Background	Library research	Research workers
2. Study of Published Church Records	Statistics	Statistician and tabulators
3. Religious Population	House-to-house canvass with schedules	Organizer of volunteer groups
		Field workers
	Statistics	Statistician and tabulators
4. The Present Churches, their Extensions and Allies	Gathering of data with schedule	Field workers
	Statistics	Statistician
5. Case Studies of Churches and Religious Agencies; and Intensive Topical Studies	Library research; study of non-statistical records	Research worker
	Statistics	Statistician and tabulators
6. Social Backgrounds	Library research	Research worker
	Statistics	Statistician and tabulator

Three types of technical workers are thus called for in addition to the director and the business manager; viz., research workers, field workers, and statisticians.

In a small survey, the technical director may be his own research worker and may share the field work with the business manager. The most highly specialized work, namely, statistics, will then go to a third worker who may be in a large measure his own tabulator. This arrangement calls for a paid force of three workers, with stenographic and filing service and the making of graphic illustrations to be provided extra. In a large survey, on the other hand, there would be one or more research workers (who would also assist in a preliminary study of results), several tabulators to assist

12 See p. 203.

the statistician, a force of field workers, and a corresponding corps of office workers under the business manager and field work supervisor.

THE ORDER OF PROCESSES

The next step is to plan all the stages of the survey in a practical sequence, so that the workers will be steadily and efficiently employed at their special tasks.

In general, work begins with existing data. These are studied while new data are being gathered. Statistics follow each phase of field work; and study of data parallels and follows each piece of statistical work.

In the first stage, for example, the director plans the schedules, assisted (as to tabulability) by the statistician. The statistician meanwhile also draws up his tabulation forms and skeletons of tables. The business manager discovers, lists, and makes his contacts with community agencies and coöperating individuals, and assembles the yearbooks and published ecclesiastical records for statistical study. The research worker locates, inventories and transcribes the existing historical and social background material that is not dependent on schedules for form.

In the second stage, the director classifies the religious agencies on the basis of the business manager's lists, districts the community on the basis of the research workers' social data, appraises and begins to study and plan the use of the historical and social data. He also plans the house-to-house canvass if it is to be conducted by the sampling method. Meanwhile the business manager sends out the schedules made in the first stage (by mail or by field workers or both); and organizes the house-to-house canvass. The statistician works on the statistical aspects of the historical and earlier social data. The research worker keeps at further social data or non-statistical case-study records.

In the third stage, the business manager conducts the house-to-house canvass. The statistician produces statistics based on published church records. Meanwhile the director continues the study of the historical and social data, and begins a written exposition and interpretation. In this the research worker now assists by predigesting data and giving it preliminary literary formulation.

In the next stage, the statistics of published church records are turned over to the director to study, the research worker assisting as before. The field data of the house-to-house canvass now come to the statistician; and the business manager, with his field workers, presses for the gathering in of the church schedules that have been previously circulated.

In the next stage, the completed statistics of the house-to-house canvass go to the director, and the data of the church schedules to the statistician. The business manager turns to field work with the church's allies. In the data, gaps now begin to appear which the research worker and field workers respectively strive to fill in promptly so that the main processes may not be held up.

In the final stage, field work is supposedly completed. The statistician works on the data last gathered; and the director, on the whole study so far as completed.

The project now enters the phase of final study in which secondary statistical processes are carried on to aid in interpretation. This phase and the interpretation fall to the director, who receives assistance in the organizing of material for report and presentation. It is now that the graphic artist is chiefly needed.

Analyzing the foregoing plan of the sequence of the survey, one finds that it depends primarily on the fact that some data already exist while others have to be gathered; and that the gathering takes longer for some data than for others; secondly, on the fact that certain data have to be gathered before the plan for gathering the rest can be made. The practical plan is simply a filling in around this skeleton of circumstance and logical necessity.

For following the plan by sequence, which would be the same whether the survey were large or small, a plan by scale must be made.

PLANNING THE SURVEY TO SCALE

Will the particular survey require seven specialists or only three? How long will it take? How much will it cost? These questions will be up at all stages; it is at this point that they get their most exact answer. For a survey of given scope and contents, it all depends on the size of the community and the bulk of the data. Fifty churches of average size will present just twice as much data as twenty-five. The survey in the first case will not take twice as long as in the other, because the planning, the making of schedule and statistical forms, the setting up of processes, and the study of general background material, will be approximately the same in either case. When, however, the time necessary for these general processes is accounted for, the additional time needed is directly proportionate to the amount of material to be handled.

An approximately accurate time estimate can be made by an experienced director who will "size up" the data and enter against each process called for in each department of the survey an assignment of hours' work and working force.

This estimate will finally determine the personnel of the survey and consequently the payroll.

Determination of Facilities

Necessary facilities will have to be determined on a like basis. What office space and equipment will be required, and what facilities of communication? What conditions as to sanitation, comfort and convenience must be provided? What technical apparatus of statistical and graphic work will be required? All these questions must be decided relative to the time-stages of the project.

Budget

The total budget required will have to be built up by entering an estimated amount to match each and every item of expenditures for personnel, facilities, and working processes, according to the time and facility schedule. There will still remain the unpredictable elements in research. As affecting costs, the chief uncertainties relate to: (1) the length of time necessary to secure data on account of inability to control voluntary coöperators; (2) the length of time required to deal with data statistically, which will depend partly on the uneven texture of the data themselves, and partly on the fact that to be dealt with fruitfully they must often be dealt with experimentally; and (3) the length of time required to interpret the data, if this is to be done originally, and with creative intelligence, and not merely mechanically. Every consideration of a fact in a relationship requires time. It is a rough maxim of research experience that it takes just as long to interpret and report a survey as it does to get the data and subject them to the preliminary statistical processes. A very liberal contingent item should therefore be entered in the budget to cover possible variations of costs on these accounts. Accidents to persons, sickness and death may be insured against, as also may loss of records by fire, theft, and in transit; and a definite item should be inserted in the budget for such insurance.

Theoretically, research ought never to be predetermined by a fixed budget. If mining operations had uncovered a vein of gold, one would not omit to take the gold out of the mine because the original estimates of cost had been exceeded. On the other hand, as nearly as possible there should be an assured income to cover every predictable item of cost; and the less imperative phases of a survey may well remain contingent until it is discovered how far its actual costs keep in step with financial resources.

Authorization

The survey plan being thus determined, both technically and as a practical enterprise, it should be adopted by formal and definite action of the official bodies concerned, subject to such elasticity of administration as may be agreed upon. The workers will then be secured, facilities will be provided, and the work will go forward with good chance of success.

Technique of Control

The conduct of a community survey constitutes a business enterprise of no small dimensions. Consequently adequate methods of checking progress, of financial accounting, and of business control, will have to be devised to care for the mass of technical labor and the product that is involved. Expert advice is important in setting up the business phase of the project, as well as the purely technical. The scheme of business control, however, should not be top-heavy or over-elaborate, but simply should be commensurate with the size of the enterprise itself. It should be definitely adopted by the bodies controlling the survey and then carefully enforced.

Termination

Probably no survey was ever finished ahead of its schedule. It is almost certain that a time will come when, for budgetary reasons, a halt will have to be called to field or statistical processes. Before this finality is reached it is most important to distinguish the relative importance of incomplete processes. Some can be finished with a little intensification of work, while others have no prospect. The former should be given the right of way and the latter scrapped so as to save the study as a whole, even at the cost of some ultimate lack of symmetry.

INTERPRETATION

Assuming that all the phases of technical research have been completed, and that interpretation of the data is now to be undertaken, two things are about equally important: first, to commit the formulation of a final unified report of results to a responsible expert, the technical director being the person naturally chosen; and, second, to subject the results to adequate discussion by a large number of interested and informed persons, especially those who have already obtained knowledge of some of the raw facts through work on departmental subcommittees. As relating to the whole community, the findings of a survey should never be put forth merely on private authority. In the case of the Springfield Church Survey, for example, a public findings conference was held immediately upon the completion of the field study and preliminary statistics. Graphic charts were prepared, and verbal reports were made on sections of the data. Later, at the end of the technical work, a two-day programizing conference was convened at which national experts were brought in to confer with local leaders as to the meaning of the survey for Springfield. Somewhat later a preliminary report was issued summarizing the simpler findings of the survey. By these means two objects were secured: (1) Group thinking was brought to bear upon the technical report. (2) First values were allowed to influence practical action while the survey's novelty and force were still fresh. As a result, a Springfield Council of Churches was organized, and a considerable number of specific projects were set up by individual churches in advance of the publication of the final survey volume.

UTILIZATION

The utilization of survey results is logically a subsequent process governed by practical, rather than by technical, considerations. Whatever particular forms it may take, the ultimate utilization of a community survey should, however, include: (1) provision for systematically bringing the results before the public—for example, through courses of study in regular schools, in classes in community schools of religious education, and in local study groups; (2) practical experimentation through the incorporation of the findings into the programs of denominational agencies, church federations, or new organizations if necessary. The overhead religious organizations of the community should systematically follow up and report upon any efforts of local churches or agencies to carry out the findings. Supplemental surveys, say, at five- or ten-year intervals, should be projected so as to carry the main points of investigation over periods of time. Even of more fundamental importance will be the acquisition by the churches of a more scientific habit of approaching their problems, and the setting up of continuous survey processes in the supervisory ecclesiastical units.

SCHEME OF STUDY

(Chapter VII)

(It is assumed that the community religious survey forms a comprehensive group of researches relating to religion in a given community.)

PLANNING THE SURVEY AS A TECHNICAL PROCESS

1. Identify the community to be surveyed.
2. Determine the units of investigation.
3. Map these units.
4. Subdivide further into racial and cultural neighborhoods.
5. Plan scope and content of survey by combining content and processes of other chapters.
6. Modify and supplement to fit particular community.

MAKING THE SUPPLEMENTARY SURVEY

1. Study historical background of community.
2. Enlarge study of religious population.
3. Study church's extensions and allies.

PLANNING AND CONDUCTING THE SURVEY AS A PRACTICAL PROJECT

I. Initiation

1. Consider practical requirements in general.
2. Take initial steps.
3. Determine the scope of necessary coöperation and coöperating agencies.
4. Decide what value to give to education through participation.
5. Secure conditional adoption by agencies concerned.

II. Organization

1. Decide upon executive aspects and form of organization.
2. Select executive and subcommittees.
3. Determine functions to be performed by employed professionals.
4. Plan order of survey processes.
5. Plan exact scale of operation.
6. Determine facilities.
7. Make budget.
8. Get final, formal authorization.
9. Secure staff.
10. Decide technique of control.
11. Provide for termination.

III. Conduct of the Survey.

See chapters ii, v and vii for methodology.

IV. Interpretation

1. Secure expert to make interpretation of results.
2. Subject results to community criticism.

V. Utilization

1. Bring results to attention of public.
2. Undertake practical applications.
3. Provide for recurrent surveys and continuous survey processes.

BIBLIOGRAPHY AND REFERENCES

Bedford (ed.), *Readings in Urban Sociology* (New York: Appleton, 1926).

Park & Burgess, *The City* (Chicago: University of Chicago Press, 1925). Especially Chapter X, "A Bibliography of the Urban Community."

Proceedings of the Twentieth Annual Meeting of the American Sociological Society (University of Chicago Press, 1926).

Bogardus, *The New Social Research* (Los Angeles: Miller, 1926).

Chapin, *Field Work and Social Research* (New York: The Century Co., 1920).

Giddings, *Scientific Study of Human Society* (Chapel Hill: University of North Carolina Press, 1924).

Lindeman, *Social Discovery* (New York: Republic Publishing Co., 1925).

Harrison, *Social Conditions in an American City, A Summary of the Findings of the Springfield Survey* (New York: Russell Sage Foundation, 1920).

Kellogg (ed.), *The Pittsburgh Survey* (New York: Russell Sage Foundation, 1914). 6 vols.

Ritchie, *How to Study Your Association and Community* (New York: Association Press, 1926).

Swift, *The Survey of the Young Men's Christian Association of the City of New York* (New York: Association Press, 1927).

World Survey; American Volume (New York: Interchurch World Movement, 1920).

Bailey & Cummings, *Statistics* (Chicago: McClurg, 1917).

Chaddock, *Principles & Methods of Statistics* (Boston: Houghton Mifflin Co., 1925).

Brinton, *Graphic Methods for Presenting Facts* (New York: Engineering Magazine Co., 1920).

Routzahn, *The A. B. C. of Exhibit Planning* (New York: Russell Sage Foundation, 1918).

THE END